Ripple Effect

Tears of the Phoenix Anthologies Presents:

Ripple Effect
A collection of fiction and art

Foreword by Rachel Caine
Edited by N. Apythia Morges and Tamela J. Ritter

RIPPLE EFFECT

"And in the Folly of My Mind" © 2008 by Theresa Rogers. "Bindings of the Dead" © 2008 by Pasquele J. Morrone. "Breathless" © 2008 by Cynthia Maves. "The Caper" © 2008 by A.J. O'Connell. "Dusk" © 2008 by Nyssa Anne Madison. "Entertaining an Angel Unawares" © 2008 by Charie La Marr. "Fairy Tale Sundered" © 2008 by Julia Katz. "Faith" © 2008 by Peg Duthie. "The Flower Song" © 2008 by Roxanne Conrad. "Free to All" © 2008 D.J. Black. "Ghosts" © 2008 by Gwyneth Cooper. "Itty Bitty Living Space" © 2008 by Aden Penn. "July 20, 2007" © 2008 by Robert Kelso. "A Jumbled Shelf" © 2008 by Jennifer Racek. "Just Another Night at the Drunken Dog" © 2008 by Matissa Evensong. "The Killer" © 2008 by Donna Beltz. "The Lady Who Cried and Flooded the Streets" © by 2008 Jason Burger. "Laissez Les Bon Temps Rouler Again" © 2008 by Charie La Marr. "Le Masque" © 2008 by Matissa Evensong. "Love Is a One-Way Street Out of Hell" © 2008 by Theresa Rogers. "Lost and Found" © 2008 by Sasha Katz. "Lucy Too" © 2008 by Tamela J. Ritter. "Lucy, Our New Spirit" © 2008 by Autumn Rose Wood. "Mud Puddles" © 2008 by Peg Duthie. "The New Job" © 2008 by Tanya Bentham. "No Place Like Home" © 2008 by Tamela J. Ritter. "Of Blood and Love" © 2008 by N. Morges. "On Order" © 2008 by Greta Cabrel. "Otherworldly Conversations" © 2008 by Caitlin Young. "The Pleasures of Mud" © 2008 by Julia Katz. "Puss in Boots" © 2008 by Tanya Bentham. "Role Models" © 2008 by S.R. Ferguson. "Saving Grace" © 2008 by Shari Smith. "Serving the Public" © 2008 by Gloria Oliver. "Solo Refrain" © 2008 by Greta Cabrel. "Staying the Course on St. Charles" © 2008 by Greta Cabrel. "Surviving" © 2008 by N. Morges. "Tears of the Phoenix" © 2008 by Autumn Rose Wood. "There You Are, Then You Go" © 2008 by Emily Moreton. "Transcendental" © 2008 by E.J. Wilson. "We Want" © 2008 by Autumn Rose Wood. "White Wall" © 2008 by Autumn Rose Wood. "Zombrarians Attack" © 2008 by Moe Biers. *** "Between Books" © 2008 by T.G. Nossack. "The Caper" © 2008 by C.A. Hiley. "A Complete Stranger" © 2008 by Yael van der Wouden. "Crack of Light" © 2008 by Yael van der Wouden. "Dreamers, Cats, and Phoenixes" © 2008 by Elizabeth S.C. Wu. "The Face of Grace" © 2008 by Pennswoods. "The Gang at City Hall" © 2008 by Elizabeth S.C. Wu. "The Inter-loaf-er" © 2008 by Bernadette Joseco. "Jarred Brain" © 2008 by Diana M. McCabe. "Jumbled Shelf 1" © 2008 by C.A. Hiley. "Jumbled Shelf 2" © 2008 by C.A. Hiley. "Jumbled Shelf 3" © 2008 by C.A. Hiley. "Jumbled Shelf 4" © 2008 by C.A. Hiley. "Large Dog" © 2008 by Yael van der Wouden. "Little Lucy" © 2008 by Pennswoods. "Lucy" © 2008 by Yael van der Wouden. "The Market" © 2008 by Emma Pocock. "Mecha-Flower" © 2008 by Silvia Barlaam. "Not Afraid Anymore" © 2008 T.G. Nossack. "The Pleasures of Mud" © 2008 by Leochi. "The Sacrifice" © 2008 by Eirik Omlie. "Temple Garden" © 2008 by Emma Pocock. "Weeping Lady" © 2008 by Kim Kiser. "Zayza" © 2008 by Jessica Sims. "Words of Wisdom" © 2008 by Diana M. McCabe. "A Whispered Conference" © 2008 by Diana M. McCabe. "You'll Have a Scar" © 2008 by Diana M. McCabe. "Zayza" © 2008 by Jessica Sims. "Zombrarian" © 2008 by Diana M. McCabe. "The Zombrarian" © 2008 by Sasha Katz *** Typewriter photo © James Steidl; manipulated by N. Morges. Puddle photo © Hidesy. *** Front cover art by Diana M. McCabe. Back cover and frontispiece art by Kim Kiser. Designed by N. Apythia Morges.

Copyright © October 2008, Tears of the Phoenix Anthologies
Printed in the United States of America
ISBN 978-0-9819198-0-5
10 9 8 7 6 5 4 3 2 1

Tears of the Phoenix
P.O. Box 30
Harrison, NY 10528
http://www.tearsofthephoenixink.org

Dedication

This book is dedicated to the city of New Orleans and to libraries and librarians everywhere.

Laissez Les Bon Temps Rouler!

Acknowledgements

This book could not have happened without the generous help of many people who offered their time and talent to turn our ideas into a fully functioning reality. We would like to thank:

— Rachel Caine for her inspiration, unwavering support, and belief in us and this project when we worried it was too big of an undertaking. Her words of encouragement kept us going through moments of insanity and self-doubt.

— The New Orleans librarians and the people at Rebuild New Orleans Public Library for their eager participation and willingness to work with us. We hope you love the outcome.

— Seale Paterson for going beyond the call of duty in rounding up other librarians and spreading the word. We are indebted to you.

— Brian from Aunt Tiki's for being such a good sport. Remember, it's all fiction (and Seale's fault).

— The Quidditch Pitch for its amazing support.

— Diana McCabe for her excellent skills as an Art Director.

— All the editors who volunteered countless hours of their lives to look for typos, examine sentence structure, and insert and delete commas.

— The many friends who offered up their expertise in areas in which we were sorely lacking. We owe you.

— Our writers and artists, without whom this book would not exist. You are an inspiration for us.

Thank you all.

Foreword
by Rachel Caine

I write the Weather Warden series, and, in those books, my main character controls the weather. You can imagine how much I wanted to be Joanne Baldwin, just for a moment or two, as I watched Hurricane Katrina careen into the Gulf Coast in 2005.

I was at a convention that weekend, and the hotel was full of hurricane refugees, since Dallas was one of the relatively close and safe destinations. The Dallas Convention Center held hundreds more, and in nearly every hotel, especially the more affordable ones, you saw the same story: people wondering what had just happened to their lives.

And at first, there seemed nothing we could do. A few acted directly—including the convention's Artist Guest of Honor, who diverted on his drive from Oklahoma to the hurricane-stricken area to pick up friends and fans who needed assistance and opened his home to be sure they had a safe place to stay. Those who didn't have room in their homes began fund-raising efforts and gathering clothes and supplies for the distribution centers. It was happening everywhere I went—at the convention, at the grocery store on my way home, in my neighborhood, at my job the next day.

It was extraordinary to see and experience, the feeling that everyone wanted to help undo this terrible thing.

After the storm passed, the true horror of what had been lost started to sink in—but like all traumas, it began to fade for those who hadn't been directly affected. After a while, the fund-raising drives ended, the collection points stopped taking donations. Refugees moved out of hotels. Some went home—some didn't.

Life, it seemed to those of us who weren't in the Gulf Coast, returned to normal.

About two years later, I was privileged to be one of the guests at Phoenix Rising, a conference focused on Harry Potter. It was held in New Orleans, near the French Quarter. The conference organizers noted that it was appropriate for the event to be held in New Orleans, which was also rising from the ashes. Nothing drove that home for me more than driving into town, passing block after block of boarded houses and shuttered businesses.

It was a terrible reminder of just how much remained to be done for this great, historic American city.

Being that the conference focused on the books of J.K. Rowling, I looked for a literary-related cause that I could promote during the event—something that would appeal to a group of people who were clearly interested in literature. During my search, I came across the Web site for the Rebuild New Orleans Public Library project...and the devastating, iconic photographs of what had been the nearly-new Martin Luther King branch, located in the worst of the devastation.

The photographs broke my heart. So did the statistics. According to the Library Foundation's Web site:

- Every branch sustained damage.
- Eight of the twelve branches were completely ruined by wind, water, and mold.
- Revenue losses forced layoffs of eighty percent of the library staff.
- While FEMA has pledged to defray the costs of rebuilding and restocking the libraries, it will take time—years, most likely.

The good news was that by the end of 2007, significant progress had been made. The Bill & Melinda Gates Foundation had funded the setup of six temporary branches while the others were being renovated. Six out of the twelve permanent locations have been reopened. New Orleans Public Library staff has more than doubled.

That doesn't mean the job is done, by any means. The Library Foundation's goal is to raise $10 million in private funds —the amount that the FEMA reimbursements won't cover.

So how does buying this book help? That's a story in itself...a pretty amazing one.

The money we raised during the conference was donated directly to the Rebuild fund. Many people made private donations after the conference as well, but the two editors of this anthology had a daring idea: They decided to put their time and energy into something that wouldn't just be a donation, but would be something in the spirit of the library itself: a collection of original fiction, poetry, and art with themes chosen by the library staff.

I wasn't one of the organizers of the effort; I was amazed and touched when I heard from the editors about what they'd put together, including all of the publication details, and even the launch events. Every single person involved in this effort did so from a true desire to help, and that's absolute magic.

Here's the important part: The proceeds of this anthology— everything beyond the cost of printing—go directly to the Rebuild NOPL program. The editors, writers, and artists have donated their time and energy. Nobody's getting paid to do this.

But all this effort means little unless someone like you pays for the collection. Those whose work fills the pages gave their time and energy; you, by buying this book, have completed the cycle and put money in the fund.

All this helps in another way, too: The librarians and staff of the New Orleans Public Library system get to see their ideas turned into reality as words on a page and pages in a book that can be shelved in the libraries where they work, in a city they've fought to keep alive for generations to come.

And that's what it's all about in the end. Books on shelves, and people reading them. History in motion.

Thank you for being part of the experience and the magic of good people doing good for others.

Rachel Caine
February 2008

New Orleans Public Library Foundation:
http://www.nutrias.org

Note from the Editor
by Tamela J. Ritter

I don't remember a time when I didn't feel a part of me belonged to New Orleans. I guess it started about the time I learned to read. From Twain's travels down the Mississippi to the vampires and witches of Rice, Williams' streetcar to Kennedy's Ignatius Reilly, the rich literary history of the place intrigued me instantly.

The first time I came to New Orleans, I felt it immediately. That piece of my soul that I hadn't even noticed was missing was there. The people I met who welcomed this lone traveler and the experiences I had as a tourist, who felt local from the first inhale of the delta wind, were life-altering. The only other time I ever felt a connection like that with a place was when I came to New York City for the first time. The lifelong reader in me loved instantly the literary history of New Orleans. The writer in me loved instantly the manic chaos of the publishing capital of the world that is New York City.

On the walls of my house, I had two pictures to represent the home of my heart and the home of my soul. They were of the New York City skyline and of an ivy-covered, wrought-iron balcony with gaslights and cobbled streets.

When September 11 happened and those buildings came down, and the world mourned, I felt that piece of my heart that was home there shatter and turn to rubble as well. Four years later, when the levees of the Mississippi broke, and the streets, homes, and lives of the Gulf Coast were drowned with grief and abandoned by the government, that piece of my soul drowned as well.

It took everything I had to go about my life with those missing pieces in me. The hardest part was the desire and the need to DO SOMETHING and knowing that nothing was enough, that nothing could be done. The hopelessness of it was overwhelming.

More so when I actually came back to New Orleans for Phoenix Rising in spring 2007 and saw firsthand how lives had changed, how people were still trying to right the wrongs. I knew I had to do something. I needed to get that piece of my soul to high ground and contribute what little I could for the people who had welcomed me so long ago.

When Apythia came to me with her idea, it was the first step, and I knew it instantly. I knew from the moment we both got the chills when the name for our endeavor came to us, as if in a dream, and then Rachel's enthusiasm matched our own, which was fate itself. We contacted Rebuild New Orleans Library and then the libraries and felt it again as each of them shared our vision for this project. Since then, every writer who has joined us, every artist who has given his or her talent, every person who has heard about us, sought us out just to wish us luck, and gave us words of encouragement has given me back my soul's home.

I hope in some way it does that for you, the reader, as well. For us, raising money was the second goal of this book—an important goal—but second to the one of showing New Orleans and their libraries that people outside of their city cared and wanted to do something to help. That we have writers and artists from as close as New Orleans and Texas and as far away as Great Britain, Austria, and New Zealand involved in the cause of New Orleans, their books, and their city has been the greatest reward for me. It has shown me what I knew instinctively all along: A book can change a life. It has mine.

All we can do in this world is share what talent, determination, and life we have with each other. Here is what we have. Enjoy!

Tamela J. Ritter
March 2008

Note from the Editor
by N. Apythia Morges

New Orleans was always a magical place in my mind, a place where Old World French met New World debauchery, a place where mysticism seemed to be in the very air one breathes.

I had always wanted to visit New Orleans but never had the chance. Tamela, who had been there many times, suggested in summer 2005 that we go there for New Year's Eve. I was so excited.

And then came Katrina.

The pictures of death and devastation left me grieving for something I never knew. The Big Easy would never be the same, and I had missed the opportunity to experience it in its full glory. Or so I thought.

Time moved on, and 2006 brought a year of events that would eventually lead to where I am now. Two of the major ones were the forming of Writers on the Rocks and the announcement of the Phoenix Rising convention in New Orleans. I was finally going to see the city I've imagined so many times as I read various books set in it. And I was going to drag Tamela (kicking and screaming at the time) to her first Harry Potter conference.

Writers on the Rocks was a critique group composed of five rebels who broke away from a much larger writers' group. One day, we got the bright idea to do a book based on the regulars of our favorite bar. This is what we now refer to as our Tears of the Phoenix test run. To say it was torture, that it required my blood, sweat, and tears, literally, is putting it mildly.

When it was finally sent to the printers, I vowed up, down, and sideways I would never do anything like that again.

We received our proof copy right before we left for New Orleans.

Relieved that mess was finished, I looked forward to a week in The Big Easy, full of fun times and sight seeing.

At the opening dinner, author Rachel Caine made a presentation on the state of the libraries in New Orleans. The facts were devastating: Libraries completely destroyed; librarians without jobs; thousands upon thousands of books, some rare and priceless, damaged beyond repair. The pictures of ruined, waterlogged books and demolished stacks produced a visceral reaction in me. As someone with eleven bookcases in her apartment, which is catty-corner to the town library, I couldn't imagine what it would be like to lose all those books.

The devastation continued to weigh on me throughout the conference. A few days after returning home, I sat on my couch flipping through our book when I had a thought. I immediately called Tamela. The conversation went something like this:

Apythia: I have an idea. You'll either love it or want to smack me upside the head.

Tamela: What?

Apythia: We should do a book for Rebuild New Orleans Public Library, just like we did for the bar, only use the librarians as inspiration and get Harry Potter fan fiction writers to try their hand at original works, and then give all the money to the library.

Tamela: (pause) Let's do it! And we can get the artists involved as well and…

About an hour later, we had the project pretty much mapped out, and Tears of the Phoenix was born. Much to her credit, Tamela only mentioned my oath to never do a book again only once or twice a day for a month or so.

The first thing we did was run the idea by Rachel, who had also made Rebuild New Orleans Public Library her charity for the year. Once we received her support and, to our very pleasant surprise, her willingness to contribute, we felt this was our chance to prove that a book can make a difference.

We got in touch with Ron at Rebuild New Orleans Public Library, who put us in contact with New Orleans Public Librarian Seale Paterson, whom we owe a drink at Aunt Tiki's next time we are in town for her help. She got the word out to other librarians, who sent us story prompts, which we then posted for writers.

A few months later, we had an unexpected onslaught of submissions of varied and compelling stories and a bunch of talented artists wanting to illustrate them.

After rounds of editing, typesetting, editing, and editing again, we sent the manuscript off to be printed.

Now here it is, nearly a year later, and we've come full circle.

My visit to New Orleans had a profound, life-changing effect on me. I never imagined when I boarded that plane that a year later, I would be writing an editor's note for a book I am so proud to have been a part of, co-running a literary charity, starting two more similar book projects, and creating a nonprofit literary magazine. All because I went to New Orleans. Because of Rachel's presentation. Because I truly believe that a book can change a life.

It is proof that the smallest thought, word, or picture can lead to a chain of events that alter your life irrevocably.

It's the Ripple Effect.

N. Apythia Morges
March 2008

Contributing Artists

Silvia Barlaam
C.A. Hiley
Bernadette Joseco
Sasha Katz
Kim Kiser
Leochi
Diana M. McCabe
T.G. Nossack
Eirik Omlie
Pennswoods
Emma Pocock
Jessica Sims
Yael van der Wouden
Elizabeth S.C. Wu

Contributing Authors

Donna Beltz
Tanya Bentham
Moe Biers
D.J. Black
Jason Burger
Greta Cabrel
Rachel Caine
Gwyneth Cooper
Peg Duthie
Matissa Evensong
S.R. Ferguson
Julia Katz
Sasha Katz
Robert Kelso
Charie La Marr

Nyssa Anne Madison
Cynthia Maves
Emily Moreton
N. Apythia Morges
Pasquale J. Morrone
A.J. O'Connell
Gloria Oliver
Aden Penn
Jennifer Racek
Tamela J. Ritter
Theresa Rogers
Shari Smith
E.J. Wilson
Autumn Rose Wood
Caitlin Young

Table of Contents

Poems

Drabbles

Flash Fiction

Flash Fiction continued

Short Stories

Appendix

List of Illustrations

Poems

We Want
by Autumn Rose Wood

We want
Fantasy to sweep away the gray dust of destruction
Casting out those clouds that hover over
our shining historical French brick home
We want
Romance to dance down our streets again
without a care or concern
Embracing us once more and trembling with passion
We want
Comedy to laugh away our tears
To hide in the cracks of our city and leap out with surprises
We want
Mystery to beckon us over the rubble of our lives
To find the clues that prove that we are all better
for surviving the tragedies
We want
Adventure to burst upon us forcing us
into achieving a greater understanding of ourselves
To climb the obstacles that have poured onto our fertile ground
We want
Triumph to remember us
To lift Louisiana and return our bright beloved
to her rightful place in America's hierarchy.
Nous Vouloir
New Orleans
C'EST LA VIE
ET
C'EST VARI

Tears of the Phoenix
by Autumn Rose Wood

Not shed, but
Healing awaits
The soothing tap of fingers finding the key
No dread, but
Anticipation
The long-held breath of the dreamer's bequest
No lead, but
Hot drippings
The bursting of a talent yet defined
Not said, but
Thought
The feelings that are trapped seek the ultimate escape
Not dead, but
Sleeping
The short nap of the cat that has swallowed her canary

The Pleasures of Mud
by Julia Katz

Thirty years old and still obsessed with mud.
People would probably think that was weird,
But fortunately for Lucy no one knows.
She hopes.

For years her guilty pleasure has been
Jumping in mud puddles during every storm.
She supposes it reminds her of childhood,
Though she never jumped in anything as a kid
Because she was a bit of a neat freak and
She didn't want to ruin her clothes.
But one rainy day in college she was
Baby sitting her nephews. They ran
Outside and started jumping and splashing in the mud.
She followed.

Much to her delight, the mud washed
Out of her clothes. And she enjoyed herself.
After that she paid a visit to her nephews
Whenever it rained to indulge their pleasure,
And her own.

Ten years later her nephews have outgrown
Mud puddle jumping. But Lucy still does it
When she can. She learned to
Like the muddy splatters on her clothes.
It's an art form, jumping in the right places
To get the best-placed splotches, and if you
Think the right way, it's really lovely.
But most importantly she likes the
Silly
Randomness
Of jumping in puddles of mud.

The Lady Who Cried and Flooded the Streets
by Jason Burger

There was a lady who cried and flooded the streets
To the sounds of Zydeco wails and Cajun beats.
The people knew she was a comin' and some made haste
But the ones who stayed were trapped, swimming in their own waste.

Some made an effort
Some tried real hard
Some left their things and
Some packed their cars

Others stood by their homes with looks of determination
And ended up on their roofs, praying for salvation.
The tears gathered force and the waves reached the shutters
Children cried as the gators peered over the gutters.

Some stayed to loot
Some stayed to save
Some were terrors and
Some were brave

Days passed and the helicopters came
Cameras peering down, inspiring national shame.
Where were the saviors, the celebrities, and aid?
A distracted government, a city betrayed.

Some tried to walk
Some tried to swim
Some rowed their boats and
Some sang hymns

They hoped for a Moses like the Hebrews in the desert
To part the seas and deliver them unhurt.
They moved in an Exodus toward the Sinai Superdome
But without a prophet, they made the journey alone.

stockings inside boots

intended for actual

contact with

sidewalks

get furry ridges

by the end

of the day

L U C Y

Mud Puddles
by Peg Duthie

The real reason Lucy doesn't like to wear pantyhose
is because they go with shoes that aren't for stomping.
Stockings inside boots intended
for actual contact with sidewalks
get furry ridges by the end of the day
circling where leather chafed the nylon.
The ridges are even less sexy than runs,
and Lucy never was one for sharpening
the tips of safety-pins to wear on her eyebrows
nor styling her hair with turquoise streaks
nor even raising her voice, not even when
exhorted to bellow and grunt during aerobics.
Yet, as much as she cherishes clean sheets, neat shelves
perfectly hemmed napkins and photographs in focus,
Lucy craves the shock of cold water
splashing her calves
and drying on her skin
as a grainy smear of runes.

Faith
by Peg Duthie

Two mornings a week, well before
her 1 p.m. shift at the library,
Imani picks up boxes addressed to Iraq
packed by her upstairs neighbor, Mrs. Cohen.
It's a thirty-minute walk from where they live
to the closest branch of the post office
and often another thirty minutes in line.
New Orleans never was a city in a rush,
but these days there aren't enough people
to wash up the wine glasses, ferry around
the FEMA file-ables, so everything takes
longer than it used to. "Far longer
than it should," some would say,
and they say so at the library, too,
and Imani hears them out, if only
because that's part of the job, to stay
at the desk, to keep answering the phone
even when the questions fail to change
or when God keeps circling *None of the above.*

For forty years, Mrs. Cohen taught history.
For seven, she's been a widow. She bakes
not only for the soldiers away from home
but also for Oneg Shabbats, the weeks
when someone can stop by on their way
to the service. The Fridays they can't,
she bakes a something anyway—a tart
or a pan of gingerbread. Imani doesn't drink
plus grape juice's not as pricey as wine,
so that's what they sip on those Friday nights
after Imani arrives with a book to read aloud.

White Wall
By Autumn Rose Wood

Orange and crimson leaking from the waterless sky
Through the thin sliver of glass
Night deepens, darkens
Looming structure is different in the darkness
Still displayed with memories
But each takes on an unformed shape
Just as complex, solid, and real
Nevertheless unfeeling

Morning rises and shines
This structure no longer shadowed
Standing without thought of consequence
Like any mundane thing
Exists, but does not live
Actually a barrier between growing beings
That is not even pure in the bright light of day

Outside the air embraces and there is no obstacle to the Heavens

Lucy, Our New Spirit
By Autumn Rose Wood

Rainy afternoons
And mud puddles
Billie Holiday sings inside her head
She might be shy, but she's not dead
She sings along
The world watches her
Still she continues on her brave new path
Nothing stops her, not even those that declare God's wrath
She laughs
Faith floats just like hope
God loves and He is not to blame that so many were left to drown
She is too busy to frown
She pounds her hammer into each new nail
"We have it in our power to begin the world over again."
She agrees with Thomas Paine
Words keep her sane
She experienced that storm's rage
Remembers the wet and cold fingers of death
Still that weather wasn't punishment for any sin
And she provides as New Orleans builds again
She is not quick to forget that God keeps His promises
She smiles at all those rainbows
She has seen the pot of Gold pouring out of Americans' eyes
and beating through their chests
Moving over and making room for all those house guests
She will not guess
What's next
She just lets it come
Keeping mum
And wiping mud from her feet
She splashes along

Drabbles

Free to All
by D.J. Black

I Will Rise

"Why shouldn't I go back? It's my home," Imani said, making her way to the library. The people needed books, and she needed them too. She needed Morrison's vision, Langston's song, McFadden's graceful clarity. Most importantly, she needed the wisdom of Angelou who told her sassiness was a virtue, and, together, they shall rise.

The crowd in front of the library surprised her, but it was the little boy sitting by himself, appearing world-weary and heartrending, looking up with liquid chocolate eyes that made her smile.

"Come, child," reaching out for his hesitant hand, "I got just the book for you."

Reading to the Dead

Kirsten walked through the doors of the library, running her fingers along the engraving there. FREE TO ALL.

Saturdays were always the same: library for her weekly book, a walk through the magnolias, cypress, and crepe myrtle-lined streets. She liked to watch the sunlight dance through the overhanging leaves onto the pages.

She walked to St. Patrick's #1 and found her bench. She sat there all day reading, and at the end of the day, she would have talked to no one, only the tomb of her beloved and her book. She had lengthy conversations with Mr. Sherlock Holmes; her beloved was still not talking.

Feed Me

Chesney was the first to hear the low rumbling. After looking for unruly children to shush, she grew suspicious of the library itself. The rumbling turned into growls as its hunger grew.

What it needed was what everyone needed—a good story. When brave children came into the starving library for Storytime was when its appetite seemed to be appeased.

It licked its lips on Mother Goose, salivated with Dick and Jane. Seuss made it happy; Silverstein made it gassy, but it's *The Lion, the Witch and the Wardrobe* that finally lulled it to sleep with a full belly.

Space Cowboy

Lanky posture, plaid boxers exposed under draggin' jeans, the tragically white youth popped his way down the damp streets looking for his whoadie posse. He had bitches to smack, vermin to gak, and homies to rep'zent. He also had an overdue library book to return.

Looking anxiously over his shoulders repeatedly, he ducked up the stairs, into the dry warmth of his childhood sanctuary. Long before he'd dreamed of being a gangsta, he'd fantasized about being a space cowboy. Late nights when his fingers weren't itchin' on his trigger, he imagined his thumb thrust to the stars, hailing his escape.

Fight for Your Rights

Jan opened the box of new books, breathing them deeply in. The smell of them made her giddy with anticipation.

Before she got to be that first person to crack the spine, a ruckus from behind the library walls disturbed her. Hesitantly putting the book down, she went to the window. An angry mob met her glance. The burning torches they carried caught her breath.

A sign told her all she needed to know: "Kill The Boy Who Lived." She ran for the doors. They would not get in her library. She would die before they got to her books.

Transcendental
by E.J. Wilson

Tara always thinks of what Ralph Waldo Emerson said: "Solitude is impractical and yet society is fatal." She agreed with that and has found her reprieve for loneliness in Nate. When he was born, she had finally gotten the best of both. She was no longer alone, but the crazy college life of too many friends, too many parties was behind her. She missed her friends; she didn't miss the chaos.

With Nate's tiny fingers in one hand and her husband Kevin's strong hand in the other, the future didn't look so bleak, no matter where they called home anymore.

Solo Refrain
by Greta Cabrel

As she trudged through the slush on University Avenue, Melody revisited her memories of spring break. She'd enjoyed the beignets, the jazz, and the tour of the Beauregard-Keyes house, with its dolls and teapots, but she'd been less happy about how she'd had to play guardian angel to her roommates. She was pleased that she'd rescued them, but she also felt they had forced her to play a role that wasn't actually hers.

"Life has a life of its own," she said aloud. She wanted to go back and see the city *without* having to look out for other people.

Staying the Course on St. Charles
by Greta Cabrel

Crystal wasn't stupid—she was well aware that she'd be collecting heftier tips if only she'd trouble herself to smile and flirt with the frat boys for whom she poured beer and the businessmen for whom she mixed martinis. She was so damned tired, however—two years of six double shifts every week did that to a woman—and yet the money barely helped her keep her head above water.

She couldn't help it—her brain insisted on *floating* phrases like that every chance it got—so she thanked the gods that her partner's sense of humor was equally fishy.

July 20, 2007
by Robert Kelso

Winn wonders how a man with one good eye could be scaffolding down a building with his partners Gloria, the deaf detective, and Dirk, the mute magistrate. Their culprit was on the run, but he was no match for the team's heightened senses.

The tip had come from the night-shift guard at the library. Arriving moments after the alarm, they wasted no time. They had to get the thief before he got to an internet connection.

He was cornered. "Give us the book!" Winn ordered.

After a scuffle, the book was released. There would be no spoilers from their sector.

Role Models
by S.R. Ferguson

Virginia Woolf would be proud, Debra thought as she added rocks to her pockets. *Dorothy Parker would have been jealous,* she thought as she tied the knots in the noose. *Sylvia Plath would have been disappointed,* she thought as she turned off the stove. *Anne Sexton would have cheered,* she thought as she rolled down the windows of her car and took a deep breath.

It was then, she thought that to emulate greatness could only be taken so far, and if she really wanted to be like the legends she so admired, perhaps first, she should actually write something.

French Quarter
By Autumn Rose Wood

Faith, that flirtatious female cabby, finally finagled Aunt Tiki's beau bartender, Brian, into a date. Yes, she dangled her bait. Saints tickets! All's fair in love and football, right? Faith swung her hair and her fanny into the bar. Brian winked while pouring Sacrez.

"Rain check?"

His carelessly tossed words broke her heart. Cheering for the home team, she felt her heart mend. She gave it to the quarterback and never drank again.

Surviving
by N. Apythia Morges

All That Glitters

Sunshine streamed through the window, illuminating the dust motes rising from the piles of debris she was sifting frantically through. It was here; she knew it had to be. Frantically she hunted, ignoring the warnings of "It's not safe" and "Keep out." Why had she flung it at him? She didn't really mean it when she said she never wanted to see him again. Now, she would give all that she had to look into his blue eyes, to wrap herself in the warmth of his arms. A glint caught her eye. It was within her reach. Her wedding band.

Tears of Rain

The first ping of a raindrop on her window made her cringe, whiskey burning her throat as she swallowed too much. The fire raced through her blood, a vain attempt to burn away the memories. She was told it was called Survivor's Guilt, but she hadn't survived. Not really. She may be alive, but that was far from living.

Rain streamed against the pane as the heavens cried. Were they tears for those they claimed? She wiped at the moisture wetting her cheeks, wondering when, if ever, it would stop being about pain and guilt and start being about healing.

Lost and Found

"I have a confession," she whispered, her hands tracing his name in the cold stone, the last memorial, the last gift she bought for him. "I was coming to tell you that day when you were stolen from me. I didn't want to leave, not without you. You see, you were going to be a daddy. But you weren't the only thing the storm stole from me." Her hand rested briefly on her abdomen. "But it gave me something. Someone." She hugged the girl to her. "This is Melody. She was left alone too. But now, we have each other."

Renewed

Rain pounded against the roof, but this time, she didn't cringe. Storms no longer caused her to drown in fear and guilt. She leaned over the wrought-iron railing and felt the warm water caress her face.

"Are you okay, Liz?"

She turned, extending her hand to the young girl who took it eagerly.

"Yes, Melody," she whispered, her arms encircling the girl. "I think I truly am okay."

Months had passed, time moved on, and she was still here. She stood there, in the cleansing rain, Melody's arms wrapped in a hug around her waist, and felt alive once again.

On Order
by Greta Cabrel

Even before the flood, Elizabeth hadn't liked seeing the words "Item missing" in the library catalog. Back then, she had usually interpreted it as someone not caring enough to do the job properly, be it shelving the item where it should have been or keeping suspect visitors under surveillance.

During her first week back at work, she had to tamp down the urge to shriek and rant each time she encountered the phrase.

During the second week, she dialed her emotions down to "numb."

As the third week began, she changed the status of every missing book to "On order."

Flash Fiction

The Caper
by A.J. O'Connell

"It wasn't an opportunity. It was a trap."

They were huddled over a table at the local bookstore's café. It was the holidays and to get to the table they were at now, they'd had to muscle their way through a throng of other people who'd decided that coffee, hot chocolate, and books were a great way to spend a chilly Sunday afternoon. Space was so tight that they hadn't bothered to remove their coats, hats, and gloves, but sat there, heads close together, whispering feverishly.

She looked up from her hot chocolate, a confection in a paper cup, topped to overflowing with whipped cream, drizzled with syrup, and finished with a stick of good, dark chocolate and gave her companion a look that meant business.

"It was a trap. We would have been caught," she repeated in a hushed voice, so as not to disturb the mother–daughter pair sipping tea barely a foot away. "You know it. We couldn't have done it today."

"Time was too short," agreed her companion. He sipped his coffee. "If we'd had a half hour more, it would have been a missed opportunity. But we couldn't have done it. Not today. It was too risky."

She nodded and stirred her drink with her stick of chocolate. The pair sat in a silence that confirmed that yes, this had been a missed opportunity, and in fact, it was the one they had been waiting for months. It fell into their laps that afternoon, and they had just turned their backs on it, opting to shy away from the risks involved, and go instead for hot chocolate.

"I guess it would have been pretty bad," she finally whispered, sucking whipped cream off the chocolate stick.

"It would *not* have been bad," he countered and leaned forward. "But the consequences would have been very bad."

Her mouth twisted a little, and she glared up through her bangs at her companion. He sighed. He knew what was coming.

"It would have been so easy though," she said. "We walked right in."

"At least we know when their annual meeting is now," he said. "We can walk right in next time."

"Oh yeah," she whispered bitterly and snapped the chocolate stick in half with her teeth. "We *will* be able to walk right in. In a year from now."

He raised both eyebrows in resignation and hunkered back down over his coffee with a loud, rumbling sigh. A college student at the next table glowered at them in annoyance.

"We could go back," she offered suddenly, the words tumbling out of her in a low hiss. "They could still be in there. It would be quick. We can still do this today."

There was another long silence, punctuated by the giggles of a group of teenaged shoppers at a nearby table and the sound of *Jingle Bells*, which was being piped into the café to encourage the generosity of the holiday spirit in the shoppers. An oversized portrait of Virginia Woolf glowered down on them from above festive, nondenominational garlands of plastic tinsel.

Finally, the man roused himself enough to look into his friend's eyes, which were glinting at him over her melting whipped cream.

"I don't want to get my library card clipped in half," he said slowly, as if to make sure she understood him. "There were already people coming out of that meeting. We would have been caught. We will certainly be caught if we go back now."

She sighed in resignation and popped the rest of her chocolate stick into her mouth, crunching on it ferociously.

"I know," she said through the mouthful of chocolate, and gave a mighty swallow. "But part of me can't stand the fact that it was the god-damned Library Association that derailed our plan. It just kind of eats my lunch that a bunch of little old blue-haired ladies got in the way."

"We didn't have a plan, dear," the man reminded her gently. "That's the problem."

"But it is what we've been waiting for," she spat, sending small bits of chocolate onto the table between them. "We've been waiting for a month to get in there while the library was unattended. The stacks were dark, for god's sake."

Her companion nodded wearily. The stacks had been complete-ly dark. It would have been so easy to slip in and slip back out. He knew this.

The chance had come to them out of the blue. They'd gone to the library to return a book—it was supposed to be open until three in the winter—and the parking lot had been completely full. That nev-er boded well, he'd pointed out, while pulling up on the side of the street. That meant there was an event. He hated events. But she was adamant. The book would be overdue unless she returned it now, and if the library was having an event, they could just walk in and walk back out again. No problem. And in any case, she thought, any chance to case the library was a chance not to be missed. The couple had spent idle moments for the last month or so talking about how to get into the building when no one was watching the stacks, how to get what they were after and then get out again, unobserved. It was a project—there was no part of the library that was unwatched during normal hours. Since they'd hatched the plan, he'd been in several times "to check out books," looking for a secure hiding place. He'd found nothing—no closets, no employee-only areas, nothing at all. And she was growing impatient and incredulous. Despite his protests that there was no place in the library for them to use as a base in their caper, she would simply not believe it.

So that day, when they waltzed up to the front door of the library, an old, venerable red, brick structure with an arched porch and big, heavy oaken doors, she was so preoccupied with double-checking her partner's surveillance that she did not see the sign.

"Damn," he said.

Her head snapped up. Tacked to the door was a sign announc-ing that although winter hours were until 3 p.m., due to the annual Library Association meeting, the branch would be closed at 1 p.m. to regular patrons.

"Well," she said, impatiently and absently, "what time is it? 12:30? We still have some time."

"Dear, it's 2:30," he said, and then got an evil look on his face and headed for the door.

"So?" she asked, and it dawned on her all at once. "Oh."

He opened the door, and she walked right through it, swooping right past an auditorium filled with the venerable patrons and spon-sors of the library, blue-haired old ladies and bald old men, all intently facing in the other direction, where the library's nervous-looking director was holding forth on the state of the library. The circulation desk beyond the auditorium doors was abandoned. The stacks were dark. The entire library staff was facing the geriatric horde. The pair was standing there, staring at each other, unable to believe their luck, when someone nearly bumped into them.

"Ooh, excuse me," squeaked a little voice.

They looked down to see a small, old lady in an ancient electric blue fur coat, her hair dyed an alarming shade of auburn, standing right next to them.

"It is much too hot in there," she said conversationally, gesturing toward the auditorium and headed outside with a significant look at the man, who obediently went to hold one of the heavy doors for her.

"People are leaving already," he murmured when he returned to his companion's side. She shot a stricken, longing look at the stacks.

He threw her book on the circulation desk, and the pair beat a tentative retreat to the lawn outside, where they paced in the cold like tigers. After a few more senior citizens emerged from the library's front doors, hobbling slightly under the weight of enormous purses, the couple made a more permanent retreat to the bookstore.

"I *really* don't want to lose my library card," he said, sipping his coffee. "Do you?"

"No," she said, throwing back her hot chocolate and promptly getting a nose full of melting whipped cream and white chocolate flakes. She swiped at it impatiently, thought for a second, and then looked up with conviction.

"Fine," she whispered in a steely voice. "Next year, when we go in, we go in earlier 'to drop off books,' as an excuse and—"

"We bring a blanket," he added eagerly, leaning so far forward their foreheads nearly touched.

"No!" she hissed. "No blanket. We travel light! We get in easy, and we get out easy."

"Right," he said. "And we don't bring library cards."

"No library cards," she agreed. "But we do have to bring books."

"But not books we checked out ourselves," he added.

"Maybe some of our own books…"

"Do *you* have any books you want to part with?" he asked pointedly.

"Right…we bring books…can we just walk out of the library with books without checking them out? Beforehand?"

"Sweetie," he whispered, frowning, "this life of crime you're planning is getting out of hand."

She nodded solemnly and wiped at the whipped-cream mustache she was developing.

"Okay," she agreed. "We wait for the annual meeting—"

"First weekend of December," he muttered.

She nodded.

"Right, and we go in earlier and we just don't bring library cards. We get into the stacks, we head upstairs, we get it, we get out."

She was still wondering how to look like she was returning books. Maybe they could grab some books from the stacks while they were in there, as a cover, in case they got caught.

He was watching the expression on her face intently.

"It has to be easy," he reminded her.

She nodded.

"Okay. I'll wear a skirt then. It doesn't get any easier than that," she said.

He looked around the table at the jeans she was wearing and smiled.

"That would make things a lot simpler," he said. "I'd wear a kilt, but I think it would draw too much attention."

She snorted into the remainder of her chocolate.

"I don't think anybody should ever have to pull a caper in a kilt, not unless they are an extra in *Braveheart*," she laughed.

"Sounds like a plan," he said and raised his coffee in a salute.

She toasted him with her sticky paper cup.

"Now all we have to do is wait a year," she said, and they both drank.

There was a fresh outburst of high-pitched laughter from the teens behind them. The man winced.

"Now," he said. "Would the criminal mastermind mind terribly if we got out of this café and browsed a bit? All this talk about books has made me want to actually look at some."

She got up, with difficulty, swigged the last of her hot chocolate and shot a look at the portrait of Virginia Woolf.

"All right," she said, edging past the irritated college student. "But don't get any ideas, mister. Having sex in the public library is one thing, but having sex with you in a chain bookstore is nothing I've ever wanted to attempt."

"Be damn near impossible," he said, inching his chair back and squeezing out from between it and their table, jostling one of the teens on purpose.

"Although tinsel and hearing Beyoncé cover *Jingle Bells* is pretty damn sexy," she grinned over her shoulder at him. He shook his head and, grinning, pitched his empty cup into a nearby trash can and headed for the shelves.

"Your strange kinks are going to get us arrested one day," he said.

She was adjusting her coat and purse after the melee that was the café.

"Then let's check out the psychology section," she said. "Maybe I can find some help in there."

Virginia Woolf's giant, disembodied head watched them head toward the big sign that read "Psychology" in sensible white block letters, her pinched face frowning after them in a mass-produced artistic rendering of disapproval.

Jingle Bells ended.

Itty Bitty Living Space
by Aden Penn

C assie nervously sticks her head in the doorway of Aunt Tiki's. Behind her, Lower Decatur bustles with midday activity. She is greeted by blessed silence and a wave from the bartender, Brian. He shouts to her before moving to dig around in a small fridge under the bar.

"It's okay, Cass. I unplugged it."

Cassie glances to the dark jukebox in the back, a handwritten "Out of Order" sign taped to the front. Laughing in happy relief, she walks in, taking her usual middle stool at the bar. There is a bottle of Negra Modelo waiting for her. Despite the sunny day, Cassie's clothes and hair are damp. It looks like she walked through a heavy downpour. Brian's eyebrows raise, and the shadow of a grin slides across his lips.

Cassie shouts back, reaching to tuck back her chocolate brown curls. Flashing Brian an errant grin, she pulls a pair of plugs out of her ears and sets them on the bar.

"Brian, you are a lifesaver."

"Were we getting rain today?"

Brian squints out the window, seeing the bright and sunny day. Not even a hint of rain to come. He sucks in his lower lip, trying to hold back laughter. For a moment, he almost feels guilty.

"Someone was blaring 'The Sky Is Crying' in their car. It broke through the plugs."

Cassie takes a long drink from her beer, glaring at the giggling bartender. Her eyes look tired. Lines of stress plague her otherwise pretty face. For a moment, Brian almost feels guilty for giving her such grief.

"I am not sure how much more I can take. I am causing more chaos than usual. There was the *Pink Cadillac* incident, which was nothing compared to the *Raspberry Beret* disaster. I used to love music, until the songs started to come to life."

She gestures wildly with her hands as she raves, finally stopping to take a breath and have more beer. Brian leans on the bar, no longer trying to hold back his amusement. What was going on wasn't really dangerous, just terribly funny.

"No one complained about the first incident."

"Yeah well, you really should remove that cover of *It's Raining Men* from the jukebox."

"Today is your last day, and then it will be over."

Those words make Cassie's face light up with joy. She tries to hold in her excitement, but she can't keep from bouncing on her seat. Brian lets the good news sink in before fixing her with a hard stare. He has to fake the serious mask his face now holds. His hazel eyes flicker with a golden light as he leans closer to her.

"And what have we learned from this situation?"

Brian is using *that* voice. The tone rattles Cassie, right down to her bones. A shame-filled heat flushes her cheeks, and she nervously fidgets with the tie on her sweatshirt. Her answer rides in on a tone of defeat.

"Djinns hate the 'itty bitty living space' line from *Aladdin*."

Le Masque
by Matissa Evensong

The city is alive, and the people are unworldly. Kirsten's painted eyes capture the scene of a Mardi Gras town at the climax of life, and her senses are so overwhelmed that she begins to *smell* the bright, colorful balloons, *see* the luscious flavor of roasted pig, *taste* the orchestra's vivacious tunes, and *hear* the fresh lavender flowers dancing as a set of blue bears hand them to her as she floats by the bakery. People are speaking in rhymes and riddles: telling lie after lie, story after story, in Pig Latin and mixed French, Italian, and Polish. It is an amazing sight, and she quickly loses herself in it.

"Come fly with me!" someone sings loudly and grabs her hand, lifting her off the streamer-littered street and onto a passing float. The float is an odd, wine-red kayak with gold spray-painted, flapping wings. Kirsten turns to smile at a seven-foot jester whose dazzling, belled hat jingles as he tips it politely in greeting. "And what might your name be?" he shouts.

"Kirsten!" she yells back, curtsying. As she bows her head, she notices that her skirt has become animated with drifting white clouds and miniature red planes doing flips and spins. "Oh my!" she shrieks, amazed.

A nearby woman with short, curly, red hair hears her and laughs, placing a Santa hat on top of Kirsten's head. "It's just magic," the girl mouths, her green eyes sparkling.

"Magic," Kirsten says in bewilderment, smiling brightly. "Magic!"

She twirls around, taking in even more unbelievable sights: a giant with a rotating head and two faces juggling baskets of singing children, flying houses, and a planet hovering above, mirroring the bizarre town. There are genies, one-dimensional characters, exotic animals, and mischievous pixies traveling the streets beside her. They cheer as the fluttering contraption goes by, and Kirsten smiles and waves like an excited child who has discovered the contagiousness of laughter.

Soon, she begins to smell oranges, strawberries, papayas, and kiwis. A bazaar suddenly appears as they turn the corner, and Kirsten skips off, entranced.

"Would you care for a golden apple?" A wrinkled, old man wearing an orange beret squints at her from narrow, black spectacles as she heads for the grape stand.

Kirsten gapes at the glittering fruit and nods her head, too astounded to speak. The man offers it to her gently, and she takes a juicy bite from it. He cackles maniacally, and it is the last sound she hears from that world. She swallows the piece in her mouth—

And the magic is lost.

Kirsten blinks frantically, hoping that her sight has just been delayed, but even hours later, she still can't see the magic. She looks around desperately for some extraordinary thing, but all she sees is an ordinary town, filled with ordinary people in an ordinary world.

She shuffles home, wondering what could have happened. "It all seemed so real," she mutters, not bothering to jump over the muddy puddles. "So alive..." The rain begins to fall from the once-white clouds, and the sun sets quickly, leaving Kirsten's new world wet and gray.

"B-b-beware—the Ides—uh, of M-March!" a man hiccups as he staggers drunkenly into the street from a nearby bar. Kirsten stops as she notices the similarity between him and the elder with the golden apple.

"Wait!" she calls, jogging to catch up. A few feet from the drunkard, Kirsten trips on a silent figure sleeping in a doorway. "My goodness, I apologize, milady!" The shadow helps her to her feet.

"Oh, it's all right," she says impassively. She glances in the direction where the old man has gone, but he is nowhere to be seen. Kirsten sighs and dusts her tattered skirt.

"Terribly sorry, uh—"

"Kirsten," she states, letting go of the soft, warm hand.

"Roderick." The hand goes to remove a red cap dotted with numerous holes. Beneath it, a pair of striking blue eyes, a thin, chiseled face, and a frail but sincere smile peek shyly.

Out of the corner of her eye, she spots the drunkard re-entering the main street and jolts in his direction.

"Hold on!" Roderick shouts after her. "I haven't properly apologized!"

"No need!" Kirsten shouts back, quickly advancing on the old man's haphazard walk. Suddenly he goes around the bend, and Kirsten slips in surprise. She watches the man entering a brightly lit shop and slowly rises from the cobblestone street. Hesitantly approaching the building, she spots an eccentric-looking sign: *Boutique de Masque.*

She is overcome with relief and excitement as she recognizes the shop's elaborate window display. "I know this boutique!" Kirsten hurriedly opens the door. "Maybe I can get back to it through here!"

"No, child," a familiar guffaw erupts from the back of the crowded room. "You cannot go back, but if you buy one of my masks, you will be able to see the magic once more."

"Just name your price, sir. I'll pay anything!" she pleads.

"You must pick a mask first, Kirsten."

She does not wonder how he knows her name, nor does she ask how he had come from the other world. Instead, she begins looking for a certain mask she had glimpsed on a passerby at the festival.

After examining each single mask, she finds the one. It is pure white and covered with sketches of black roses, sequins, and loose glitter. A small bouquet of soft, wispy feathers sticks out from above the left eye and a cascade of tiny, blossoming roses lines the same side.

"This one," she whispers, staring in awe. The man nods, a mad gleam in his eyes. She empties her purse and dances gleefully to a wall of mirrors. Kirsten takes her time adjusting the mask so it fits perfectly and is amazed to witness the change in her appearance. Her hair appears neater and lustrous, her figure, trim and elegant. And her eyes are sharp and alluring. She scurries out of the shop, wondering what else will change.

But everything seems colorless and dark. The sky is black; the puddles look like tar, and the moon is looming and spiteful.

"Kirsten!" Roderick moves toward her tentatively, unsure that it is truly her.

"Roderick?" Kirsten hears him, but does not see.

"I'm right here," he answers, standing in front of her with concerned eyes. "Can't you see me?"

She reaches out but feels nothing. "No."

"What happened?" he asks, dragging his fingers over the sparkling surface of her mask. "Why are you wearing this?"

"I..." Kirsten doesn't know what to say. "I don't know. I guess I just wanted to live in a better world."

"But you are!" Roderick answers, startled. "Take a look around, and you'll see all the incredible things this world has to offer." He takes her hand, and though Kirsten can't see him or consciously feel him, she knows where he is leading her and follows.

They walk to a small hill above town, and he pulls the mask off, throwing it to the ground. It shatters, and he stares into her bright, inquisitive eyes. Her face is pallid but soft and full of hope. Her thin mouth gapes as she sees him standing in front of her, the great world and sunset behind him, realizing that he is no ordinary boy, and this is no ordinary world.

Lost and Found
by Sasha Katz

The air is warm and stale, and it smells of mildew. Dust motes are drifting lazily across the beams of sunlight from the tall windows, but it's not quite enough light for my liking. Not being a very social creature, I have decided to spend my free Saturday in the cavernous old oak library. It's peaceful here, and I have nothing better to do.

The story I'm reading has just gotten to an exciting part, and, for seemingly no reason at all, I look up. I do not know what pulled me from the book I was so absorbed in, but there, three desks from my left, sits a loaf of bread. It is an unremarkable loaf of plain, white bread, and yet there it is, on a desk in the middle of a large and mostly empty library, completely alone. Just sitting there. *This should not be here*, I think. *Should I throw it away? But what if someone comes looking for it? I don't want to be accused of stealing someone's bread.* These thoughts plague me as the minutes roll by, and I sit, frozen by indecision.

I conjecture that I am making too much out of nothing. I try to concentrate on the book in front of me but quickly realize that continued studies are a futile cause, as my thoughts, as well as my eyes, keep wandering back to that loaf of bread, just three desks away. My mind is rapidly concocting parables and tales of intrigue centered on this one loaf of bread. *Is this manna from the heavens left for the learned downtrodden? Is someone missing it right now, regretting the sandwiches that will never be? Or was it left by some moneyed personage who will never even notice it is gone?*

I can take it no more. *Let me turn this loaf over to the authorities and be done with it!* I stand up and walk slowly over toward the bread, trying not to look too intent on reaching it. To my disappointment, I spot no one concealed in the rows of bookshelves, my last hope of

reprieve gone. This bread is my responsibility now. Taking a deep breath, I pick up this accursed loaf by the excess plastic at the opening of the bag. It has never been opened. My mind still reeling, I carry the loaf as quickly as I can manage, while still looking nonchalant about the whole mess.

At the tall front desk, a harsh-looking librarian in cat's-eye glasses is peering down at me. I explain that the bread was left on a table, and that maybe she would want to put it in lost and found for a day or two. She admonishes me, even after my repeated attempts at explaining my disassociation with said loaf. After listening to her lecture on food-damage to books, I thank her and excuse myself, leaving the loaf in the hands of fate.

It only now occurs to me that I may have done the wrong thing. *Would it not have been fitting for me to take the loaf? If not just for a bit of closure? Will I always be left wondering how the story ended, as much a mystery as it began? Did the bespectacled librarian throw it away? Did the mysterious loaf end up in lost and found? What role did I play in the grander scheme of things?* I can only speculate.

Love Is a One-Way Street Out of Hell
by Theresa Rogers

I try to lift my arm, but it is clear my sleeve has other plans. I squint at the table, and the quick shine of a spilled and congealed drink flashes as I turn my head to and fro. "This place is vile."

"Yeah, well." He lifts his glass, and the contents disappear into the wide open cavity he calls his mouth.

"then wave bye-bye"

"I keep my eyes on the crack of the light I see around the door and move

toward it."

I rip my sleeve up. I don't touch the fabric. "I suppose this all has a purpose." I reach for my glass, but at the last minute, I let it be. Who knows what lurks on the rim? I don't. I can't even *see* the rim. The only way I can tell my glass is there at all is because when someone walks in, for a brief moment, the sun dazzles off it.

"Chesney, does everything in your life have to have a purpose?"

"Lately, yes." I cross my arms and jiggle my foot, but he can't see me, so what's the point? "This," I wave my hand around, "being one of the reasons why it never worked." I stand up. "I'm getting the hell out of here. I can't even *see* you. Or *anything.*" I move and trip over—something.

He catches me, damn him. I'd push him away if I didn't think it might mean my own demise.

He rights me and chuckles. "You'd rather we meet at Aunt Tiki's?"

"You know I would. Brian knows what he's doing. At least there you can tell whether or not your drink has a *drink* in it."

He holds up his glass. I think. "What do you *think* is in there?"

"I don't even know what you ordered me. It could be camel spit for all I know."

"Then you didn't even drink any of it." He reaches for my glass and gets it on the first try. What is he, nocturnal?

"Can you see me?"

"Yes."

"Then wave bye-bye." I keep my eyes on the crack of light I see around the door and move toward it. With very few stumbles over whatever is piled on the floor, I make it. Just as I reach for the latch, a large hand closes around my wrist. I jerk my hand away.

"You all right, hon? You're lookin' a little unsteady on yer feet."

"Oh, for..." I shove my way past, and the bar spits me out onto the street.

Where, again, I can't see a thing. The light stabs my eyes until they water. *Damn* Ray for making me meet him in this subterranean cellar! Well, damn *me* for going.

When I can see without weeping, I walk north. My car is somewhere in that direction. I knew I should have written down the cross street. I wander for a while here and there. More people are disgorged from other bars. We wander together.

I turn down a street and immediately see my mistake. Before I can correct it, it's on me. *Large dog,* I think, before I am made intimate with the sidewalk.

"Brutus! Down!"

No need for the "down," as I'm about as far in that direction as I can be.

"Lady, you all right?"

I squint upward and see a hand directed at me. I take it. My involvement with the pavement becomes much less personal.

"Curtis, ma'am, but you can call me Quickbeam."

I stand. "Of course I can. Chesney Forbanter, but you can call me Moonlight." The dog growls. "Or not." I back away, trying my best not to look as though I did.

"Oh, he don't bite."

"But he does, apparently, jump." I take another step back.

He takes the dog by the collar. "You lookin' for something?"

"I looked for a drink, but I couldn't see it, and it didn't go so well. So now I'm looking for my car, and that isn't going so well, either."

"Nice lady like you drinkin' before noon?"

"No, nice lady like me peeling my sleeve off a vile table before noon. Person she met doing the drinking." I hold up my arm and inspect the damage. Something brown. I put my arm back down.

He sucks air in through his teeth. "That's vile. You're right." He laughs. "You at Reggie's?"

Large dog, I think
!!!
before I am made intimate
with the sidewalk.

I narrow my eyes. "Seems to be a man magnet. A fetid cesspool of testosterone. Know the place, do you?"

"I know the owner. He's my brother. Reg."

"Yeah. Um." I suppose my face could get redder if I smeared it with paint. I look him in the eyes. Nice eyes—brown and warm. The curve of his mouth suggests the lazy muggishness of summer evenings when lightning bugs float over the lawn. Or the boys who smash those lightning bugs.

He laughs again. "So I know what kinda place it is. Good brother, crappy bar owner. Aunt Tiki's is better; you want a dive that don't follow you home."

"Now that's just what *I* said. Nobody's sleeve has to be sacrificed at Brian's bar. You must be from here to know about Auntie's."

"Born and raised right here in Lower Decatur." He looks around. "What's your car look like?"

"Fast. Sleek. The kind of car you drive that just screams *cool*. You know. A 1976 VW Rabbit."

This time he laughs a long time. I like his teeth. They are uneven. I can see them all the way back in his mouth. But it's the laugh that gets me. I want to take that laugh in my hands and pull it, shake it out around me like a blanket. Never mind looks. Never mind job. Never mind relatives. I want a man who can laugh like that. Who makes *me* laugh like that.

The dog pulls, and he takes a fast step forward. "What color?"

"A sort of...um...yellow."

"A real *bright* yellow?"

"Well, yes. Except for the parts that are sort of a rust color."

The dog tries to bound forward again. "If I let go a him, you gonna be all right?"

I put my hands out in front of me. "Yeah. Sure."

The hound is released, and he runs right by me to the corner. "That was rather anti-climactic."

"You wanna meet my sidewalk again?"

"Oh no, once is usually enough. I'm pretty good with names."

He holds his hand out to me. No rings. I take it. *A complete stranger!* a voice in me says. *His hand is warm*, another voice says.

"I seen a sorta bright yellow rusty VW Rabbit just this way." He walks forward, and I walk beside him like I've done it all my life.

Just Another Night at the Drunken Dog
by Matissa Evensong

The huge oak doors to the Drunken Dog tavern swung open with a groan. From the windy, late fall night came one dark gray-skinned and silvery white-haired Drow with one flighty-looking nymph and a four-inch-tall, emerald-green blur. The Drow looked around then headed straight for the bar. The nymph smiled charmingly around at all the hunched, bulky figures and glided toward the stage where a young bard was playing a haphazard tune on a harp. The green blur, a fairy, began to circle around the head of a weary-looking soldier, giggling.

"You mind taming your familiar?" the bartender asked the Drow as he slammed a mug of ale down in front of her.

"Not my familiar," the Drow answered, watching the man through her bangs. "The squirrel is mine." And, indeed, there was a squirrel curled up on the rafter above the Drow's head.

"Hey!" the bartender shouted to the fairy. "Stop harassing the patrons."

"Zayza!" the Drow yelled. "I swear to Chaos if you *don't stop,* I'm getting my Sphinx hair net!"

The green blur zipped over to the Drow. "You ruin all my fun, Aisling," she pouted in a high-pitched huff.

"You couldn't sleep with him anyway; you're four inches tall." Aisling eyed the nymph weaving between the tables, starting to hum while she swung her hips. "If she starts dancing, Chaos help me, I'll kill her. All I want is a drink and a meal. But you two keep getting me kicked out of every Chaos-blessed tavern in the world."

"Then why do you stay with us?" Zayza settled on Aisling's shoulder. "You could just ditch us."

"And watch you two get killed?" she grunted. "Yes, exactly the way to go about redeeming my soul."

"Well, that's your problem," the fairy snorted. "I can't believe you got tricked into giving your soul to a demon. I thought Mages were supposed to be better than that."

"Sure, announce to the whole tavern I'm soulless. Thanks so much, Zayza," Aisling growled, ready to sic her familiar on the pixie.

"You're welcome. Can I go flirt with that half-elf now?"

"Just don't get us kicked out," Aisling muttered. That's when she heard it, the startling air of a gypsy song. She dropped her head to the bar and groaned. She peeked out from under an arm to see the least-welcomed sight in the world: Phaedra, the nymph, was going to dance.

Within minutes, Phaedra was weaving through the tables, singing about swimming in a stream with only the water as her covering and wiggling her hips to tempt men. Aisling knew Phaedra didn't mean to make every man in the tavern stare and drool, but gods, that stupid, built-in need to show off that all nymphs had was going to be the death of her. And if she died without a soul, Aisling didn't want to think about it. The hooting began when Phaedra draped herself over the same half-elf Zayza was hitting on.

"Hey!" The high-pitched shout split the air. "Back *off*, Phaedra!"

"You buzz off, *gnat*. I'm trying to perform."

"This is going to get ugly," Aisling muttered and dumped a handful of gold coins onto the bar. "That'll cover what's going to happen soon and one more mug of ale." She raised the drink to her lips and listened to the fight that was almost scripted.

"Perform?! Perform?! You're trying to steal my man!"

"He's not yours, short stuff; he can't be. He's human-sized!"

"So? That doesn't mean you need to shuffle in here, waving your hips and shoving your breasts in his face!"

"I was doing the Kajia Majio, for your information, not a shuffle," Phaedra snapped, a hand shooting out to grab the fairy. Of course there was no way she could catch the fey. She chasing the little green shape all over the tavern. This meant knocking into tables, people, and whatever was hanging on the walls. When the bartender glared at Aisling, she finished her ale and rose to her feet. She picked up her dark oak staff from the floor. She slammed the bottom against the floorboards twice, and Phaedra froze as if struck.

"You said you wouldn't do that again," Phaedra countered fear-

fully. Aisling raised one eyebrow. "You *promised!*"

"Actually, I believe she said only if you don't make her mad," Zayza hummed, wings glowing golden-green as she darted around Phaedra's head. "Guess you made her mad."

Aisling whistled once, and Zayza screamed.

"Not fair!" Zayza yelled, banging against the door, trying to escape the red squirrel that was stalking the pixie. "You promised you wouldn't sic him on me!"

"Only if you didn't make her mad," Phaedra retorted as she opened the door for the fairy who zipped out to escape the squirrel. She glared at Aisling as she strode out of the tavern. Aisling followed. On the way, she felt the reassuring weight of her familiar drop onto her shoulder.

"Sorry about the mess," she called to the barkeep and then slammed the door.

Saving Grace
by Shari Smith

I'd been following Grace for an hour now, watching her work, and I had to admit, she had style.

She had a confident stride for such a petite woman. Her waist-length, mousey hair always appeared to be billowing behind her, no matter which way the wind blew, and she never looked uncomfortable in the long, black leather coat that hung from her shoulders. She wore no makeup or jewelry; she possessed nothing but piercing gray eyes.

She clamped her strong hand on my shoulder as I crossed the street and yanked me back to the curb. There were honking horns and screeching brakes, and she looked at me as if I was a foolish child who had carelessly let go of her mother's hand to skip across a busy road.

I didn't know why I was still following her. I did know that she seemed to be permanently overcast on this, the brightest of days, and yet she paused beside a pile of crumpled newspapers in a doorway and extended her hand to the homeless man within. Carrying a shadow with you wherever you go must help you see what other people find so easy to ignore. The old tramp got to his feet and gave her a nod of gratitude.

She walked on, and we both followed her. She had a magnetic pull. A powerful gust of wind sent her coattails flapping behind her. On the other side of the street, the air was still.

She passed by a young woman, who was busy rummaging in her purse, and deliberately bumped right into her. The woman staggered backward and scowled at Grace before opening her mouth to tell her to watch where she's going. There was a loud crash, and we turned to see a plant pot had been knocked off a windowsill high above.

"I was standing there! Oh my god, you just saved my life."

Grace smiled at her and nodded back to the spot where the pot landed.

"Look again."

That's when I saw the woman's body, broken and bloody on the pavement. There she was, dead on the ground, and there she was again, standing at my side.

We all looked to Grace for an explanation.

"You were killed by a falling plant pot." She turned to the homeless man. "You just had enough and gave up the fight." And finally, she looked me in the eye. "And you should really look before stepping out into the road."

Grace turned and strode around the corner into a side street and walked all the way down it, even though it was a dead end.

We wondered what was going to happen now. Grace turned as soon as she reached the wall closing off the end of the side street and leaned back against it, arms folded across her chest. She looked faintly bored.

"So, what now?" the young woman asked anxiously.

The ever-present wind picked up, and the dreariness was washed out by dazzling, white light. I turned and saw the light fading away, the wind becoming a mild breeze, and a figure stepping forward. He was dressed in pale blue and had large, white-feathered wings, like those of a swan, folded neatly at his back.

We all looked at him and then back to Grace. The dark figure turned her gray eyes to the young woman and nodded toward the man I could only describe as an angel.

"You're with him. Go on."

The woman looked at peace as she smiled with relief at Grace, who still looked immensely disinterested, and then approached the angel. The feathered wings spread and enveloped her as she stepped into his arms.

Another brilliant flash of light as the wind picked up again signified the departure of the angel and the arrival of another. This one was a kindly looking elderly woman wearing pale yellow and stretching out her elegant wings behind her.

We remaining two souls, pulled from our dead or dying bodies that afternoon, looked again at Grace for direction as the wind died down.

"You," Grace said as she looked at the homeless man. "She's yours. Get going."

The vagrant shuffled toward his angel, and the light swallowed them both up. The blustery swirl of wind snaked around the two of them, and the light faded into nothing.

We were left with the dreariness we had wandered in before, beneath the black cloud, and Grace finally introduced herself.

"I'm Grace. What do you want to go by?"

"My name's Anne," I said as I wondered why the light had gone and the angels with it.

"No," Grace said, "come up with something else."

"What?" I blinked as I looked behind me to the spot where the two angels had appeared moments earlier. "I don't understand. Why aren't I going with them?"

I turned back to Grace for an explanation and saw the reason. She stood before me, knowing smile on her face and black leather coat spread wide behind her like the wings of a bat.

"I think you know why."

Short Stories

Lucy Too
by Tamela J. Ritter

Crystal couldn't really call what she was doing "running away," could she? No, in order for her to be running away, she'd have to have something she was running from, a place she was running to, and more importantly, someone to miss her when she was gone. No, Crystal wasn't running away. She was just getting away.

A year and a half before when she moved to Houston, that had been running away, and, as it turned out, no one came looking for her at all. So when she escaped for her first trip to New Orleans, she wasn't looking for anything or anyone. Just herself. She knew she had left bits of herself somewhere, and New Orleans was as good a place as any to begin the search for where those bits had migrated.

She was not off to a good start as she drove along I-10 and couldn't find the French Quarter. If she couldn't even find that, what hope was there for her? Being young and not speaking any French, she drove by the signs that advised exiting for *Vieux Carré* several times before she took a chance and wound up somewhere close to Esplanade Boulevard. After that, she was in the Quarter, and there was no turning back.

The minute she got out of her car, she felt it. The rightness of New Orleans washed over her. The pieces of her that were missing—she felt them at her fingertips, but she also felt pieces she didn't even know she had lost. The sense of *home* shrouded her skin and raised the hair on her arms and neck. She *belonged* here, and there was nothing she couldn't become, nothing she couldn't do. Except find a place to stay.

This trip was to be an adventure. One doesn't call ahead on a quest. There is no making of reservations for voyages into the unknown. Sadly, there were also "No Vacancies" and atrocious prices for spontaneity and flights of fancy. And while she pretended she liked living on the edge, she was also practical—and poor.

Swallowing hard, an anxiety attack creeping up from the pit of her stomach, she continued to explore the Quarter. If she were going to be sleeping in her car, she'd like to at least see the neighborhood first.

She was not one to fall in love easily, but then again, they don't call it The Big Easy for nothing! She loved it all: the cracked, crooked sidewalks, the ivy spinning around the ironworks, the tropical-colored houses, and the gates that sometimes gave the average passerby a peek into the stunning foliaged courtyards that were like secret gardens for her fertile imagination.

The shops were quaint, and she spent hours just looking at things that were as foreign to her as if she were in another country. After visiting a curio place that sold everything from a lighter to a coffee mug with a bare-breasted, beaded woman, she strayed away from the tourist traps and made her way to the French Market, which, of course, is another sort of tourist trap altogether, but hopped up on sugar from the beignets at Café Du Monde, she wasn't complaining. Unfortunately, the amount of caffeine in her chicory coffee wasn't helping her anxiety over lodgings any as she strolled down North Peters Street.

Looking back, she couldn't even recall what it was that made her stop walking and move in closer. This was always how it was with her and her shopping. She liked to look, and then sometimes, although thankfully for her purse, very rarely, a piece would call out to her. A talisman would announce itself, and she would be forced to take it into her hand, to feel it, to sense it, and, finally, to own it. The thing that stopped her was not the talisman, but definitely a distant cousin. All the pieces were exquisite in the crimson and maroon walls of the African Tribal Shop. It was a tiny enclave of a shop, but it was well-stocked with art, and she got sucked in happily.

It was a long time before she noticed the eyes watching her. The only other person in the shop was studying her with curiosity overflowing from her milk chocolate eyes. She had to be about six years old, gauging by the missing front teeth in her smile when she finally caught Crystal's attention. The brown- and black-print sarong hung to her knees, and the beads in her three oddly placed braids jangled as she approached Crystal. Leaning in close, she whispered, "Is your name Lucy?"

Crystal didn't know exactly why she did what she did next; maybe it was just that this little girl was so cute she didn't want to disappoint her. Maybe she got caught up in the girl's serious tone and forgot who she was. Or perhaps it was that she saw the playful sparkles in the child's eyes and wanted desperately to play as well. Whatever it was, it made her lean down, cover her mouth as if astonished, and whisper, "How did you know?"

The girl squealed with glee. "I'm Lucy too," she proclaimed through her giggle.

"No," Crystal exclaimed. "That's impossible. I'm Lucy."

The giggling was uncontrollable now. Little Lucy doubled over, and Crystal got caught up in the mirth as well. It was then that she saw out of the corner of her eye the piece that she was meant to have. It was a figure sculpted from a dark wood of two people standing across from each other; their limbs intertwined and woven in such a way to look like a whirlwind. At first, she thought of lovers and wondered with her freshly broken heart why this piece would call to her. As she stared at it though, it wasn't about the people, it was about the energy they created, the give and take, the ebb and flow that inspired her. She almost forgot about the little girl with the bangles in her hair.

"Is your name really Lucy?"

Crystal tore her eyes from the piece and looked at the girl, faking effrontery. "Of course. Why would anyone lie about a name like that? If I were going to pretend to be someone else, I would be," she thought for a moment, "Sophia, Julianna, Anastasia, Lorelei, Boston, Detroit, Pitt—"

"Detroit. You wouldn't want a name like Detroit," little Lucy spurted out between the fingers covering her mouth and her hysteria.

"Well, what would your name be if it could be anything?" Crystal asked.

The girl thought for a long time before she answered, "Lucy."

Crystal smiled wider and held out her hand. "Well, then, Lucy it is."

The little girl stood up straight and took Crystal's hand. "Nice to meet you, Lucy."

"You too, Lucy."

"So Lucy," Crystal said. "What are you doing here all alone?"

Lucy looked confused. "Why shouldn't I be here? I live here."

Crystal laughed. "No, not in New Orleans, in this shop."

Lucy still looked perplexed but didn't have time to ask any more questions; they hadn't noticed the entrance of another person. Not until she spoke, "Imani, leave the nice customer alone."

The little girl instantly stopped laughing and scuttled away. Crystal's heart broke for a moment, then the little girl appeared again for a second, winked, mouthed *Lucy,* and disappeared.

"Oh, she wasn't bothering me," Crystal said.

"My niece," the woman said in a strong French accent, "is a rambunctious ball of energy that I just could not live without."

The pride and tenderness in the woman's voice warmed Crystal to her. She asked about the piece that she had discovered and found out that it was from Kenya and meant for artists and writers to stimulate their creativity. "Are you an artist?" the woman asked.

Crystal shrugged her shoulders and was instantly ashamed of herself for the gesture. "I have been, but my imagination has been... well...parched lately."

"Oh, then you must have this. I insist. It will be good for you." She handed it to Crystal.

Crystal agreed and felt reassured by the woman's promise. They concluded the transaction by credit card because Crystal didn't want to know how much her inspiration was going to cost her.

While the woman rang up the order, Crystal asked, "Do you know of any affordable places around here that have a vacancy?"

The woman thought for just a moment. "Yes, I think I do. It isn't in the Quarter; it's about a mile or two out, The Mazant Guest House. An old mansion filled with antiques and plants. It's where I send my family when they come to visit. Close, but not too close," she said with a laugh in her deep, delicate voice.

"It sounds perfect; do you know what they go for?"

"I think you can get a room for sixteen."

"Sixteen *dollars?*" Crystal asked, not trusting her hearing. All the places she had found that had vacancies wanted more than $100.

"If you want a private bath, I think those run you twenty-four. Would you like to call them?"

"Yes please," Crystal said.

Five minutes later, she had a room for twenty-four dollars, a brand-new, probably overpriced muse, and a brighter outlook on life in general. Being so excited that things had worked out, she almost forgot her new friend. She was just walking out when she remembered. "Bye, Lucy," she called.

The little girl was instantly there, waving madly. "Bye, Lucy!"

Crystal spent the next two days investigating all of New Orleans. The Mazant Guest House was not only cheap; it was also cool in a bohemian, free-spirited way. The rooms were a study in period and function, antique furniture and musty bedding. The bathtub was huge and ornate with brass workings and claw feet. Besides all that, they also provided bikes for their guests. So every day, she would ride into the Quarter and investigate a different part of the city she was soon beginning to call her city.

She knew the first night that the craze of Bourbon Street wasn't for her, but she did enjoy the dizzying multitudes of musical venues and spent one night following the flow of music among jazz, blues, and classic rock cover bands. Food was another source of instant connection to the city. Of course she had heard about Cajun dishes and knew a fair share about Southern kitchens since moving to Texas, but she had no idea that there were—at least in her investigations—nineteen different recipes for gumbo.

All these things made her fall in love with the city, but what really made her yearn to be a part of it was the people. Not the tourists who weren't hard to spot, not the beer-bellied men trying to recapture some past idiotic glory by pelting her with beads from balconies and shouting out lewd comments. No, it was the locals: The waiter who, in that slow time between the lunch and dinner rush, sat with her and talked endlessly about tattoos and vampires; the cab driver who, for no extra charge, took her on a tour, showing her Louis Armstrong Park and where to find the cemeteries she *just had* to visit the following day, finally depositing her at a club she never would have found without his instruction, where she heard the best fusion jazz band play until the wee hours. But it was little Imani, who wanted to be a Lucy, and her aunt, who helped her when she didn't need to, that she loved the most.

It was the fate of the town that she cherished. Fate that put her in the hands of people who seemed to know what she needed and seemed to know she'd never ask.

The night before the trip ended, she walked out of the Voodoo shop full of the fortune she had just heard, picking out the pieces that meant nothing, looking for the bits that would guide her, not noticing or caring really that it had begun to rain while she was in the other world.

She heard a familiar giggling coming from an empty side street she was approaching. She turned, and there was her Lucy, jumping and splashing in the large mud puddles. Her aunt stood on the sidewalk, just amazed at the energy and vigor the child invested in the project. Crystal, too, was mesmerized.

Little Lucy turned and saw Crystal, and her gleeful look reached its apex. "Lucy! Lucy! Come on! Jump!"

For a shining moment, Crystal imagined herself running, jumping, abandoning everything she'd been taught—all the lessons she'd learned from the time she was six until now. Then reality crashed down, and she smiled, raised her hand in the air. "Have fun, Lucy!"

She walked around the corner with a heavy heart. She should have said more; she should have told Lucy to always stay this way, to never let people tell her it was not ladylike or that she was too old, too responsible, too anything. Never let a woman who was too wrapped up in her own stunted growth to join you get you down...

She barely knew she had stopped, barely knew she had turned around. But when she found herself covered in water, laughing uncontrollably in the rain-soaked streets of a town that knew her better then she knew herself, kicking off her sensible shoes and jumping in muck, she knew she had found her true talisman, the piece that was missing. Her inner Lucy.

Of Blood and Love
by N. Apythia Morges

With an unexplained feeling of defeat, as if she knew her expectations for this trip had already shattered into nothing but dust—even though she'd only been in New Orleans a grand total of three hours—Elizabeth Keller sighed heavily and pulled out the complimentary map she had received when she checked in at the conference.

"Hey," she said to her coworkers who were checking out the menu at Muriel's in Jackson Square, "I'm feeling tired." They had had to get up at three that morning to catch their flight. "I'm going to head back to the hotel and take a nap before the kick-off dinner."

"Want us to come along?" asked Jane. The concern in her eyes let Elizabeth know Jane wasn't buying her excuse.

"Are you sure you can find your way back?" Kirsten asked over her shoulder, turning her head from the lunch options.

"I'll be fine. It's a straight walk, and I've got my trusty map in case I manage to get lost." She waved the paper. "You two enjoy the afternoon. I'll see you back at the hotel."

Ignoring Jane's questioning look, Elizabeth turned and walked away. The wrong way. She wasn't overly concerned about her lack of direction. After ten years navigating the streets of Manhattan, New Orleans with its quaint street signs and beautiful wrought-iron balconies felt welcoming—and much smaller than she expected.

She didn't really want to go back to the hotel, but she wasn't feeling up to socializing. Truth was, she didn't know what she felt right now, other than an unrelenting sense that something was going to happen, something that made her uneasy.

Wandering the European-esque streets, sightseeing, and window shopping were doing nothing to elevate the feeling of impending...

something. Instead, the air seemed to settle heavier around her, the sun shining not as brightly as it had a few moments ago.

What is wrong with me? she chastised herself. *I am finally in the city I've dreamt about visiting for years, and I feel like jumping the next plane back to New York.*

Determined to shake her mood, she began to walk with a purpose as she made her way back to Chartres Street. Serendipity always seemed to have its way with her, and today was no different. Tripping over a nonexistent crack in the sidewalk, she rolled her eyes at herself, spotting the sign above her head: Bottom of the Cup Tearoom.

Figuring a nice cup of tea would help, she opened the door, a bell jingling gently, and entered a small room filled with jars of unique blends of leaves, herbs, and flowers. Inhaling deeply, she ventured toward the shelf, looking for the perfect mixture. As she crossed to the other side of the room, she noticed a narrow archway with a tiny sign above it that said "Readings."

"Excuse me," she asked the blonde behind the counter. "What type of readings do you do?"

The one thing Elizabeth had been looking forward to was getting her cards read by an objective outsider. A tarot reader herself, she was having problems understanding what the cards were trying to tell her. She knew better than to read her own cards; it was Tarot Reading 101. You can't be objective about your own life. But her usual readers were insistent that her life was fine and, with hard work, she would get what she wanted.

She didn't believe that. She had begun to have a nagging feeling during the past three months that there was something important she was overlooking, something keeping her from feeling confident about the new path her life had taken. She looked down at the now-empty ring finger on her left hand and pushed back the numbness that threatened to overtake her. It was better than the pain, but she had worked too hard to begin to feel again to dare to think of the past.

She refocused her attention on the blonde who was listing the various types of readings available.

"I'd like a tarot reading please," Elizabeth interrupted. The request surprised her; she had been leaning toward a tea leaf reading, but the cards felt right, and she'd learned long ago to trust her instincts.

She was led back a narrow, dark hall. Instead of doorways, the walls were broken by little caverns closed off with floor-length curtains. The receptionist pulled the floral material back, exposing a small wall-to-wall table with a typical office chair on each side. The room was no more than three feet wide. Elizabeth sat down, her eyes adjusting to the dimness of the lone desk lamp as the curtain closed behind her.

"Hello," said a soft voice.

Elizabeth looked up to find a woman about her own age, with long, curly, dark hair and intelligent hazel eyes taking the seat across from her and felt instantly at ease.

"I'm Creola Dejean," the woman said, extending her hand.

The moment Elizabeth's hand brushed Creola's, a tingle ran up Elizabeth's arm. The psychic's eyes went wide, and Elizabeth tried to pull away, but Creola's hand held firm, her face full of the surprise that Elizabeth was sure was etched on her own as well.

Elizabeth froze, fearing to even breathe as the tingling increased. Just when Elizabeth was about to start shaking from the energy strumming through her, Creola withdrew her hand with a shaky breath.

"Well, that was unusual," Creola said.

"What was that?" Elizabeth asked breathlessly. While she believed the cards could be a tool to figure out a problem in the here and now, she didn't truly believe in psychics who could see the future. But she did believe in energy and the ability to tap into it, though for what use, she wasn't sure.

"I'm…I'm not entirely certain," Creola hedged. "I'd rather take a look at the cards before I say anything."

Elizabeth nodded. Cards were familiar; they were her friends. "I should tell you," she asserted, "that I read cards as well."

"I know," Creola said with a twitch of her lips. "I've been expecting you since January."

Elizabeth started. It was now May, but January was when she had booked this trip. It was the same day she had signed the papers that ended her not-so-happily-ever-after marriage.

"Breathe, Elizabeth."

The sound of her name, which she was certain she hadn't given, spoken with a thick Creole accent helped pull her from the precipice of her past. Inhaling deeply, she let the familiar scent of smoldering sage sooth her.

"It's not your imagination," Creola continued. "You're just blocked."

"Excuse me?" Elizabeth said, stopping mid-reach for the cards Creola had set before her.

"You can feel it, can't you? Just out of your reach?"

Elizabeth nodded.

"I believe the Powers That Be have chosen me to pass their message on to you." She gestured toward the cards. "Let's see if we can make them happy."

Elizabeth slid the cards closer before gathering them in her hands and shuffling the slightly oversized deck. She had to force herself to focus on her question, but the problem was that there were as many questions in her head as cards in her hands. She finally settled on "What do I need to know?"

Cutting the cards into three piles, she pushed the middle one toward Creola, whose lips twitched again.

"A middle-of-the-road woman," she said, before continuing more seriously. "Your desire to keep the peace and make those around you happy will definitely be tested."

Silently, she flipped over the first card. The Three of Swords: betrayal and heartbreak. Elizabeth willed herself not to glance at her ringless finger.

The next card was The Hanged Man. Creola looked disapprovingly toward Elizabeth's wrist while Elizabeth pulled her long sleeve lower over her secret shame.

Ten of Swords. Elizabeth only nodded, embarrassed that her pain was so obvious.

Creola placed the next three cards: The Hermit, Page of Cups, and Death.

She smiled gently at Elizabeth.

"It's not so good to withdraw so much. You will need to reach out to others, to open yourself to them," she warned. "Change is coming. You are about to be reborn. All the events of the past year have been preparing you for this metamorphosis."

Knight of Swords, The Magician, Seven of Cups.

"You will have to make a choice soon between them." She gestured to the Knight and the Magician. "Neither is as he seems, but both need you to secure their victory."

"Who are they and what victory?" Elizabeth asked.

Instead of answering, Creola pulled three more cards: The Devil, The Emperor, The Lovers.

Creola sucked in a breath before raising her eyes to Elizabeth.

Elizabeth stared at the cards. She knew what they meant on the surface: The Devil—the corruptor—would challenge the ruler, and The Lover—obviously meant for her—would be shackled to both, forced to choose, but it would be a choice of consequence. The sense of unease settled heavy in her chest, making breathing difficult.

"Do you understand?" asked Creola.

"Yes...no...I..." Elizabeth started and then paused, taking a breath to collect herself. "I will have to choose between the two, but I don't know who they are or what this is about."

"You do know," Creola encouraged. "But like I said, you are blocked."

She tossed the final three cards: The Tower, Judgment, and The World, reversed.

The impact of the cards knocked the breath out of Elizabeth as she recalled what she had seen that night her life was running from her in crimson rivulets against the white tile floor. *It had only been a hallucination*, she repeated. *It was loss of blood, and my mind wasn't right.* It was what she had chanted to herself night after night when she would scream herself awake. *Just a dream.* But suddenly, she wasn't so sure.

The next two days past in a cacophony of voices and static, like a radio with bad reception, but Elizabeth didn't attempt to tune in to the happenings around her. She felt safer in her numbness, life reduced to white noise in the background.

"Liza, talk to us," Jane pleaded.

Elizabeth forced her eyes to focus and was surprised to find herself on a bench in Jackson Square at twilight with Jane on one side and Kirsten on the other. She didn't remember leaving the conference center. Looking at the concern painted on the faces of her friends, she felt guilty for making them worry, but she didn't know what to tell them that wouldn't have them on the phone to her psychologist before the words completely passed her lips. She feigned cluelessness. "What about?"

Jane's eyes narrowed, but it was Kirsten who spoke. "How about the fact that you haven't spoken since Thursday," she prompted.

"I've spoken—" Elizabeth started, only to be interrupted.

"'Yes,' 'no,' 'fine,' and 'whatever' do not qualify as conversation," Kirsten countered.

"Seriously, Liza," Jane continued, "it's like you're in a fog, like it was when…when…" She didn't finish the sentence, but Elizabeth knew what the missing words were: *when Drew left you, and you tried to end the pain with a bottle of pills and a box cutter.*

"I'm sorry," Elizabeth whispered. "But I swear it isn't like that at all. I'm not suicidal; I've just got a lot on my mind."

"Such as?" Kirsten snapped, making Elizabeth wonder if she really cared about the answer. Elizabeth tried to remember the last time they really talked and drew a blank.

"It's nothing, really," Elizabeth said soothingly. "I'm just taking in all the material from the conference and thinking of how to apply it to upcoming projects."

"Fonts are not *that* interesting," Jane contradicted. "Even to you."

Before Elizabeth could answer, a shadow fell over her. She looked up to see what had cast it and stopped breathing. There, backlit by the streetlight, was an impossibly gorgeous man, with chiseled features and designer suit, obviously some model or actor or something.

The stranger locked eyes with her, an alluring smile spreading across his face. He nodded slightly toward her, a mere tip of his head and then…was gone. She blinked and tried to refocus, searching the crowded square for a man who should be so easy to spot among the tourists in their jeans and baseball caps.

"Hello? Liza!" Kirsten snapped her fingers in front of Elizabeth's face, who ignored her, still seeking out the mysterious man. Kirsten sighed, throwing her hands up in frustration. "I give up. I'm out of here."

"Kirsten," Jane said, exasperated, but Kirsten only shook her head as she stalked away.

Elizabeth thought she caught a glimpse of that long, honeyed hair in the crowd and started off in the opposite direction of Kirsten, but a hand on her bicep stopped her.

"Where are *you* going?" Jane asked, clearly annoyed.

Elizabeth tried to look around her dearest friend, who was blocking her path, but once again, the mystery man had disappeared from her sight.

"Damn it!"

"That's it!" Jane declared. "I can't deal with you *and* Kirsten. I don't know what the hell is up with you, but we are going to find a bar and start drinking until you spill all your secrets."

"Where is she?" Kirsten spat out impatiently, not even bothering to greet Elizabeth as she stormed through the bar and over to their table.

"Bathroom," Elizabeth sighed. She didn't know what she had done to Kirsten, but it was obvious the woman was highly annoyed with her.

Kirsten scanned the room. Apparently satisfied that Jane was truly not in hearing distance, Kirsten turned on Elizabeth.

"I don't know what the hell your problem is, Elizabeth," she hissed. "But I am sick and tired of poor, old you getting treated like you're some fragile flower just because you got dumped. What the hell makes you so special? I'm going to give you some advice: Suck it up," she suggested, "before you use up all your friends' patience. That poor, broken girl act won't work forever, not even with the men."

Elizabeth just stared, shocked at the animosity and harsh words coming from someone she considered a friend. She focused on the tone, because she didn't want to think of the words. She didn't want to think about why she was so fragile. "Dumped" Kirsten had called it—like Elizabeth was some cheerleader the quarterback broke up with before Homecoming—but Elizabeth likened it to having her heart torn out, shredded to pieces, then stomped upon, leaving nothing but a jagged, painful hole and a wish for death. "Dumped" wasn't sufficient enough to describe the emotional torture she'd been through.

Jane reappeared at the table, swaying a little thanks to the— Elizabeth counted the cups on the table—four Hurricanes Jane had consumed while Elizabeth sipped absently on her single vodka and Coke.

"What's up, be-yotch?" Jane greeted Kirsten. "You know, you were totally harsh back there! Elizabeth has some funky shit going on. The least you could do is cut her some slack. I mean, broken heart, horrible nightmares, and freaky tarot readings…who wouldn't be a little fucked up over that?"

"What in the bloody hell are you talking about?" Kirsten asked. "Never mind, I don't want to know." She waved her hand dismissively. "You promised you'd take me to your favorite jazz club, and I want to go tonight. Now. Alone."

Her frosty tone made Elizabeth cringe, but she figured she deserved it.

"Come on, Liza!" Jane said, tugging on her hand. "Let's go scope out some hot musicians."

"Which part of 'alone' didn't you get?" Kirsten asked bitingly.

"I think I'll pass," Elizabeth demurred. "It's been a long day. I think I'll head back to the hotel."

"Come on!" Jane whined. "You haven't experienced New Orleans until you've been to a jazz club, and I promised to show you all of the city."

"Yes, you did," Elizabeth conceded, "but you don't need to do it all at once. We're here for four more days. There is plenty of time. You two go have fun." She flashed Jane an encouraging smile, not wanting her problems to interfere with her friend's fun.

Kirsten just grunted as she locked arms with a fairly drunk Jane, leading her out onto Bourbon Street, completely ignoring Elizabeth.

Elizabeth sighed as she watched the retreating figures. *So much for a girls' vacation.*

"Excuse me," purred a deep voice in her ear. "May I join you?"

Elizabeth looked up, prepared to tell the would-be player that she wasn't interested in the game, when she realized it was the man she had seen in Jackson Square.

"Sure," she said breathlessly.

"My name is Tristan," he said, his smooth voice caressing her skin.

"Elizabeth." She offered her hand to him and was surprised when he raised it to his lips and placed a chaste kiss against her knuckles.

"What a beautiful name for such a beautiful woman," he said, a French accent slightly evident in his melodic lilt.

Elizabeth rolled her eyes. She knew she was not beautiful, nor was her name. She felt slightly disappointed that this specimen of perfection would use such a trite line on her. But then again, she mused, this was probably a man not used to having to impress any woman. *They probably fall at his feet.*

"You do not believe me?"

"Whatever," she answered with a shrug, taking a deep swig of her drink. Drowning her sorrows was starting to look like her best option for the night. She wondered how hard it would be to find her way back to the W Hotel if she got completely wasted.

He reached for her chin, and she jerked back, his hand lingering so near, but not touching, her cheek.

"I see," he said.

"Look," she started, "I am not interested in whatever game you are playing, so I suggest you move on."

"I am not him," Tristan said softly.

"Pardon me?"

"I am not the man who hurt you."

"Who says I've been hurt?"

He raised an eyebrow as if it were obvious.

Elizabeth, refusing to acknowledge his questioning look, narrowed her eyes and took a deep gulp, draining the remains of her drink and cursing the fact she'd have to get up to get another.

"Will you walk with me?"

Elizabeth sighed heavily. "I thought I already made it clear that I wasn't interested. Find another girl to torture."

"Torture?" He seemed genuinely perplexed at the word choice.

She rolled her eyes. "I am not completely oblivious. You are a gorgeous man, and you obviously know it. I am an average woman who is quite possibly on the verge of her second nervous breakdown, so I would appreciate it very much if you would just find someone else to be the next notch on your bedpost."

"Have I done something to offend you?" He seemed serious.

Elizabeth looked at him, not understanding the sincerity in his emerald gaze. She stared into his eyes, entranced by the openness she saw within them. She found her reasons for doubting him evaporating like puddles after a summer rain. She wanted, desperately, to believe his interest was sincere. Perhaps she had been unfair. Perhaps she judged him too hastily.

"No, not yet," she answered slowly. No matter what she wanted, she had been a stranger to hope too long to welcome it back so easily.

He cupped her cheek in his palm, and this time she did not object. His skin felt so cool, so good against her skin, warmed with the alcohol flowing through her veins.

"I swear to you, there are no games." His eyes penetrated hers, and she felt exposed before him, as if he were privy to her most intimate thoughts, the ones she only dared to examine in the deepest of night when she was alone in body and mind. She found herself wanting frantically for his words to bear true. "Will you give me a chance?"

"For what?"

"To prove I am not him?"

She eyed him speculatively; he was too perceptive for his own good. "I am well aware that you are not—" she said, unable to fill in the missing name. Her chest suddenly felt tight as if being squeezed.

"Well, now that that is settled"—a grin lit up his perfect face—

"perhaps you will give me a chance to prove it, just in case there is any lingering doubt."

Elizabeth sighed, feeling the objection flee her body. She was suddenly weary and not nearly intoxicated enough for her tastes. She was tired of constantly being on her guard. Staring into his deep green eyes, she surrendered, deciding thought was overrated and losing one's self in a drunken fog with a beautiful man who, for some reason, exhibited an interest in her may not be a bad thing. Her chest tightened, but she chose to ignore it. Drew was not coming back. It was time for her to move on. *There could be worse options than the man before me,* she mused, knowing the vodka was further influencing her thoughts but not caring in the least. *This was New Orleans. Wasn't the whole point of coming here to have an escape from my life?*

"Make it good," she said, standing and gesturing for Tristan to lead the way.

"Okay," Elizabeth said, dragging out the word, "why me?" It was approaching three in the morning, and she was pleasantly intoxicated: emotionally numb yet physically charged. It was the best she had felt in nearly a year, though she chose not to think about that too much.

"Why you what?"

Elizabeth found his questions frustrating and hard to decipher in her drunken haze. "Out of all the beautiful women in New Orleans, why did you choose plain, old me?"

"You are neither plain nor old," he laughed. "Quite the contrary, actually."

"Forgive me if I find that hard to believe coming from Mr. Calvin Klein model."

He chuckled. "If you only knew what all the other men in this establishment were thinking of you in this moment."

"So you can read minds now?"

He smirked, raising an eyebrow. That look caused a feeling deep within Elizabeth that she hadn't felt since…well, for a long time.

"But of course," he leered. "Shall I tell you what you are thinking?"

What she was thinking were thoughts not appropriate to have for a complete stranger, thoughts she hadn't had since her finger was relieved of its diamond, her wrists relieved of their blood. "By all means," she gestured.

He gently cupped her face between his cool palms. "You're wondering if I can take away the pain, if I can make you forget, for just one night."

"Can you?" She meant her voice to be filled with derision, but wistfulness had managed to creep in.

"I'd like to try."

The snarling was so close, too close. She crouched even lower in the wet grass, her head cradled protectively in her shaking hands. A second growl, even more evil, sent shivers down her spine. The two monsters collided in a rush of gnashing teeth and preternatural strength battling over her, her blood. She looked at her wrists, the old wounds pouring red down her raised forearm. It was the key, and they were coming for it. She could hear the heavy breathing and scraping of nonhuman feet against the stones as the distance between them shrank. Glowing eyes locked on hers.

Her scream ended abruptly as Elizabeth jolted up in bed.

Strong hands encircled her shoulders, gently drawing her back into bed. A velvet voice whispered reassurances as sleep quickly reclaimed her.

She groaned as consciousness, followed by an overly loud zydeco band filling her ears, wrenched her from sleep. She pulled the cover over her head to block out the offending sunlight then immediately sat up. This was not her hotel room, which faced west and was, mercifully, overlooked by the morning sun. A quick survey of the strange room confirmed she was alone and that she was naked. She moaned as the memories of the night before resurfaced: Tristan and her walking, arm and arm, through the square, coffee and beignets at Café Du Monde, a short drive out of the city in his too-flashy-for-her-taste foreign ride. More vodka, more caresses, more…everything.

She fought back feelings of self-loathing, heightened by the fact she had awoken alone. Spying her clothing flung around the room, she slid out of bed and quickly dressed, already testing excuses for her absence last night in her head, secretly hoping Jane and Kirsten had their own indiscretions to deal with.

Surveying the room one last time to make sure she had all her belongings, she spotted a piece of…*was that really parchment?*…stuck to the door.

My Dearest Elizabeth,

You will never comprehend the depth of my regret at having to leave you to awake alone this morning. If I could change circumstances so that I could have held you as you rose to consciousness, I would have done all in my power to make it so. Please believe me, and please believe that I want nothing more than to see you again tonight. I ask that you meet me in the square, under the lamp post where you first saw me. I will make this up to you.

Yours,

Tristan

She reread the beautiful script before folding the letter and stuffing it in her purse, deciding to think about it later. Right now, she wanted to return to the hotel, to wash off the feeling of morning-after regret that clung to her, that polluted her skin and irritated that still-raw wound in her heart that would never heal. A sense of betrayal weighed her down. *What have I done?*

She barely stifled the scream that threatened to erupt from her mouth when she opened the hotel door and found Drew perched on the edge of her bed. Her heart seared with pain as if freshly stabbed by a sharp blade; her knees weakened and she braced herself in the doorjamb to keep from sinking to the floor. It had been nearly a year since she had glanced upon the vision of the man she had loved more than her own life. And now he was here, before her, flesh and blood. She couldn't decide whether to run to or from him.

"Liza," he whispered, his arms held wide in a welcoming embrace.

"What are you doing here? How did you know where to find me? How did you get into this room?" The questions flowed from her like water in a fountain.

"Jane," he said simply.

She felt the blood drain from her face. Jane was someone she trusted, someone she felt she could confide in. The knowledge that her friend had been in contact with the person responsible for the gaping hole in her being, had told him where to find her, had Elizabeth blinking back tears.

Drew lowered his arms, a look of sorrow haunting his handsome features. Elizabeth ached to comfort him, even now, even after he had stood before her and told her that he didn't love her, didn't want her, that she was nothing more than a convenience to him. The memory of their last conversation together in Central Park, where she begged him not to leave her, promised to do whatever he wanted if he would just stay, and the feeling of utter desolation that engulfed her as she watched him walk away. Still bleeding from his stabbing words, the memories became too much, and her face was awash in fresh tears for an old pain.

"Oh god, I am so very sorry, love," he said as he swept to her side, holding her tightly to him. "I know you can never forgive me for what I have done. I never wanted to hurt you. I thought…I thought if you could just move on, forget about me, find someone else, you would be safe. But I was wrong. Oh god, was I wrong."

His words flowed over her but didn't penetrate; they merely crashed against her skin as their joined tears trailed down her cheeks. She felt herself split in two as the part that wanted so desperately to believe him, to accept that the pain was unintentional, battled with the part that knew she would never survive being in his presence again only to watch him walk out the door once more.

Fighting her instinct, she somehow extracted herself from his embrace and walked to the far side of the room. Settling in the high-back chair in the corner, she wrapped her arms tight around her, trying to contain the emotion that threatened to overspill, not trusting what might happen to her in the aftermath.

Drew sighed wearily as he sat down on the side of the bed directly in front of her. "I don't expect you to love me, or even trust me after what I did to you," he ventured.

Elizabeth snorted derisively.

"When I heard what happened, what my leaving drove you to do—" He seemed unable to continue. After a few moments, he spoke again, his voice hoarse with regret and other unshed emotions. "You have to believe that I only left out of fear for your safety. I honestly thought you were better off without me. I was willing to give you up, the one good thing in nearly 300 years in my life, because I didn't want to see you hurt. Yet, ironically, it was my actions that almost took you away from me permanently."

Elizabeth balked at his explanation, but then froze. *Three hundred years?* Her mind flashed to her dream, of two immortal enemies locked in deathly peril. Her breath caught as she looked at him.

"It's time you knew the truth," he began. "I worked so hard to hide it from you, to protect you from my life, but it was of no use. My heart belonged to you the moment I met you; both my enemies and I knew that. I was a fool to think setting you free would guarantee your safety. You must believe me when I tell you I did it all for you."

As he reached to encase her slim, shaking hand in his two large ones, closing his eyes as if to savor the feel of them, she sat perfectly still as though she could freeze time, stay forever in that moment with his hands on hers and never have to face the hurt she knew would come when he withdrew his touch.

"Liza, I am not what you think I am," he resumed, his eyes boring into her, though she refused to meet them until he gently lifted her chin with his index finger. "All those business trips I went on every few weeks, the late-night meetings, the early morning phone calls…I wasn't having an affair; I swear. I was…I am…I'm a werewolf," he confessed, his eyes drilling into hers as if he could make her feel the truth of it if he could just reach deep enough. "I'm *the* werewolf, actually. For the last 100 years, I have been ruler of the largest, most influential pack in the United States."

Her mind railed at the ridiculousness of it all while her heart ached to believe him, to believe that he didn't betray her, that he still might love her.

"There is only one other that matches my influence in the preternatural community in this country, and it has been during the past three years that he has decided to openly declare war against me," he continued. "That was why I had to let you go, to make you believe there was no hope of a future between us. I needed you to be safe somewhere that was away from me. From him."

It was what she had wanted so desperately to hear this past year, that her marriage didn't end because her husband no longer wanted her, no longer deemed her worthy, but because some outside power was forcing them apart. But though she might personally doubt her sanity at times, she was never so touched in the head to believe in werewolves. After all, she had lived in the same house with him for nearly five years, surely she would have noticed. *But what about all those business trips?* a voice in her head asked. *He was rarely home for more than a few days at a time before taking off again.*

"Why are you here?" she asked again, not knowing what else to say.

"He has found you," he said succinctly, as if those few words answered everything.

"Who?"

"Tristan," he growled.

She was relieved her eyes had been trained on their entwined fingers on her lap, for she didn't want her face to betray the thoughts swarming in her mind.

"And who is Tristan?" she asked as nonchalantly as she could manage, which was much better than she expected.

"He is a vampire," he spat the word out like poison. "He wishes to defeat me to join our people in an army so powerful that it will sweep across the country, enslaving all humans to his whim."

"A vampire," she muttered to herself. Elizabeth began to wonder if she was dreaming. Perhaps she had still not awakened from the night before, and her mind was playing a cruel joke on her, parading Drew before her only to take him away when she opened her eyes. What other explanation could there be for all this strange talk of vampires and werewolves and world domination? The realization that this was obviously just her imagination settled around her as burning tears escaped her closed eyes. She felt Drew's finger trace their tracks.

"What are these for?" he asked gently.

"This is just a hallucination, a cruel nightmare," she said, her voice cracking as she suspected she hadn't been wrong about the possibility of having another nervous breakdown. "I'll eventually wake up, and you'll still be gone."

He pulled her to him, wrapping her small frame in his muscular arms. "I'm not going anywhere, love," he promised. "I know I can never be forgiven for what I have done to you, but I promise I will do everything I can to never hurt you again."

He pulled back from her to look into her eyes, and she whimpered at the loss. Cradling her face in his palms, he forced her to look at him. "What have I done to you?"

Elizabeth could see the regret in his eyes through the blur of her tears, and it only made her cry harder. Giving up, knowing she would hate herself for it later, when he was replaced with the wound of his absence, she threw her arms around him, and he pulled her onto his lap, allowing her to sob on his shoulder.

When her shuddering weeping subsided to sniffling, she realized he was holding her to him tightly, one hand cupping her head toward his shoulder, the other making comforting circles across her back. She sighed involuntarily at the exquisite sense of rightness she felt in his arms. She knew she would do anything to stay there.

"Are you feeling better?" he whispered into her hair.

She nodded.

"Do you believe that I am not a hallucination now? That I'm here to stay?"

She hesitated at the second question, and his arms wrapped tighter around her. "I will not give you up again," he said. "Tell me what I need to do to make you believe me, to believe you are the only person I want. There never was another. My life is worthless without you."

Looking up into his chocolate eyes, reddened with emotion, she had no doubt of his sincerity. "As mine is without you."

He gently ran his thumb over the raised scar on her wrist. "Promise me," he said, choking on the words, "promise me that you will never, ever do this to yourself again."

She wanted to promise him that, but she couldn't. She knew she wouldn't be able to live through his leaving again. "I promise to try," she hedged.

"That's not good enough."

"That's all I can offer right now."

She picked up his hand that wasn't caressing her back and lightly traced lines on it. It was strong and thick and so different from the cool, long, nearly delicate fingers of the man whose hands stroked her last night.

She stiffened in his arms as the impact of the night before hit her. She had had sex for the first time since Drew had left with a complete stranger. A stranger named Tristan. "Tell me about Tristan," she whispered.

"Tristan," he hissed. "I don't know much about him before the 1400s. I do know he was one of the first to leave France for the New World. The Inquisition was making it difficult for anyone preternatural at the time, especially blood drinkers, as the humans tended to stay locked up in their homes, especially once dark descended. He made a new life and a new army for himself here in what was to become New Orleans. He's remained here ever since, easily thwarting any attempt at takeover from any other vampire clan."

Right, she thought wearily. *Last night's lover is supposed to be a vampire and the love of my life a werewolf. And I am obviously touched in the head,* she mused. Part of her wished this was a dream; otherwise, she would have to consider that perhaps Drew was no more mentally stable than she. "What does this have to do with you?" she asked.

"Werewolves and vampires are mortal enemies," he said as if it were common fact, and she was silly for not knowing it.

"Oh." What else could she say?

Seeming to take pity on her, he explained. "Tristan has set himself up as the despot by ruthlessly destroying any competition. He's grown restless now, though. In looking for new enemies, he's decided that it's only natural for him to lord over the entire preternatural community, starting with his strongest opposition, the werewolves."

"Starting with you," she corrected.

"Yes, starting with me."

"Why?"

"Just as he rules the vampires, I lead the werewolves, only I am more a president than a dictator."

She raised an eyebrow. "A president werewolf?"

He smiled. "I am less bloodthirsty, but I will do what I must to protect the pack as I have for centuries. I did not ask to be in charge; it just happened over the years."

"Werewolf," she repeated, not sure whether to play along. "How could I not have known?"

"I've hidden myself among humans for hundreds of years, Liza. You would have never known if I could have prevented it." He sounded so sure of himself.

"The business trips?"

"Pack business. Full moons," he shrugged.

"Full moons," she picked up. "So you get all furry and race around Central Park?"

"Not Central Park, but yes."

"Is that the only time?"

"No," he said. "I am old enough and strong enough to change at will. Sometimes, when emotions become too unbearable or if one of us gets seriously hurt, it can force a change."

The ringing of her cell phone interrupted them. She reluctantly extracted herself from his embrace and picked through her purse until she found it. Not recognizing the number, she answered with a hesitant, "Hello."

"My darling Elizabeth." Tristan's voice slid over her, forcing her to remember what it felt like to have his body against hers. "I was so disappointed to see that you had left. I would never have ventured away from your side if it were not a matter of utmost importance.

Please allow me to make up for my uncouth behavior."

"Tristan, I—" The phone was suddenly wrenched from her hand.

"You stay the hell away from her," Drew growled into the cell. She watched as anger raged across his face and then, suddenly, his face went pale as the blood drained away. He looked at her, so shocked, so hurt, and she knew Tristan had told Drew about the night before.

"You will *never* touch her again." Each word was forced out through clenched teeth as Drew was shaking slightly with rage again. "You want me? Fine. Tonight. Lafayette Cemetery." Pause. "I am going to enjoy killing you."

Her phone shattered against the wall.

"Drew!" She turned to see him convulsing, a low growl emanating from deep in his chest. She backed away, suddenly realizing that perhaps Drew might not be delusional after all.

"Get out," he snarled.

"No." Werewolf or not, she wasn't leaving his side.

"Damn it, Elizabeth." He took a deep breath, eyes tightly shut, hands clenched in fists. "I need you to go until I regain control. Go find Jane."

He was practically vibrating, seemingly growing larger before her. Self-preservation finally kicked in, and she stumbled out of the room.

She pounded on Jane's door across the hall, and when she didn't answer, Elizabeth pulled out the extra keycard and slid it in the lock. "Jane, Kirsten," she called out, barging in the room and stopping short.

Her scream echoed through the room before her mind fully comprehended what her eyes saw. Jane was lying naked and lifeless on the bed, her dulled eyes staring at Elizabeth. Pairs of pink punctures decorated her wrists, neck, and, Elizabeth noted, feeling faint, her upper thighs. Kirsten was on the other bed, her throat torn out.

Elizabeth crumpled, but she never collapsed onto the floor. Instead, strong, familiar hands caught her. Drew cradled her against his chest, and she buried her face against his neck, turning away from the horror. She barely noticed the door had been torn from its hinges as Drew ran with her through the hallway and down the stairs, not stopping until they reached his car less than a minute later.

Elizabeth was shaking as Drew settled her in, securing her seat belt. He bolted to the other door, and the car was racing down Interstate 10 before she exhaled. The vision of Jane and Kirsten had been burned like a sunspot before her eyes, so that Elizabeth could see little else. It wasn't until Drew was easing her out of the car that she realized they had stopped in front of a cluster of small cabins surrounded by swampland.

"What's wrong?" rumbled a deep voice. Elizabeth looked up with a start to find Kevin, Drew's best friend and the best man at their wedding, standing before them.

"Tristan. He killed Jane and Kirsten, and he…he," Drew looked at her hopelessly and then back to Kevin. A silent moment passed between them before Kevin let out a long breath.

"Let's get her inside," Kevin said. "Then we can talk."

Drew wrapped his arm around her waist, guiding her uncooperative legs up the steps and across the kitchen to a tiny bedroom in the back, closing the door behind them.

"Elizabeth. Elizabeth, look at me."

She raised empty eyes toward him, and he crushed her to him.

"It's real," she muttered against his chest. "They're dead."

"I'm sorry," Drew whispered. "I never meant for you to get involved in this."

"So you really are a…a werewolf?" The word felt foreign, heavy on her tongue. "And Tristan—" She felt him stiffen in her arms.

He slowly withdrew from her. "We have to talk about it," he said, though the clenching of his jaw and the hard set of his features made it obvious he didn't want to. "I need to know what happened. Everything that happened."

"I am so sorry, Drew," she started, the words coming out in a rushed jumble. "I don't know why I did it. I hadn't been with anyone since you, and—"

"Hush," he said, resting a finger against her lips. "I cannot fault you for being with another man, not when I pushed you away so you could do just that," he said, his tone clearly at a conflict with his words.

Elizabeth bit her lip and looked down, contrite.

He raised her head toward his. "I need to know if he bit you."

She felt the heat flood her face as she looked away.

"Did he draw blood?" Drew asked in a strangled voice.

She shook her head.

"Thank god," he exhaled, pulling her into a crushing embrace before peppering her face with kisses. When his lips finally closed on hers, all was forgotten in the rush of senses. He was her drug, and she was getting her first fix after months of withdrawal.

"Do you want him?" Drew asked, leaving her lips for the sensitive area beneath her ear.

"No." The answer was breathy but absolute.

"Do you want anyone else?" His lips brushed her collarbone.

"Just you."

"Tell me to stop. Tell me to leave, and I will," he said against her skin.

"No. Never."

"You should," he continued. "I don't deserve you. I've done nothing but cause you pain, put you in danger—"

She silenced his argument with a kiss, telling him with her body what she couldn't say in words. As long as he would have her, she was his.

She awoke to an empty bed, again. She blinked at the bright afternoon sunshine flooding through the small window and remembered where she was and why. *Drew.* She scrambled out of bed, dressing haphazardly, when whispered voices from the other side of the door caught her attention.

"You can't be stupid enough to actually go, let alone by yourself." Kevin was whispering, his disbelief obvious.

"This has to end," Drew countered.

"It will, but don't be stupid," Kevin implored. "The pack is going to be there."

She could hear Drew suck in a breath to argue, but Kevin cut him off. "You can't be such a fool as to believe that Tristan will show up alone, that this isn't a trap."

"Kevin, he *seduced* her. He used her to get to me. The game has gone on long enough."

"What if this isn't about you?" a new voice quietly interjected. Elizabeth recognized it as Tara's, Kevin's wife.

"What do you mean?" Drew asked.

"In the battle of light and darkness, the blood of the lover will anoint the king and he shall rule supreme for all eternity," Tara recited. "What if it is her blood? What if she is the lover?"

Elizabeth's stomach lurched. With a clarity lacking for so long, her mind linked the puzzle pieces until the picture was whole before her. The Lover. The Devil. The Emperor. The Dreams. Vampire. Werewolf. Blood. She knew what would happen tonight at the cemetery, what she would have to do.

"When do we leave for the cemetery?" she asked, stepping into the kitchen with the others, who went still at her presence.

"You are not going anywhere near that place," Drew protested, rising from the table and coming to her side, taking her in his arms. "You are going back to New York before sunset."

"Like hell I am," Elizabeth said, pushing him away, startling him with uncharacteristic aggressiveness. "You need me." She calmly walked to the counter and pulled the fillet knife from the butcher block. "Shall we do this now? How much blood do you need?"

"What do you think you are doing?"

"You need my blood, and I am giving it to you," she said plainly.

"Elizabeth!" The knife was torn from her hand and thrown across the room before she could blink. "You promised me you wouldn't hurt yourself again!"

"Maybe she is right," Tara offered. "Her blood may be what it takes for you to defeat Tristan."

"I will not allow her to sacrifice herself for me," Drew declared.

"Would you rather she sacrifice herself for you or be a victim of Tristan?" Tara asked quietly.

"Neither. She will be safely away in New York," Drew said adamantly.

"Drew," Kevin began.

"No!" he said with a finality that left Tara and Kevin looking at each other in hopelessness. "She gets on that plane in an hour."

With a quick kiss, he stalked out of the cabin, leaving Elizabeth to watch his receding back.

"This is suicidal," said Kevin, grimacing. "I'm going to go talk to him. You should get her to the airport," he directed to Tara.

"I'm not going—"

"Fine," Tara said, talking over Elizabeth. "I'll be back in a few hours."

Tara grabbed Elizabeth by the arm and directed her out of the cabin and toward the Volkswagen in the driveway. "Get in."

"No!"

"Get in." Tara's words were harsh, but her eyes were pleading, as if willing Elizabeth to read her thoughts.

Sighing disgruntledly, Elizabeth slid into the passenger's seat, slamming the door shut. By the time she had her seat belt in place, they were navigating the road, and the cabin was out of sight.

"I am not going back to New York. I will not leave him," Elizabeth declared.

"No, you're not," Tara agreed, stunning Elizabeth. "But he needs to think you are."

Elizabeth's fingers clenched at the corner of the tomb, her knuckles white as she tried to remain still, to not let the scene unfolding before her cause her to scream or turn and run.

These aren't monsters, she chanted. *They are people; they are Drew's friends.* But staring at the wall of wolves larger than any found in the wild, she had trouble remembering that. Others were standing on the side of the wolves, still in human form, including Drew, Kevin, and Tara.

Across from them, Tristan was smirking, flanked by at least twenty inhumanly beautiful creatures, some smiling nastily, sharp fangs glinting in the moonlight. "You are outnumbered Andres," he drawled. "Surrender now, and I might make the death of your people quick and painless."

"Let's skip the small talk and get to the killing," Drew countered. Elizabeth sucked in a breath at the cold indifference in his voice.

"I'd say someone was angry that I bedded his wife, oh I mean ex-wife," Tristan mused. "Whyever did you discard such a beautiful, eager woman?"

Drew growled, and Kevin placed a hand on his shoulder in warning.

"Did she tell you she begged me to take her? That she screamed my name until she was hoarse with pleasure?"

Drew moved so fast he was just a blur to Elizabeth. Suddenly the air was filled with snarls and screams, growls and groans as the divided lines came together in a rush of fangs and claws.

Too terrified to watch, too mesmerized to look away, Elizabeth froze, wishing she knew what was happening, who was hurt, who was winning. The battle raged on for an eternity, or so it felt to Elizabeth, still crouched in her hiding place. A noise to her left alerted her that some of the fighters had broken away from the main confrontation. Adjusting herself so she could see the combatants but remain hidden, Elizabeth peered around a headstone to see Tristan flip Drew, now in some half-man/half-wolf metamorphosis, onto the top of a tomb, pinning him there, fangs bared.

"No!" Elizabeth screamed, running toward them.

Both men froze, looking at her. The distraction was enough to allow Drew to throw Tristan off him. Tristan snarled, charging him, as they once again locked in combat.

Elizabeth withdrew the fillet knife from her back pocket, the one Tara had given her, its blade reflecting the moonlight, catching the men's attention. She held Drew's gaze as she dragged the blade across her bared wrist, reopening her scar in a river of crimson.

Tristan came at her with inhuman speed, his eyes lost to blood-lust.

"No!" she heard Drew yell from behind her as sharp claws dug into her shoulder, creating new streams of red as he pulled her toward him.

She screamed, fighting back as Drew tightened his hold on her, unintentionally widening the wounds. He looked startled at her reaction until he saw what had happened, what *he* had done. Her blood coated his hand as he extracted his claws from her skin, horrified that he had hurt her. She sank to her knees, weak from fear and blood loss.

"You've truly lost her now," Tristan laughed. "Look at her. She will never let you touch her again. She sees you for the monster you truly are."

Elizabeth looked at Drew's tortured face and tried to tell him that it wasn't true, but her mouth was too heavy to move, and the world was growing dimmer.

"Don't worry, I'll make sure she is safe once you are dead," Tristan said.

A scream rent the air as Elizabeth succumbed to blackness.

A rhythmic beeping eroded the blissful nothingness Elizabeth had been floating in, forcing her mind to consciousness. She opened her eyes and then quickly shut them against the glaring white light.

"You're awake."

Her eyes shot open at the relief evident in her favorite voice. Drew sat in a plastic hospital chair, his hands wrapped around hers.

"I thought...I thought I killed you," he whispered, his face awash in self-hatred.

"You're alive," she whispered back, in awe.

"I told you I would never leave you again."

"And Tristan?"

His face turned stony. "He will never bother you again." Drew paused, as if debating whether to continue. "It was because of you, because your blood anointed me."

"The Lovers," she whispered, astonished.

They sat in silence, too many words to speak, but little to say. Elizabeth fought the drugs to stay conscious, not wanting to miss a moment with Drew.

"Sleep," he urged gently. "I'll be here when you wake."

"Promise?" she asked, her voice light as her eyelids fluttered shut.

"For eternity," he answered.

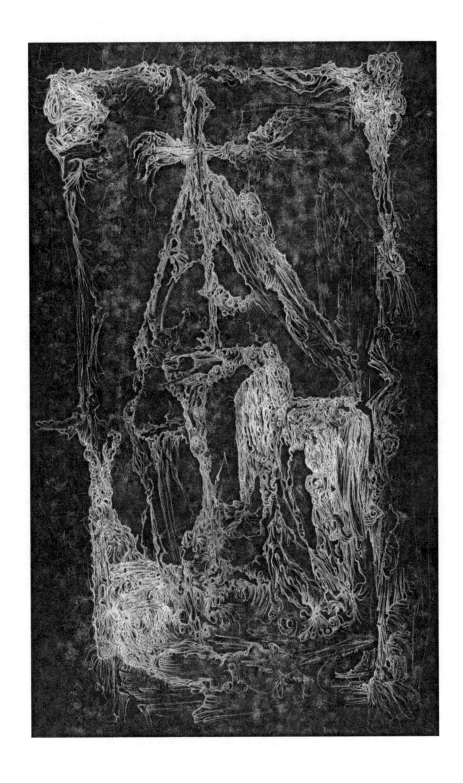

Laissez Les Bon Temps Rouler Again
by Charie La Marr

Diana Martinez tripped as she entered Aunt Tiki's, falling flat on her face. The bag of paperback books she was carrying spilled out across the floor. Brian, the bartender, scanned the titles with amusement as he continued to wipe glasses behind the bar. Romance novels: the single girl's best friend—well, one of them, anyway.

"Damnit, Brian! Will you get that freaking step fixed?" Diana swore as she brushed her hair out of her face and gathered up the books, shoving them back into the bag.

"It ain't the step, Diana; it's you. Why don't you give up those spiked heels of yours and get yourself some sensible shoes? Some of the ones like my mother wears?"

Diana scrambled to her feet, nursing her skinned knee. Another pair of stockings ruined. "Bite me, Brian. There's nothing wrong with my shoes. You know good and well I trip coming in here at least once a week. It's the step, Brian; the step is broken."

The bartender laughed. "Yeah, but the thing is, nobody else trips. It's the shoes, Diana. Lose the *Sex and the City* heels. You're too damn clumsy for that kind of shoe."

A hand reached out for her. Diana reached up demurely and took it. "Forgive the one who tends to the bar, *cherie,* I was a witness to the whole thing. I noticed you the moment you came in. The problem was with the step, not the lovely red shoes. If you should like to sue, I would be delighted to serve as your witness."

The accent was definitely French. Diana was almost afraid to look and see if the face was half as hot as the voice. She snuck a peek. It was even better than she expected. Dark hair with a shot of gray at the temples and tiny laugh lines in the corner of eyes the color of

Wedgwood porcelain. Teeth as white as blinding snow. And he was holding her hand.

"Listen, Pierre," Brian said. "If that klutz tries to sue us, I'll produce a hundred witnesses who'll testify she's about as graceful as the Saints' center Bronco Washington and just about as good looking. She comes in here and trips all the time. Trust me. It's the shoes."

"Yeah, well I do not," Diana said defiantly. "And I happen to know a couple of the Saintsations pretty well. In fact, I even tried out for the team once. I would have made it, too, but I was too short. So keep your rude comments to yourself, Brian. Mr...was about to buy me a drink."

The gentleman flushed a deep red. She liked that about him. A guy not afraid to show his emotions. "Ah, of course! Shall we share a bottle of champagne?"

Diana laughed. "Yeah, right. The last time Aunt Tiki's saw a bottle of champagne, they used it to toast the sailing of the *Titanic*. And we all know how that turned out. That was the same day they last washed the bar, too. A vodka martini would be fine." She glanced at Brian. "Grey Goose, please. In one of those clean glasses you hide for the good customers, if you don't mind. And two cherries."

"Make that two," the man said. "Only an olive for mine. Is this something American? Cherries in a martini?"

"I read once where the original martini had a cherry in it. I read a lot. But anyway, I just like cherries." She held out her hand. "Diana Martinez. And you are?"

"Forgive me, I haven't yet introduced myself. Gregory Matieu. And the pleasure is all mine, I assure you." He brought her free hand to his lips and kissed it lightly. "Come now; let's find a nice quiet booth where we can talk. Something tells me you are someone I would like to get to know better."

"We're talking about the back booth then. It's the only place in the joint where Brian can't spy. Brian, bring the martinis back there. Toot sweet." She giggled at her new friend. "I threw that in for you. You're French, right?"

His eyes sparkled as he laughed. Two more points for the stranger. "No, Belgian. But that is close enough. Most of us speak French there. The real difference is in our chocolate. We make the best chocolate in the world."

The way he said it, it had three syllables. Choc-o-late. She could easily fall for this guy.

"So what's a guy from Belgium doing in New Orleans these days?" she asked as she slid into the booth. "We aren't exactly at our tourist best yet. And Mardi Gras isn't for months."

"I thought I was here strictly on business," he said, "but then a lovely young lady literally fell into my life. Now it looks as though some pleasure may be included in this trip. So tell me what it is you do, dear one? Why all the books?"

"Oh, those! I'm a book reviewer. I work for *Romance Monthly*. I do a little editing on the side, too. And I teach creative writing in a local high school. At least, I did until the hurricane. The school hasn't reopened yet. But I get by on the money from the book reviews and the editing."

Brian set the martinis on the table and walked away. They toasted before taking a sip. "It must have been terrible for you, dear lady. The storm and all. Did you lose much?"

"Just about everything," she sighed. "But I do have my Yorkie, Brontë. I just bundled her in my coat and took her with me. I had to hide her at the shelter for three days. Brontë's my baby. I couldn't decide which one of the Brontë sisters to name her after, so I just named her Brontë.

"We live with Jacques and Jacqueline, a couple of street mimes. They're out most of the day so I get a lot of work done. Then there's Serena, she's an exotic dancer, so she works nights and sleeps when Jacques and Jacqueline are out. And lastly, there's Evan. He's a baker, so he's getting up when Serena gets in. They just trade places in the bed. It's kind of nuts, but I've actually gotten used to sleeping in a hammock, and Brontë hasn't fallen out in months. It was the best we could do. There was no way I was leaving New Orleans."

"A hammock! Oh, my dear! How terrible that sounds! So hard on one's back!"

"We all get along great. On Sundays, Serena dances for the Saints, so sometimes we get football tickets. And Evan always brings home great leftovers from the bakery. On a good day, J and J can pull down a couple hundred with the mime thing. So if I manage to write a couple dozen reviews a month and edit a couple books on the side, we're doing great. Better than most. It's a little crowded, but we share a lot of stuff. In fact I have a confession to make. I had to meet a publisher today to pick up a batch of books to review and I grabbed Serena's shoes by mistake. These are actually her favorite stripper heels."

A look of surprise crossed his face. "No! I would never have guessed!"

"Yep. Serena usually has these on while she's wrapped around a pole naked somewhere." They laughed as they drank.

"So, now I've told you about my merry band. What brings you to our fair city?"

"Actually, we have something in common. I am a reporter. I have traveled the world—mostly covering wars. But this time, I volunteered for a different kind of assignment. I wanted to see what happened here, firsthand."

"Well, you won't see much sitting in Aunt Tiki's. Quite honestly, this place looked this bad before the storm." She chuckled. "No offense, Brian."

Brian yelled from the bar, "Hey, you can always take your business elsewhere, sister. You aren't exactly making us a bundle here. Mostly, you just take up space so you can read your books in peace."

The man at the table seemed suddenly edgy. He finished his martini and ordered two more. Brian hurried them over to the table, pausing to look over his shoulder at the guy. He heard the remark about the journalist, and there was definitely something Brian didn't like about him. He didn't look like a journalist; there was no camera, and none of those vests with all the zippered pockets for film and stuff. Honestly, Brian thought he looked like some guy in a B movie.

Some new customers entered the bar. The bartender shrugged and went over to help them. Diana was doing fine anyway, batting her eyelashes like Madame Butterfly and flirting like Charo with a bunch of sailors on shore leave.

"So tell me of your fair city, Diana. I know it took a terrible hit from the Hurricane Katrina. It must have been terrible for all of you. Your Mayor, he is a good spokesperson for you. He has done a lot to help. In fact, I understand he is having a press conference at City Hall tomorrow. Do you know where City Hall is, Diana Martinez?"

"Of course I do. On Perdito Street. Are you going to be covering it? Is that why you are here?"

The man made some motion underneath the table, as though he was reaching for something in his jacket pocket. He looked her in the eyes. His friendly expression quickly changed to steel.

"We shall both be there, Diana, my dear. You see, I represent a certain faction who believes The Mayor has been rather hard on them. He has been very critical of the construction of the levees, and I am afraid that has been very bad for my client's business ventures of late. Nobody wants to hire the company who made those levees, not as long as your Mayor is shooting his mouth off. Well, tomorrow that will end. An irate citizen of this fair city will assassinate The Mayor. That, of course, will be you."

Diana started to stand. "That's what you think, mister. I'm not killing anybody."

She heard the familiar click of the hammer of a gun pulling back and locking into place. "No, you are not killing anyone, but I am. You will just take the blame. Now sit down. We will finish our drinks, and then we'll leave together. Two strangers who have found each other in the city and who are enjoying each other's company during a night out on the town."

With her hands shaking, Diana finished the drink in a single gulp. She reached across the seat for the bag of books, tucking one down the seat of the banquette and hoping her companion didn't notice. He held her close as they walked passed the bar. "'Night, Brian. Gregory asked me to show him around Bourbon Street."

As he dragged Diana down the street, Gregory laughed maniacally. "Tomorrow at noon, you will be found holding the gun that killed your mayor, and I will be out of the country by way of a tramp steamer leaving at one from your lovely port of Orleans."

"A tramp steamer, huh? What's that? A boat full of hookers? Kind of like a singles cruise?"

Around the corner, he shoved her into the backseat of a car and quickly bound and gagged her. She tried to keep up with the turns as they drove, but quickly lost track. She thought they were heading north, but she couldn't be sure. When the car stopped, he dragged her into a small building and threw her on a cot.

"There," he said. "Better than your hammock. Now get some sleep; we have a lot to do in the morning."

Around midnight, Jacqueline and Jacques arrived home from a busy day of street performing. Business was picking up somewhat. They cleared almost $125 between them. On a good day before the storm, they could have done twice that much by lunch. Half of the time people paid them not to mime. Now, nobody seemed to care if they built imaginary boxes around them or pretended to be pulling on the end of a never-ending rope.

The apartment was dark and empty. Evan was out on a date, which meant he'd get no sleep before he went to work, and Serena was off dancing somewhere. Jacques stepped in a puddle and almost slipped as he turned on the lights. His mime balance held him upright.

"Brontë! Where the hell is that damn flea-bag dog? Shit! How can such a little dog make such big puddles? Diana? Get in here and clean up after your dog!"

There was no answer. Only the sad little dog, dragging its blankie and whimpering to be fed. With the apartment dark and from the looks of things, Diana hadn't been home all day. Usually, she was either stretched out on the couch with books all over the place or busy at her laptop at the tiny desk they shared.

"That's strange," Jacqueline said. "She was going to meet with that lady from that book publisher this afternoon and pick up a new batch of books to review. I wonder what happened to her, Brontë?"

Jacques pulled a note off the back of the door. "Maybe this will tell us, huh?" He read it. "Diana, I want my damn shoes back, you bitch. Serena." It looks like Diana took the wrong shoes this morning again. Maybe she's still sitting down at Aunt Tiki's reading. You know how she gets when she's involved in one of those teary romance books she reads."

Jacqueline got out the phone book. "I think we should call. After all, Brontë has been here alone all day, and it isn't like Diana to leave her alone that long."

They caught Brian just leaving. "I don't know, Jax, she was here earlier, around six. She had two martinis with this guy named Gregory. He had a French accent, and he picked her up off the floor when she tripped in those damn heels she wears. Next thing I know, the two of them are heading arm in arm for Bourbon Street like long-lost lovers. You mean she never came home?"

"No," Jacqueline said. "And it's just not like her. The dog's been locked up all day. Did she say anything when she left? Maybe the guy was kidnapping her! Did she write a note on a napkin or something? People do that when they're getting kidnapped, don't they?"

"Sure, they ask the kidnapper if they can borrow a pen." Brian said sarcastically. "But hold on, I'll look."

He returned to the phone a few moments later. From the sound of his voice, the news was bad. "She left those damn red heels under the table. That means she was barefoot when she left. And there's one of those trashy books she's always reading stuck in the banquette."

"What's it called?" Jacqueline asked.

"*Married at City Hall*. Jeez, what a stupid book! There's a picture on the cover of this couple standing in front of a judge. She has a little veil on and she's carrying a bouquet of flowers. The guy looks like he's about to bolt. I would, too. The girl looks like Donna Reed."

"Who's that? Never mind. City Hall, City Hall. She's trying to tell us something about City Hall. Let me think. Hey, isn't there supposed to be a big deal at City Hall tomorrow? The Mayor is going to start naming names and start some lawsuits or something?" Jacqueline held the phone so Jacques could hear, too.

"What's that got to do with Diana?" Jacques asked.

"I don't know," Brian said, "But I think we need a plan. It looks like this Gregory guy is up to something, and Diana is in it up to her ears. I'll be right over. Start thinking."

"And don't forget to bring those shoes," Jacqueline yelled into the phone. "Serena wants them back!"

By the time Brian arrived at the apartment, Evan was home from his date and already got someone to cover for him at work. Between lifting heavy sacks of flour at the bakery and weights at the gym, Evan was a solid, muscular guy—the kind of guy wife-beater T-shirts actually looked good on.

His girlfriend, April, was a good, solid 200 pounds and about three-quarters of the way through a full-body tattoo job, although nobody dared ask her which quarter was left to cover with ink. She owned a motorcycle and hung out with a local biker gang called The Saints—what else?

Brontë was in the corner whimpering until Evan went over and picked the little dog up. She snuggled under his beard.

"Look," Evan said. "From what I hear, this is going to be a really big thing tomorrow. Lots of press and lots of people standing around. We've got a lot of ground to cover. We're going to need all the help we can get."

Jacqueline raised her hand. "I think I can get Max, that blind trumpet player who plays on the street corner over near Aunt Tiki's. He can help."

Brian sighed. "He's blind, Jax. What good can he do? Should we make him the lookout or something?"

Jacqueline chuckled. "He ain't blind, you moron. It's a gig, that's all. People feel sorry for blind musicians and they give them money, you know, like José Feliciano."

April's eyes widened, making the yellow stars tattooed around them look even bigger. "José Feliciano isn't blind? I used to love that guy. He sang that Spanish Christmas carol, right? I love that song!" She started humming the song to herself.

Evan almost hit her with the dog. "She was just making an example, April. Max isn't blind, José is."

"Oh," she said with disappointment. "Well anyway, I can get some of the bikers to help out. Some of them know Diana, and we can make up pictures for the others so they know what she looks like."

Jacques shook his head. "How are they going to fit in? Bikers... at a mayoral press conference? Won't that look kind of strange?"

"Nah," replied April. "Most of them are only weekend bikers. Eddie Green actually used to work for the Mayor, until that little incident with the marijuana in his desk drawer. Anyway, they can loiter around in suits and ties. I know! We can get some of those coiled white key chains and stick them inside their ears. Make them look like Agent Smith from *The Matrix*."

Evan hugged her. "April, you know, you aren't so dumb after all. That's a great idea! How many do you think we can get?"

She smiled sweetly at him. "As many as they have at the dollar store. Oh! You mean how many Agent Smiths! I'll start making some calls. In the meantime, you run down to the dollar store and get us some of those key chains in white. As many as they have. Sunglasses, too. They always wear sunglasses. And take that dog. It smells like she needs a walk."

Evan took off with the dog while April started working the phones. "So who are we supposed to be?" Jacques asked. We can't exactly go around dressed as mimes. We'll stand out like...mimes. We don't have a permit to work down there anyway."

"You can be tourists," Brian said. "You still have those Bermuda shorts and that funny shirt from that masquerade party at the bar, right? You must have some Mardi Gras beads lying around here someplace. A pair of sunglasses, a goofy hat, and a couple shopping bags from some stores and you'll be fine."

Jacqueline clicked her cell phone closed. "Max is in. He has five other guys, too. Deaf Paulie, Blind Mike, those two one-legged twins who tap dance, and Crazy Mitch. But Mitch says he won't do it unless he can wear his Spider-Man costume."

Brian shook his head. "You mean the two-legged twins who tap dance aren't really two-legged?"

"Sure they are," Jacqueline said. "But they can outrun you in a footrace anytime. Those two can move! So it's cool about the Spider-Man costume? I told Max, whatever."

The sun was beginning to rise when Serena stormed through the door. "Where is that bitch Diana? If she ever touches my best red fuck-me heels again, I'll kill her!"

It took Brian about ten minutes to calm her down, return her shoes, and explain what happened to Diana.

"Oh!" said Serena. "I know what I want to be. I have this really hot cat suit. Just like Emma Peel used to wear—you know in *The Avengers?* I loved it with Emma Peel, but I hated it with that other girl, Tara something. Brian, if I wear the cat suit, would you be John Steed? You know, with the bowler hat, the carnation in your lapel, and the umbrella?"

To see Serena in that cat suit, Brian would have agreed to go as the Queen Mother.

"Hey," Serena added. "I know these two girls from the Saint-sations. They moonlight as Strip-o-Grams. They get a lot of calls for the cop thing. You know, they bust into a bachelor party claiming somebody complained about the noise. They get everybody up against the wall and start frisking—"

"Okay! We get the idea," Brian said. "Call them. Have them in uniform and ready to go by eight."

So it was set. April rounded up six bikers to dress up like Agent Smith and wear coiled white key chains in their ears. Serena got hold of two cops who were at least double-Ds and barely fit into their uniforms. One of them brought along Billy Joe Stewart, her boyfriend and, appropriately enough, tight end from the Saints, who was dressed in cutoff jeans and a T-shirt that said "If you're close enough to read this shirt, Fuck Off!" Jacqueline and Jacques rounded up the two blind trumpet players, a deaf beggar who wasn't really deaf, the tap dancing twins with two legs between them, and a weird old guy dressed like Spider-Man. Evan came up with two friends from the bakery who looked like they had serious cocaine habits, but it turned out to be just flour.

Serena poured herself into the cat suit and even managed to do a little version of the Emma Peel flip with her hair. Brian obligingly put a carnation in his jacket and put on a bowler hat, which looked more like a hat some clown wore in a Mardi Gras parade. He twirled the umbrella playfully and stared at Serena's ass. Jacques and Jacqueline made dorky-looking tourists. They would fit right into the crowd. April and Evan somehow came up with a baby carriage, which they filled with water balloons.

"So what are we going to use for weapons?" Serena asked. "At least Brian has the umbrella. And the fake blind guys have canes. What are the Agent Smith guys going to use?"

They shifted nervously and looked at April. "It's kind of a don't-ask-don't-tell thing, but don't worry about them, they're well-armed. The double-D cops have nightsticks. Billy Joe has his football skills. And have you ever been garroted with a string of Mardi Gras beads? Everybody else can pick stuff up along the way. Just blend into the crowd and look for Diana. If you find her, just start screaming."

Brian checked his watch. "It's zero-eight hundred hours now. I figure we should start leaving at zero-ten hundred hours; a couple should leave every fifteen minutes. We don't want to attract a lot of attention to ourselves. The press conference starts at zero twelve hundred hours."

One of the double-Ds smacked him. "We'll start leaving at ten o'clock. The press conference starts at noon, you boob."

Brian started to say something, but bit his tongue. "Okay," he said, "that works for me."

By 11:30, the gang was scattered throughout the crowd at City Hall. Surprisingly, they blended in pretty well. They wandered slowly through the gathering, occasionally giving each other the pre-designated sign. They thumbed their noses at each other just like Paul Newman and Robert Redford did in *The Sting*. Evan loved that movie. It was his idea to use the sign. Serena thought the gesture looked obscene.

As April and Evan strolled through the crowd with the baby carriage, there was a tiny squeak from inside. Evan pulled the top back. Inside, Brontë wiggled her little ears and grinned happily, surrounded by a batch of water balloons. "Shit, April, you brought the damn dog? Tell me you didn't!"

"There she is," April said, pointing to the carriage. "I couldn't leave her home alone, Evan. She was so traumatized when she found out Diana was kidnapped. It's no problem. Once people look at the two of us, they're scared to look inside the carriage anyway. And Brontë's being a perfect angel. We may need her to sniff Diana out. Dogs are good at that, right?"

"Yeah," he said. "Bloodhounds are. Not Yorkshire Terriers. The only thing they're good for is tearing up blankies and peeing. Well, it's too late now. She's here. Just try to keep her quiet. We have to find Diana before something happens."

About ten after twelve, the gang noticed a commotion. It was Diana, dressed in a baggy sweatsuit and wearing the ugliest orange and pink sneakers anyone had ever seen. Serena gloated. *That's what she got for taking the red fuck-me shoes without permission.* Everyone took up positions as they watched the man push her forward in the crowd.

"Mr. Mayor! Mr. Mayor!" Diana called out. "Diana Martinez from *Romance Monthly*, sir. I have a question for you. When do you plan on returning books to our libraries? People need reading material, Mr. Mayor. Quite frankly, television is kind of depressing lately. Supplying the libraries with some good romance novels would do wonders for a community already severely depressed."

The Mayor whispered to one of his aides and turned to answer her. *People are still looking for places to sleep and this nut job wants romance novels?* he thought.

He cleared his throat. "Yes, um, I see your point, Miss Gonzalez, but—"

"Martinez," she called out. "It's Miss Martinez. Diana Martinez from *Romance Monthly*."

"Yes, Miss Martinez. Well, I have a committee currently studying the best ways to bring literature back to New Orleans' public libraries, but I'm afraid we have to prioritize, and right now food and shelter are our main priorities."

"So you're saying literature doesn't matter, Mr. Mayor? From Thomas Paine's famous pamphlets to the Declaration of Independence, our country has always treated literature with the utmost respect and dignity. What would this country have been without *The Midnight Ride of Paul Revere? Tom Sawyer? The Valley of the Dolls? Peyton Place?* I demand you prioritize bringing literature back to New Orleans! I demand a committee headed by our own famous citizen Anne Rice to examine the possibilities and bring books back as quickly as possible!"

By this time, the crowd was starting to get ugly. That's when Billy Joe noticed the gun to Diana's back and went in for the tackle. He got Gregory low, just around the knees. At the same moment, Serena jumped on the guy's shoulders and wrapped her thighs around his arms.

Brian watched in amazement. He didn't realize pole dancers had such strong legs. The blind guys started smacking him with their canes, and Jacques and Jacqueline used their Mardi Gras beads to bind his hands. April pelted him with water balloons. Even Brontë jumped out of the baby carriage, firmly planting her tiny teeth in his upper thigh, wagging her tail proudly.

Diana wiggled out of the pile and stood. "Mr. Mayor! This man was here to kill you! He was hired by some of those cheap laborers who put up those crappy levees and nearly drowned us all. He kidnapped me last night at Aunt Tiki's over on Decatur Street, and he was going to pin it on me while he hopped a Carnival Cruise Lines boat to the Bahamas. He said his name was Gregory Matieu, and he was Belgian. But don't you believe a word of it."

"Hey, I recognize him!" said one of the real guys with the white coils in their ears. "That's Estoban Cubana! He's a freelance hit man and paid assassin. He's on every Most Wanted list in the world! Interpol has been looking for that guy for years."

Billy Joe stood up proudly. "Yeah, well this time he messed with the wrong guys." He glanced over at the double-D cup cops. "And girls."

Within a moment, Estoban was handcuffed and led away. The Mayor led Diana onto the stage and held her hand high over her head while she clutched Brontë with the other. "Ladies and gentlemen, this little lady is a true New Orleans hero. She saved my life today. And I promise you, Diana Martinez, I will do everything I can to get books to New Orleans as fast as possible."

"Mr. Mayor!" A hand went up in the crowd. It was a tourist dressed exactly like Jacques and Jacqueline. "I happen to be an executive at a big New York book publisher, and I'll see to it a truckload of books is delivered here by the end of the week. And I'll call some of my competitors and get them to match my donation!"

Diana smiled and waved her hands at the crowd. All she really wanted to do was go home and crawl into her hammock and sleep for about week.

Brian slipped behind her and wrapped an arm around her waist. "Hey, babe. This is City Hall. We got the Mayor here and everything, how about me and you—"

"Not if you were the last man on earth, Brian. But Emma Peel over there looks kind of hot to trot."

As Brian went over to see what Serena had on her mind, Diana scooped up Brontë and shook hands with the Mayor. "Glad everything worked out for you, sir. You just keep on doing what you do best. Laissez les bon temps rouler again!"

Fairy Tale Sundered
by Julia Katz

It was three o'clock on Christmas afternoon, and Tara Kane found herself doing homework. Seated at her desk wedged in next to the couch in the living room of their small apartment, she pored over her paper on the intricacies of cataloguing for what would hopefully be her last class in library studies that semester.

In the background, she could hear the television narrating Ralphie's exploits as he tried to get his coveted Red Ryder air rifle for what had to be the fourth time that day. Her husband, Kevin, and their son Nate, oblivious to the fact that watching *A Christmas Story* over and over again was a monotonous pastime, were still in their pajamas, comfortably curled on the couch watching it. Kevin insisted on keeping this family tradition alive. Since he had moved half a country away from his family at her behest, she thought it would be best to keep her opinions to herself.

But she had to stop thinking about that, or she would never finish her paper. She shook her head and returned her attention to the Dewey Decimal System and Library of Congress subject headings.

"I miss snow," Kevin said, pulling Tara from her scholarly thoughts on Dewey. "There should be snow on Christmas. At least it should be cold."

"I thought you hated snow," Tara replied. "When we lived in Boston, you spent half your time in the winter complaining about how hard it was to shovel, how difficult it made driving, and how you could never walk more than two feet without falling on your bum."

"I do hate snow," Kevin amended. "One of the reasons I was so willing to move here was to get away from it. But there should be snow on Christmas. It's just one of those things I grew up with, and I miss it today."

"Maybe we can have your mom send us some? Nate would be the only kid on the block with a snowman."

"Nah, neither FedEx nor Santa could get it here before it would melt," Kevin sighed gloomily. "Besides, I talked to Dad last night, and they don't have any snow either. It's just cold and windy. Dad thinks their ears'll probably freeze off their heads when they walk around Copley Square tonight. Come to think of it, I miss that too. It was a nice family tradition to walk around and see all the Christmas lights."

"Maybe we can go walk around the French Quarter tonight. It's not Copley Square, but it'll be lovely, and we can take some comfort from our ears not falling off," Tara said as sat down next to Kevin, all thoughts of finishing her paper forgotten.

"Well, it'll tire Nate out, so maybe he'll go to sleep without the usual fuss," Kevin replied, looking at his son who was engrossed in the movie, oblivious to the discussion around him. He seemed to be giving the idea some serious thought. "Sure, we can walk around the French Quarter, but only if you admit Boston's utter superiority to New Orleans."

"Fine, so long as you remember that you live here now, you will live here forever and ever, and the Saints can take the Patriots any day of the week."

But the idle boast sounded hollow to her. Tara wasn't about to admit it just then, but for the past two years, she'd been frustrated with the city she grew up in. For five years, she and Kevin had a house near the London Avenue Canal with three floors, a backyard, and a porch swing. They had loved it there, passing lazy evenings wandering the streets or just sitting on the porch together. But that was before Katrina, before their home had been almost entirely destroyed in the hurricane. The roof had blown off and a tree had fallen through the front wall into the living room. Worst of all, the house had been flooded up to the second floor.

In the two years since that fateful week, Kevin and Tara had been working tirelessly to repair the home they once had. They managed to replace a few of the walls and brace the others, as well as repair the roof and the floor on the ground level, but that was it. There was still so much to be done, but they had simply run out of money to pay for it. Kevin's teacher's salary wasn't much, and though Tara worked at a local library a few nights a week, they still had to pay off college loans and Tara's tuition for school. Both FEMA and their insurance company were dragging their heels on providing assistance. As a result, repairing the house was put on hold. Now, they lived in a two-bedroom apartment in Pearl River, a suburb about an hour away from the city itself. She missed city life and all that it had to offer. Driving so long to get everywhere almost made her cry on a regular basis. Right at that moment, Tara would have given anything to be living just about anywhere else.

February 25 was turning into a rough day. Tara had done miserably on her Research Methods for Libraries and Information Centers exam that morning and, unfortunately, couldn't shake the feeling that she was a failure who would never get a job and move on with her life. That afternoon she had gone to the grocery store and purchased a week's worth of food, only to have one of the bags split en route to the car, spilling groceries everywhere.

At around four in the afternoon, Tara was setting Nate up with a movie and worrying about her husband, who was a half hour late getting home. Kevin usually called when something held him up. So when the phone finally did ring, the FEMA representative was the last person she wanted to hear from.

"Hello?..Yes, this is Tara Kane...What do you mean I can't appeal it?"

This was just another in a series of disappointing contacts with FEMA. When they first applied for aid, they were denied due to a mistake on FEMA's end. Tara had spent three nerve-wracking weeks doing nothing but waiting for someone to finally show up at the house, yet they claimed she had refused entry to the inspectors who came to survey the damage. When she and Kevin realized the error, Tara had to spend two days waiting in a stuffy auditorium with Nate to prove that she had, in fact, cooperated completely with the inspector. The mistake was cleared up, and Tara was sent home to wait for official notice that she had been turned down for benefits.

"I'm sorry, Mrs. Kane," said the voice on the other end of her telephone. "But FEMA policy states that you must appeal a decision within the first forty days after the decision has been made. You and your husband missed that deadline."

"But you said I couldn't appeal until I got the notice that I was officially turned down, and I didn't get the notice until last month, and it's been nearly two years!"

"I'm sorry, ma'am; it's policy."

"Policy? *Policy?* This is entirely your fault! You told me I couldn't appeal until you sent the notice, you didn't send the notice in time, so now I get screwed? That is fifteen kinds of ridiculous. You have to take the appeal, you have to! We did everything exactly the way you told us to!" she screamed, completely losing her patience with this man.

"I'm sorry, but there's nothing I can do."

"You're sorry? You're not the one with a house to repair and no way to pay for it; you're sorry. You'll be sorry when I'm done with you. I should come over to…wherever you are and throw things at you…you…GAH!" She hung up the phone. "FEMA…Fix Everything My Ass."

Two hours later she was still furious at the nameless FEMA agent who called. The phone rang several times, but she was so upset that she wasn't in the mood to talk to anyone else. Then the door opened, and Kevin walked in.

"Kevin, you're late!" Tara began to shout at him, stopped in mid-sentence when she saw him awkwardly remove his coat, revealing a blue sling. "Oh my stars, what happened to your arm?"

"It got sprained. I was trying to break up a fight between two seniors, and I got knocked into a locker."

"Great," Tara muttered. "Exactly how I wanted this day to end." She sighed and went to hang up her husband's coat.

After dinner that evening, Tara curled up in Kevin's favorite chair to enjoy her favorite book, something she hadn't been able to do for some time. Three chapters into her reading, the phone rang, and she was pleasantly surprised to hear her father-in-law's voice on the other end.

"Hi, Dad. How are you tonight?" she asked.

"I'm still alive, so I guess that's something. And how are you?"

"I've been better."

"I'm sorry to hear that. How's Kevin's arm feeling?"

"It still hurts him, but he'll be fine in about a month. Hang on… how did you hear about Kevin's arm?"

"He called me from the hospital," he replied. "He said he tried to call you but the line was busy. Who was so important you couldn't talk to your poor wounded husband?" he teased.

"The stupid FEMA guy," she said. "He said we can't appeal, even though we did exactly what they told us to do."

"That must be frustrating." The teasing tone was gone, replaced by one of sympathy and concern.

"Ugh. Frustrating is an understatement. I hate this damn apartment; I want our house and our old life back."

"Don't worry, dear," he replied. "I know you hate to hear this, but just relax a bit and things will work out in the end."

"How can you possibly know that, Dad?"

"Because they always do."

"I'll believe that when we're back in our old house," she said with a reluctant smile. "How's your semester going?"

His tone became cheerful again. "Great, thanks for asking. I'm teaching a course on romance literature of the Renaissance. Who knew there was so much to say about it? Well, I did, because I wrote a book about it, but my students are really getting into it. It really is a fascinating subject, perfect fodder for a dorky old romantic like me. See what you did?" he chuckled. "Now you've got me going on about literature and my book."

"Sounds wonderful, Dad. I know we've got a copy here, and I promise to read it when things calm down a bit."

"Well don't rush on my account. You know, this book really is one of my favorites. I might even enter it in a competition here at the university."

"You should! I hope you win!"

"So do I," he laughed. "Well darling, it's getting late, so I should get some sleep."

"Sure Dad, thanks for listening to me whine about my life."

"Oh, it's my pleasure dear. Sweet dreams."

With that, he hung up the phone and Tara, in a much better mood, returned to her book.

"Mommy, what are you doing?" Nate asked, pausing from his game of crashing his Hot Wheels cars together on the tiled floor in the kitchen.

"I'm researching," Tara replied, picking her son up and sitting him on her lap. Behind her, the window to their apartment was open, allowing an occasional late May breeze to waft in. Having made no progress at all with her insurance company, FEMA, or the Red Cross, Tara had spent the past several months attempting to find other ways to obtain money to repair her destroyed home.

"But I thought you only had to do that for school, and you're done with school," Nate said.

"Well, sometimes, you have to research for life too. I'm trying to find people to help us fix our old house," replied Tara.

"Mommy, don't people want to help us?"

Tara forced herself to smile reassuringly.

"Of course they do, sweetie. The problem is that a lot of other people need help, too. So we're kind of in a help line."

"So, they'll help us when it's our turn in line, right?"

I hope so, Tara thought to herself. *But how do you explain bureaucracy and red tape and politics to a kindergartner?* "Yes dear, but we've been waiting in line for a very long time, so I'm trying to see if there are any shorter lines we can wait in."

"I hope you find one." And with that, Nate went back to his toys.

Tara, meanwhile, continued her work. They'd managed to save enough to replace one more of the house's walls, but the final wall still remained, as did the first-floor ceiling, the joint work, and the second floor. To make matters worse, the contractor who did the first contract skipped town, taking several deposits (mercifully not theirs) with him, and the Road Home Program had an enormous waiting list. Tara was really starting to believe that nothing short of a miracle would fix her home now.

Nate was extremely excited. He couldn't concentrate all day, which was very inconvenient to his teachers. By the time Kevin picked him up from school, he was nearly jumping out of his skin, knowing that when he got home, his grandparents would be there to greet him…with presents.

"Grandpa Alex! Grandma Ginny!" Nate screamed as he opened the door and ran into their arms, not bothering to take off his jacket or backpack. "What'd you bring me?"

His grandmother chuckled. "Why don't you go into your room and see?"

Nate disappeared into his room and emerged a few seconds later, clutching a package wrapped in red and gold paper, which he was quickly tearing off.

"Dinosaurs! Thanks, Grandma and Grandpa!"

Tara was excited about the visit, too, but she was better at controlling her glee than her six-year-old. She hadn't seen her in-laws since they came to visit shortly after Katrina, and she wondered what had prompted their sudden appearance.

"How's your book selling, Dad?" Kevin asked during dinner.

"Brilliantly, thank you," he replied. "It's among the top sellers by Harvard professors, and I didn't even have to force my students to buy it."

"That's wonderful, Dad," said Tara.

"It really is," Ginny replied. "It's nice to see all of Alex's hard work paying off, in more ways than one."

"What do you mean?" Tara asked.

"Well, do you remember me mentioning the contest in which my book was entered?"

"Yeah," Kevin said. "You said the English department gives…" Realization seemed to dawn on him, and he dropped his fork. "No way."

"Yes way."

"What?" demanded Nate.

"Yeah, what?" further demanded Tara.

"The English department," replied Alex, "gives $150,000 to the faculty member with the highest quality of research."

The same realization dawned on Tara. "No way." Tara stared, openmouthed, at her grinning father-in-law.

Nate looked at each person at the table in turn and continued to demand, "What?" until his grandfather explained it to him.

"My job gave me a lot of money because I did the best work on my research project."

"Cool!" Nate said.

"What are you going to do with it?" stammered Kevin, who was beginning to recover from the shock.

"Help you fix your house, of course," answered Ginny.

"Oh, Mom, Dad, you can't!" said Tara. "You earned that, we can't possibly take it. You should have it."

"Nonsense, dear," said Alex in a voice that brooked no arguments. "We have enough money for what we need. You, on the other hand, do not."

"Dad," said Kevin, getting up to hug his parents, "we can't thank you enough. I don't even know how to begin."

"Well I do," said Alex. "You can get your house fixed and move out of this tiny apartment. Then you can invite us to visit."

"Yeah…of course…anytime you want. Often. You can come often," stammered Kevin.

"Well, maybe not that often," said Ginny. She smiled and winked at Tara.

Tara was relieved. Her father-in-law had turned out to be right. Things did work out in the end, and she finally got her miracle.

Breathless
by Cynthia Maves

The lieutenant paused at the window to watch the sun-darkened woman before moving to knock on the frame of the open door. The sun shone upon her dark curls as she stirred a pot on the stove. She stood with a quiet confidence, shoulders back and eyes bright, and she was not at all what he expected. In his description, the patrolman had failed to mention that she was young, beautiful, and self-assured. He moved to the doorway, raised his hand to knock, only to be greeted by the woman's intense hazel eyes.

"Ms. Dejean?"

"I am," the woman replied with a nod.

"I am Lieutenant Levine with the New Orleans Police Department. I'm afraid that I may be in need of your service," he said.

Again, the woman nodded. "Yes, you are, Lieutenant. You are quite afraid. The real question is, are you afraid of me or what I am about to do?"

He felt unsettled by her forwardness. He really hadn't meant it that way, but there was no doubt as to the woman's accuracy. He *was* afraid, and if he were honest, he would admit to being afraid of this entire situation, the woman included. He had expected to meet an aging, possibly demented woman, not the intense beauty before him. He had also expected to be able to discount her abilities, but something about this woman felt genuine and sincere. The entire situation terrified him.

The lieutenant felt his entire body stiffen in defiance, but forced himself to forge ahead. "To tell the truth, Ms. Dejean, it is probably a little of both," he chuckled, hoping that it would ease the way for the remainder of his answer. "You should probably know that this was not my idea. My orders are to request your assistance, so I'm here. I'm not really sure what they expect you to be able to tell us though."

"Are you a man of faith, Mr. Levine?" she asked.

"Um, no, ma'am. I am not," he stuttered before taking a calming breath and continuing, "I believe in that which I can see with my own eyes and touch with my own hands. Life is filled with too many fabrications and downright deceptions to believe anything else."

Ms. Dejean gestured for him to sit at the table, and he thought her smile looked almost sympathetic. She placed two bowls of gumbo on the table, then sat opposite him.

"I was born a psychic, lieutenant. I have no choice but to acknowledge the existence of the spiritual world. My mother was Haitian, raised by her mother to be a powerful Voodoo priestess, and my father was a devout Irish Catholic. I have been surrounded and influenced by spirituality my entire life. If you cannot accept its existence, however, why did you come to me? You would never believe any answers I provide you."

"Patrolman Brou gave your name to my superior. I am told that he spoke very highly of you," the officer replied.

A beautiful smile transformed her previously serious countenance. "Louis and I have known each other for decades now. He is a wonderful man." Ms. Dejean paused, her eyes narrowed. He felt as if she were trying to evaluate his very soul. "I will accept your offer, Mr. Levine, so as not to disappoint *mon cher* Louis, but our work together will be difficult."

He set down his spoon and felt a genuine smile break upon his face. "I will do my best to keep an open mind, Ms. Dejean."

"*Oui, bien.* Now finish your meal and I will accompany you to the scene."

"What? Now?" he sputtered.

"Of course now. Time is of the essence, my good man, is it not? It takes time to gather all of the clues. One little insignificant-looking clue could make the difference, am I not correct?" she said, sipping at her own soup.

"You are," he agreed hesitantly, unsure why she felt the need to tell this to him of all people.

"Then it is important that we start gathering our clues as soon as possible I would think. *Piti a piti, zozo fait son nid,*" she continued.

"My apologies, Ms. Dejean, but I do not understand French."

"It means, 'Little by little the bird builds its nest,'" she explained.

She had a valid point, the lieutenant conceded with a nod. He then turned his concentration to the bowl before him. His hostess was an excellent cook.

As soon as the meal was finished and the table cleared, he ushered her into his car. Ms. Dejean sat silently as he drove from her home in the French Quarter to the Garden District. He shared the location and general description of the crime scene with her as he drove but was careful not to divulge specific details. If she was to prove him wrong about the world of the paranormal, she was going to have to do it of her own accord, not from clever manipulation of information he himself had provided.

The scene inside the residence looked very much as it had days before. The evidence had been collected, labeled, and taken away, yet the markers remained. The uncomfortable weight in the air he had felt on his previous visits was still present as well. The shoe prints of the investigators, evident in the thin layer of dust that clung to everything, and the stifling heat of the room caused by the closed windows, were the only obvious changes.

His eyes then fell on the woman at his side as he surveyed the room. Beads of sweat had formed on her forehead. As she surveyed the room, she unbuttoned her short-sleeve blouse to reveal a tank top underneath. The woman was lovely and voluptuous, all curves. This errant thought was cut short, however, when she suddenly turned and caught his stare.

"Can you feel it?" she asked.

"What? Can I feel what?" he asked, hoping that she did not mean his sudden, unprofessional surge of attraction.

"Do you feel anything odd about this house? Anything different? Unusual?"

He had felt a great many things since they had arrived in this house, but most of them would not be considered unusual. The attraction he'd felt flare was easily explained by the presence of Ms. Dejean. The heat, although oppressive, was obviously a result of the closed windows and the glaring sun.

"There's a weight to the air, as if the house is trying to literally suck the air from your lungs. Sounds ridiculous though, doesn't it?" he replied, looking down at his shifting feet. His discomfort at voicing such an absurd confession would not allow him to meet her eyes.

"No, it doesn't sound ridiculous," she said firmly. "That's exactly what I am feeling."

Slowly, she walked around the room. At several different spots, her eyes closed, and a pained expression overwhelmed her beautiful features. Once, near the doorway, she gasped as if all of the air had suddenly been sucked from her lungs. She recovered as soon as she opened her eyes, though, and continued her odd exploration through the hall and other rooms of the house.

He tried to wait patiently as Ms. Dejean finished her slow inspection of the house, but found it difficult. The strange heaviness they had discussed upon arriving affected him more than he felt comfortable admitting, especially now that he had admitted to feeling it at all. He felt as if something ominous could happen at any moment. Logically, he knew that it was a ridiculous notion, but his body refused to agree. It refused to abandon its ready-to-pounce stance, and his shoulders and neck were beginning to ache.

"Are you familiar with Voodoo?" she asked when she finally returned to him in the bedroom.

"I am aware that it is a practiced religion here, but beyond that... well, nothing," he admitted.

"I'd be happy to explain the fundamental concepts, as I think it may be important, but would you mind if we moved the discussion somewhere else? I'm feeling very ill at ease in here," she said.

He heaved a sigh of relief. "Happily. I think we passed a café just up the road. That should be comfortable enough, no?"

"Let's go then," she said.

Ms. Dejean patiently explained the rather confusing fundamental concepts and practices of the Voodoo religion over a couple of lemonades. Even as she spoke, the cool liquid started to ease away the tension the lieutenant had felt at the victim's residence. His companion's lilting voice shared stories of the Voodoo god, Bondye, and the spirits, called Iwa, and how they mount people to channel through them. Such concepts would usually only annoy him, but as her words washed over him, they soothed away the last of his remaining tension.

"I believe we are dealing with a very powerful priest or priestess in this case, and not the usual practitioner either. This is most definitely Petro at work," she concluded.

"Petro? You mean you know this person?" he asked, straightening in his seat.

Her laughter floated on the humid air. "No. Petro is a rarely used form of Voodoo. It is the black magic side of the religion," she explained so calmly that he thought she may as well be giving him a weather report.

"Black magic? You think that this man was killed by magic?" he asked, unable to hide his disbelief.

"Yes, that is what I'm saying," she replied, her features hardening.

He raised an eyebrow in response but said nothing.

"I'll need to look over my materials, however, to be sure. It will require some time, a few days, most likely," she said.

As unlikely as he thought this theory was, Lieutenant Levine nodded his consent. It was the only possible lead he had at the moment. Besides, it couldn't hurt to hear what the woman had to say. Perhaps her magical theory could give him an idea as to what had really happened.

Three days later, they met again at the café. Over fresh lemonades, Ms. Dejean shared the outcome of her research, the visions she'd experienced while inside the residence, and finally her theory as to what had occurred. She told him that in several places within the bedroom, her heart had raced, and she had seen the victim in her mind's eye.

"He was holding his chest, and I could feel his loss of breath because I, too, felt as if my breath had been robbed from my lungs," she said. "I felt an overwhelming sense of fear and guilt at those moments. I think the victim felt guilty due to some perceived wrongdoing on his part, and he feared that this was his recompense."

The lieutenant rolled those thoughts around in his head. "The victim was recently divorced. He'd been having an affair and was caught by his wife. In the end, he lost his mistress as well, due to the fact that she'd been unaware that he was married. He took up residence at the crime scene after his wife threw him out of their marital home. We've investigated both the wife and the mistress though, and while they both have motivation, each has a sound alibi for the night in question."

"No one would have to be present for the powers to work. They would need only to have contacted a priest or priestess," she replied.

"And how do you propose we determine that?" Lieutenant Levine challenged. "Are we just supposed to go through the telephone book and expect whoever answers to reveal their client list?"

"Of course not," his companion replied, rolling her eyes and placing her lemonade down on the table with a thud. "Besides, very few people would dare to perform services as dark as these, and considering the fact that I think this person has already killed someone, we would do well not to arouse their suspicions or upset them."

The lieutenant shot his companion another skeptical look but once again said nothing.

"All inquiries will need to be extremely discreet," she added, sounding as if she were speaking to a challenged child.

Later that afternoon, Lieutenant Levine sat at his desk documenting his latest meeting with the mysterious Ms. Dejean and pondered the situation. The fact that he was even continuing along this vein of investigation left him baffled. Normally, he would have put a halt to such a farce long before this point, yet Ms. Dejean seemed so confident and there was just something about her that seemed so genuine to him. He hoped against hope that in this one instance he would not be proved wrong. He didn't really want to discover that he had allowed himself to be deceived just because he found this woman so intriguing.

At his first available opportunity, the lieutenant approached Patrolman Brou. He had been the one to involve Ms. Dejean in the investigation in the first place, therefore, he was the most logical person with whom to start this "discreet" search.

"Officer Brou? May I have a minute, please?"

The officer looked up from his report. "Certainly, sir."

"Ms. Dejean would like to talk to some Voodoo practitioners regarding the Armand case. I was hoping that you might have some ideas as to where we should start," he said as haughtily as he could in an effort to cover how ridiculous he felt asking for such information.

"Practitioners, sir? Just ordinary followers or priests and priestesses?" Brou asked, his eyes widening in surprise.

"Priests and priestesses, I believe," he said.

The patrolman pulled a sheet a paper from the drawer and wrote a list of names. "These are not all priests or priestesses, but those that aren't are close with some. They are all trustworthy people, sir. They'll help you, if they can, and they will understand the need for confidentiality in your investigation," he said, handing the page to the lieutenant.

"Thank you, Brou. This should be very helpful," he said with a slight smile, then folded the paper and placed it in his pocket. As first attempts went, the lieutenant was satisfied with the results.

Over the next several days, the lieutenant located and spoke to the people on Brou's list. He also met regularly with Ms. Dejean to compare notes and discuss their progress, or, more appropriately, lack of progress. They each had spoken to several people, but the only result they had achieved through their efforts so far was to shorten the suspect list as the people they spoke with were ruled out.

"I want to go back to the house again," Ms. Dejean announced on the seventh day into their search.

"Why?"

"I had a dream last night about the victim. It was similar to my visions in the house, but this time an image of a woman kept appearing, too. There was a second woman as well. She had red hair, but that's about all I can recall about her. I only saw her once. If they appear in the house as well, then I'll feel much more confident that they are connected with this man's death," she said, bouncing slightly in her chair.

"A redhead? Are you sure you can't remember anything else?"

He had purposely not revealed any specifics of the case, and he was sure that he had never described the two women involved in the victim's divorce. Ms. Dejean could not possibly know that the man's wife had red hair.

"No. It was nothing more than a glimpse, like a flash of a picture in a fast-moving slide show," she replied, her face scrunched up as she tried to remember.

"What about the other woman? What did she look like?" he asked.

"She was a dark woman, darker than me. She was very thin too, almost skeletal. She kept smiling, but not in a way that could ever be considered kind or beautiful. She looked...malevolent. Please, I'd very much like to see if either of these images appears from within the house," she said.

Pulling his cell phone from his pocket, he called the station to clear the order as they left the café. Back inside the house, Ms. Dejean wandered through the rooms, much as she had done on her first visit. Occasionally, he could see the evidence of the house's influence over her, but eventually, she just looked at him with saddened eyes and shook her head.

"Nothing. Not one glimpse of the women here."

"Do you think that you might be able to construct a picture of the dark woman with the help of an artist?" the lieutenant asked.

"I could certainly try, I suppose," she replied. Her slight smile softened her dejected tone.

The following day the lieutenant brought Ms. Dejean to the station to meet with the sketch artist. One by one she looked through the faces, eyes, noses, and lips, discarding this one, accepting that one, and replacing yet another. A multitude of slight reactions flashed across her face as she concentrated on finding the perfect match and he soon lost himself in the mesmerizing display. Her soft exclamation of "it's her" finally broke into his awareness, and he was shocked to discover that he had lost almost an hour in quiet appreciation of her beauty.

He glanced at the artist's rendering, but his attention was drawn away by a harsh exclamation from behind him. "That looks like Madame Emiline."

The lieutenant turned around just in time to see Ms. Dejean rush past him to embrace Patrolman Brou.

"Mon cher, Louis! *Comment allez-vous?"*

The patrolman released her with a chuckle. *"Oui, bien. Et tu?"*

"I'm sorry to interrupt," the lieutenant burst in, suddenly feeling much more jealous than he should over their camaraderie, and not apologetic in the least. "Did you say that you recognize this woman?"

The officer before him straightened at once. "Yes, sir. She looks like Madame Emiline, a woman in the neighborhood where we," he nodded toward Ms. Dejean, "grew up."

"Madame Emiline was a friend of Mother's, but this doesn't resemble the woman I remember at all, Louis. She was plump and extremely friendly and generous," Ms. Dejean countered.

"One 'n' the same, *ma chere,* yet very different. The years have not been kind to her," the patrolman replied.

"We need to talk to her, Ms. Dejean," the lieutenant said, the hard tone of his voice even surprising himself.

"Sir, if I may, proceed with caution. She's a right nasty piece a work these days," Patrolman Brou offered with hesitation.

"We will, and thank you for your help," Lieutenant Levine replied with genuine gratitude.

Ms. Dejean abruptly stopped at the edge of the walk. She looked pale and troubled.

"Louis was right. This is a very dark place. Tread lightly, lieutenant," her voice trembled slightly, and her chest rose and fell visibly with each breath.

He nodded in understanding and offered her his arm, then led her toward the house.

He knocked on the door, which opened to reveal a woman. The woman's resemblance to the picture of Ms. Dejean's dream woman was striking. Her eyes narrowed dangerously when the lieutenant confirmed her identity as Madame Emiline. She glared as her eyes fell upon the woman on his arm.

"I am a very busy woman, so state your business quickly, man. Your disbelief darkens my doorway and isn't welcome here," Madame Emiline snapped.

"I apologize for the imposition, but this is very important. We are looking for a Mrs. Violet Armand. We found your name in her date book. It appears that you met with her shortly before she left town. I hoped that you might have a telephone number or some way to reach where she is staying," the lieutenant stated in his best professional air.

"She called me, but I wasn't able to make our meeting. As I said, I am a very busy woman. I'm afraid I can't help you," she replied in the same sharp tone she had used to greet them.

Lieutenant Levine pulled a business card from his pocket and thrust it toward the insolent woman. "If you remember anything that you may have forgotten or if you hear from her, please let me know. I can't stress enough how important it is that I locate her, Madame Emiline."

"Oh, I will certainly remember you, Mr. Levine," she said, grabbing the card from him and glancing down at the name. She then leveled her eyes on his companion. "Your choice of company is very disappointing, Miss Dejean," she added with a sneer. The old woman then shut the door on them.

Back in the car, Ms. Dejean turned toward him. "Was her name really in that woman's date book?"

"No. It was just a hunch," he chuckled.

Over the next few days, Lieutenant Levine repeatedly left messages for Mrs. Armand. She had gone on vacation just before her ex-husband's death and showed no signs of returning soon. He wanted to know why she had contacted Madame Emiline, and his frustration was rising with each unreturned call. Adding to his frustration, he had not been feeling well. Several times, he felt short of breath. The whole situation was unnerving.

He finally received a small measure of success on the fourth day following his visit to Madame Emiline, when Mrs. Armand answered his calls. Of course, at first she denied any knowledge of Madame Emiline, but when confronted with the old woman's confession, she admitted to having contacted her. Mrs. Armand refused to cooperate further, however, claiming that she did not have to reveal the reason for their contact based on religious reasons.

The lieutenant let out a heavy sigh. "Mrs. Armand, there are two problems with that statement. The first is that I know you are an active member of St. Mary's Assumption Catholic Church. Secondly, the act of murder would undeniably overrule religious confidentiality," he snapped over the long-distance connection.

That certainly got the woman's attention. "Murder? What on earth are you talking about? I don't know anything about a murder."

"Your husband, Mrs. Armand. I've already spoken to you about it once."

"Ex-husband, Lieutenant Levine, and yes, I remember your last call," she said, her voice shrill and accusing, "but the nurse said that they thought it was a heart attack. It certainly wouldn't be surprising, I mean, honestly, a man *his* age carrying on with a twenty-five-year-old girl!"

"It was an attack; I'll agree with you there, although I have reason to believe that it was something much more sinister than a heart attack," the lieutenant said. "I can have you summoned for questioning if necessary, Mrs. Armand, though I think we would both rather it not come down to that. Now, I'm only going to ask one more time, why did you contact Madame Emiline?"

"Fine. Fine. She has a reputation of helping scorned women. I wanted her assistance in getting back at him, for this horrible scandal he brought upon us. You know, a genital rash or something."

"Well, it sounds like you certainly got your wish...or something," he scoffed.

"No. It wasn't like that. I never asked for his death. I wouldn't do that, lieutenant!" she screamed, starting to sound hysterical.

"We shall see, Mrs. Armand. Make sure you stay close to your phone. I may need more information," he stated firmly.

"I will. I promise. Good day, Lieutenant Levine."

Madame Emiline had misled him, not that he was exactly surprised. It seemed he needed to pay her another visit. Perhaps the knowledge that he had spoken with Mrs. Armand would make her more cooperative.

He had just started up Madame Emiline's front walk when he felt the air flee from his lungs again, much stronger this time than previous episodes. He fell to his knees and clutched at his chest. He was just beginning to black out when it finally let up, allowing him to once more fill his lungs. He was so thrown by the experience that it took him a few minutes to realize that a pair of hands were resting on his shoulders.

"Are you okay?" a familiar feminine voice asked, filled with concern.

"Yes. I am now," he gasped, his voice sounding raspy to his own ears.

"I was just leaving Louis' house when I saw you. What are you doing here?" Ms. Dejean asked.

"I heard from Mrs. Armand. She did contract work from Madame Emiline. The woman lied to us," he replied.

"Can you stand?"

He stood up and turned to face her. "Thank you. I'm fine now."

The young woman looked unconvinced but did not protest. Instead, she held out a brightly colored pouch tied to a loop of thin rope. "Put it on. It may help you. Now, come on. I'll go with you."

Together, they trekked up the path and knocked on the door. It flew open almost immediately, as if the woman was expecting them. Her malicious smile did nothing to alleviate the feeling of dread that washed over him upon seeing her.

"I told you, you aren't welcome here," Madame Emiline said, still smiling that nasty smile.

"Yes, you did. You also said that you didn't meet with Mrs. Armand, but I know differently, Madame. What did you do to Henry Armand?" he demanded.

The old woman suddenly thrust out her right arm, something soft clutched in her hand. It looked harmless enough, like a street child's doll, but as she squeezed the doll, he once more felt the air rush from his lungs. For several seconds he gasped unsuccessfully for air as Ms. Dejean just stared down at him with widened eyes. Recovering from her shock, she jumped forward and shoved the elderly woman just hard enough to knock her off balance. The doll fell to the floor as Madame Emiline struggled to regain her footing, and the lieutenant choked on the rush of air as the pressure released. Not giving the woman a chance to recover, Ms. Dejean grabbed his arm, and they ran for his car.

"You drive. I'll never be able to if she does that again," the lieutenant said as he tossed her his keys.

She drove to her house, quickly ushered him inside, and gave him a glass of cold water. He sat at the table sipping the water and trying to digest all that had just happened. It didn't feel real. An hour earlier, he would have vehemently denied that it was even possible to incapacitate someone without laying a finger on them. Yet, it had happened. He had seen it. He had felt it.

"Thank you, Ms. Dejean. I don't know what I would have done without your help today," he said, looking her in the eye.

"It's Margaret, and you're welcome," she replied, flashing him the most beautiful smile he had ever seen.

"In that case, Margaret, I'm Andrew," he said. Then, he lifted the pouch from under his shirt. "Now, can you tell me what this is?"

Margaret sighed. "It's a juju bag, a form of protection. My people have a proverb: *Pranne garde vaut mie passé mande pardon*, which means, 'It is better to take care beforehand than to ask pardon afterward.' I had hoped to take the initiative before Madame Emiline found an opportunity to harm us. She is very powerful. Unfortunately, it didn't seem to help much just now."

"Thank you for your thoughtfulness and concern. It is much appreciated," he said, smiling at her.

The next morning, Lieutenant Levine went into the station, prepared to file a report on his encounter with Madame Emiline. He was rather sure that his superior would recommend a psychiatric evaluation after reading it, but he still felt the need to document the altercation. The woman was down-right dangerous! However, Patrolman Brou stood waiting for him at his desk. The fellow officer waited as he got settled, then handed him a folded newspaper. A short entry was circled in the obituary column.

He felt as if his heart had jumped into his throat. He had not had another attack of breathlessness since leaving Madame Emiline's house the previous day. What if she had turned her attention to Margaret, thinking Margaret had led him to her? Would Margaret's knowledge of Voodoo be able to protect her? Would the woman hesitate to kill again? That last question he felt confident that he could answer with a resounding no, and he silently pleaded for the listing to be anyone other than Margaret Dejean. Finally focusing on the paper in his hand, he read the words, "Emiline Boujean, known to many as Madame Emiline..."

"I thought you would want to know," Brou said.

"Thank you."

It was over. After the events the previous day, Lieutenant Levine felt convinced that Madame Emiline was responsible for Henry Armand's death, but the truth of that crime had died with the old woman. He would never know exactly what she had done to him, or why. He would never have the opportunity to try again to get the woman to confess. The official cause of death would be listed as a heart attack.

One thing he did know. He needed to call Margaret. She too would want to know, and he still needed at least some of his questions answered.

The Flower Song
by Rachel Caine

If there was one thing Paul Lance hated most, it was the silence on Nelson's World. It was a clean planet, with just a bit more oxygen and a bit less gravity than his home world, but you'd never mistake it for Earth. Earth was busy, noisy, cluttered, trampled—used up. He'd never seen a field of flowers, except in ancient vids and still museum paintings, until he'd gotten off the ship here.

Most colonists had cried in joy at the sight of the gorgeous golden blanket of petals.

He didn't. He'd found it vaguely unsettling with nothing in his ears but the wind. Even on the ship there'd been a subtle mechanical hum, and of course packing a hundred colonists in a relatively small ship meant that it was never really quiet.

Nelson's World was beautiful, but he really couldn't stand the fact that it was never, ever *loud*.

He took to playing his earpods after the first day (and night) of unbearable silence, pouring music into his empty head to keep busy. He'd already earned a reputation on the trip of being sarcastic and a bit standoffish from the other settlers, so nobody really minded if he stopped forcing himself to respond to their half-hearted attempts at conversation. The Company's music library was extensive, and he intended to go through every single song in it if he had to.

He was here not because he wanted to be, but because he was getting paid. Period. If he'd had his way, he'd have stayed on Earth, but the Company had made it clear that if he wanted to keep his job, he had to join one of the colonies. It was a new internal rule for all Company physicians and scientists—they wanted to make sure they were seeding their colonies with specialists, not just environmental refugees.

Paul Lance was a doctor, and he went where the company sent him, whether he liked it or not. After six months on Nelson's World, fighting his own sense of oppression and anxiety about this place, he was ready to tell the Company where to shove it and hop the next supply vessel back home, damn the consequences.

He sat at the top of a hill, drinking his morning coffee and looking out at the unspoiled wilderness—which was, in truth, not so very wild. Nelson's World was a gentle sort of place, all flowers and trees and fields, a few mountains to the north. He heard there was harsher desert a few thousand kilometers away, and he'd seen the vast oceans from orbit, but what he could see from the hill was likely to be all he'd ever see of Nelson's World. Doctors were valuable commodities. They didn't go exploring off into the wild. Someone might break a toe while he was gone.

His earpods were blasting an old Pink Garters song, one of his favorites, straight into his brain. As he sipped his hot liquid breakfast, a tiny green screen appeared in front of his eyes, overlaying the scene, with a red blinking dot directly behind him, closing in at a deliberate pace. He'd set the earpods to alert him if anything came near him while the music was engaged—a useful precaution on a strange planet—and so he wasn't surprised when someone else arrived at the top of the hill, coffee cup in hand, and thumped down breathlessly next to him.

Pause, he told the music, and it politely did.

"Dr. Lance," said Dr. Maribel Ouima, the colony's geologist. She was a tall, strong-featured woman who favored severe hairstyles and no-nonsense jumpsuits; it wasn't her fault that those things flattered her. She was about his own age—thirty—and he knew she was, like him, pressed into service by the Company. She had family back on Earth, which was something he hadn't had to sacrifice to make his own move. She wore the picture of her two little boys in a locket around her neck, and he knew she counted the days to her home furlough. "Mind if I join you?"

"You already did," Lance shrugged. "Doesn't matter now, does it?"

"Well, look who spilled a little nasty in his coffee this morning!"

"Sorry." He was, actually. He liked Ouima, and she was a fellow sufferer. He knew she missed Earth terribly, too. "Bad night."

The look she sent him over the top of her coffee cup was bright. Piercing. "Still bothering you?" She knew about his hatred of the silence, which was, even now, beginning to press in on him like an invisible hand. Ouima's voice wasn't big enough to fill that void.

Nothing was.

"No," he lied. "Just couldn't sleep. You know Nelson's World, wild parties all night long…"

She laughed, a bright shiver on the still air. "Life must be different on South Street than on East Street. My neighbors couldn't stay up past dark if you paid them genuine E-dollars. They tell me the quiet makes them sleepy."

It didn't do anything like that for him. "What've you got on today, Ouima?"

"A blockbuster day of exciting geologic documentation, just over that ridge." She pointed off to the east, near where the sun was cresting the hill. "There's a ravine there, looks like it was cut by the stream running through it. Great place to see the developmental layers, maybe find some fossils if I'm lucky."

"Fossils?"

"I know we haven't seen any animal or insect life, but there has to be some; this amount and variety of plant life can't sustain itself without something fitting into that ecological niche. Right? There have to be herbivores, since there's such an abundance of plant life. And that means predators."

Of course she was right. Lance nodded slowly. It was part of the general oppression of Nelson's World, that absence of life. No buzzing bees, no calling birds. Not a rustle in the grass that couldn't be accounted for by wind.

"Mind if I join you?" he asked her suddenly. Ouima sent him an odd look. "I've got no patients. I'll switch on the hologram alert pad before I go. But I'd like to get at least that far out of town."

"I don't blame you," she said, and looked over her shoulder. Behind them, at the bottom of the hill in a gentle bowl, surrounded by nodding yellow flowers, was the town. It didn't have a name yet; there was a contest of sorts to come up with the final designation, but for now, it was just The Town. With more than 500 colonists all holding strong opinions about how it should be named, Lance didn't figure it would be called anything but The Town for several lifetimes. "It's just too damn quiet down there."

She was talking about the lack of human-generated excitement, not the kind of silence that bothered Lance, but he nodded anyway. It *was* too quiet. People were polite, hard-working, grateful for this new chance at a life where they wouldn't be poisoned by the world around them. For a chance to conceive and raise children who wouldn't remember the old ways.

It was probably sick of him to miss those old, cluttered, polluted streets, but then again, he wasn't trying to escape from it. He just wanted to keep his job.

"All right," Ouima said. "You clear it with Administration, and we'll be on the road in half an hour. But no whining if you can't keep up."

"Me?" He arched an eyebrow at her. "Never."

Lance took the emergency medical kit with him, a flat palm-sized box that slipped easily into the side pocket of his trousers. He also checked a weapon out of the armory. Ouima, as far as he knew, never went armed, and nobody else bothered either, but if he was going exploring, he wanted to be prepared.

He was aware, from the smirks he got at Admin, that it was probably a stupid idea, but since he had Pink Garters blasting in his earpods again, he didn't really care what anybody said to him.

He met Ouima on the outskirts of town, just beyond the clean, ordered boundaries of East Street. She had a heavy pack on her back, which made him feel unprepared until she smiled and said, "I always plan to be stranded. Emergency shelter, food concentrates for a week, water, tools, comms. And my toolkit and comp, of course."

Of course. He wished he'd thought to bring all that, but he supposed, since she didn't send him back to do it, that she had enough for them both.

Ouima had long legs, and she set a brisk pace out of town, up the hill, and down into what they called the East Field, which was marked for cultivation as soon as they finished the botany tests to see what would grow well there. It'd be a pity to see the flowers go, Lance thought. They really were beautiful. But the town needed to become self-sufficient for most of its food supplies, and that meant cultivating the land.

Walking through the flowers was a surprising experience, because Lance could have sworn that he could *hear* something. But that was impossible, especially over the earpods. He paused the music, but no other sound became clear to him. He had the sense of hearing *something*, but all he actually heard was...nothing.

The flowers had a sweet scent, a little like fresh-baked cake, and golden pollen thickened the air with every step as the disturbed flowers released clouds of the stuff. "Hope you're not allergic!" Ouima called back. "Don't worry, it's not dangerous, at least according to the botanists."

Lance didn't actually trust the botanists.

They crossed the field in a surprisingly short amount of time, arriving in the shadow of some tall trees, not unlike pines. Conifers, anyway, though the needles were more feathery, like tiny ferns, and were dark green with a faint coppery sheen in the light.

Lance kept his earpods on. If Ouima talked, he didn't hear.

The trees lasted for almost an hour, a dense canopy of shadow but clear open space at ground level. Little underbrush. The fallen needles made a soft cushion beneath their feet, and Lance imagined that the hush—had his music not been echoing in his head—would have been profound. Ouima stopped once to swig water and handed him a bottle as well; he felt pleasantly warm, not thirsty until the liquid touched his tongue, and then he drank half the contents.

The end of the trees marked a dramatic change—rocks. A disordered jumble of color and shape, with a few plants clinging to life in the crevices. The broken landscape sloped down, and the cloying smell of the trees was blown away by cool air and the heavy smell of water.

Ouima tapped her ear. *Pause,* Lance instructed the music, and the silence fell like a sodden blanket.

"Okay," Ouima said. "Here's where it gets a bit tricky. Watch your step, there are plenty of loose rocks, and it's a long way down. Keep your earpods off. I want you to be able to hear me scream when I fall."

She flashed him a dazzling smile, hitched the pack to a more comfortable angle, and set off through the maze of boulders. Lance followed.

No sound of birds or animals, no metal, no people. Nothing but wind rustling through trees and whispering through the rocks. Even the tiny sounds of Ouima's feet on gravel seemed huge. Lance gritted his teeth and followed, wiping sweat from his forehead. The sound of lapping water grew louder and louder, until they arrived at the edge of the ravine.

Lance leaned over. The descent was only about twenty feet, and there was plenty of damp sand at the edges of the stream. The water glimmered silver in the sunlight, frothing white where it hit fallen stones.

"Right," Ouima said. "Down we go." She took off the pack and got out a thin, flexible rope that she wrapped around a large boulder; the rope's ends immediately fused together. She handed Lance a pair of thin, padded gloves. "Don't burn your hands."

Climbing down was tougher than he'd thought, and his biceps and triceps burned with strain as he lowered himself hand over hand down the rope. The gloves were friction models, designed to grip tight, so he couldn't slide easily. His scrabbling boots kicked loose pieces of rock on the way down, which fell with a constant rattle.

His feet touched down at last on the damp sand, and he let go of the rope with a sigh of relief.

Ouima's descent was as graceful and natural as a spider on a line of silk. She hopped down the last few feet, landing lightly on the balls of her feet, and gave him another smile, breathing hard. "Okay?"

He gave her a sarcastic thumbs up. "Can I turn the music back on now?"

"Knock yourself out, doctor."

Play, he subvocalized.

Nothing happened. His heart rate spiked, and he forced himself to take a calming breath. *Play. Play, dammit!*

The silence was, quite literally, deafening. It seemed to soak into his skin, crawl down his throat. He was choking on it. Hard to breathe....

"Lance!" Ouima saw him stagger and was quickly at his side, easing him down to a sitting position. "Lance, what the hell?"

"Play," he said aloud. "Play, play, *play!*" It almost came out as a sob. *Speak clearly,* he told himself. *The earpods can't understand if you don't.*

"Not working?" Ouima took a flat display from her pocket, something small enough to fit in her palm, and consulted it. "No power. Your earpods are down."

"Can't be," he gasped. "Powered by—"

"Biochemical, I know, but trust me, they're down." She turned the display face out toward him.

Blank.

"All our electricals are down," she said. "Comms, too. Everything."

"How is that possible?"

"It isn't," Ouima said. "Right?"

Not as far as he knew. Granted, he wasn't an engineer, but he knew the earpod technology. It was constantly recharged by simple biochemical interactions, and as long as the body was living, the earpods were too.

Something else was happening. He didn't realize it at first, but he was having trouble hearing Ouima's voice. "Lance?" she said, and he identified it more by the shape of her lips than the sound. "Can you hear me? Say something."

"I'm going deaf," he said. His voice felt raw in his throat, but he wasn't sure if he was speaking at all; there was a faint buzz in his ears, nothing more. "Ouima? What's happening?"

She shook her head, and he saw alarm in her eyes. It wasn't just him, then. It was happening to her as well. She tapped her ear. "Can't hear!"

The silence was white and featureless. Ouima's mouth was moving, but he couldn't hear her. It was all...gone. Completely empty. He reached out and grabbed her, and she pushed him away. He fell against the wall, and his head hit stone with a jarring crunch that he felt rather than heard.

Ouima, bending over him, blocking out the light. *Lance?* Her lips were moving.

The silence was brilliant, white, and terrifying.

I'll get help! He read her lips, saw the panic in her face. She jumped for the dangling rope and swarmed up, leaving him alone, drowning in the white silence.

Dying in it.

Lance rolled over and crawled across the sand, trying to get to the rope. His head felt sick and wrong, and the wet, hot, sticky feeling across the back of his neck had to be blood, not sweat....There was a *thing* lying in the sand, near the base of the rocks. A white crystal, and it was glittering in the light.

It was vibrating, a faint motion that made it hard to fix his eyes on it. He felt that the silence was pouring out of that thing.

Lance reached out for it. It felt warm, sharp, alive under his fingers.

Noise exploded over him in a deafening roar. Screaming, horrible screaming. Crashes. Metal tearing. The sound of death and war.

He pulled away from the crystal, and the silence closed in again. The artifact vibrated faster. There was a smear of his blood on its sharp edges.

Anything, he thought. *Anything but the silence.*

He picked it up.

The city was beautiful. Nelson's World's blue sky, Nelson's World's fields of flowers, but the *city*—a tall, glittering sculpture of crystal and steel. It wasn't designed along human sensibilities. The inhabitants of Nelson's World, whoever they might be, didn't favor square corners or ordered lines. It felt like a city that had grown up naturally from the ground—directed, maybe, but not built.

Lance stood in the empty field and watched as it was destroyed.

Now that he could *hear,* he understood. Everything vibrated on Nelson's World, on frequencies that human ears couldn't pick up—deep hums from the trees, shrill soprano chirps from grass rubbing together.

But it was the flowers that sang the loudest.

The inhabitants of the city fought them with fire, burning out every single bloom that approached the no-man's-land of empty ground, but the flowers adapted. As they died, they blew their pollen into the air, and within hours, dozens more sprouted. The cycle sped up, the harder the city fought.

It was too much for the creatures who'd built this lovely city. They fought a constant battle, but they were losing. It couldn't be won, not long-term, and Lance felt their despair, their fear.

This was the last outpost on Nelson's World. How he knew, he couldn't have said, but the vibrations from the crystal carried more than sound, more than language. They carried waves of knowledge. Of history. These people—entities, anyway—were strangers here, immigrants like the humans were now, and the flowers—slow to notice, but implacable in their rage—were going to kill them.

Eventually, the inhabitants fell behind in their eradication program, and the flowers sprang up in the dozens. Enough to begin a deadly cycle of reproduction and vibration. The city began to shatter—small cracks at first, then deeper ones as the flowers' song grew and reached a fever pitch. The sound—the scream—was deafening, enough to break not only the city but also the exoskeletal bodies of those who inhabited it.

It was murder, and the flowers were the killers.

Lance felt tears slide down his face as the screaming reached a terrible pitch, and the towers began to shatter, explode, fall in flame and smoke.

The flowers covered the remains in a breathtaking swarm, splintering them into finer and finer shards, until there was nothing left but a field of nodding yellow blossoms, with the bones of a

city under their roots.

What he was holding in his hand was a piece of that city. A piece of history, embedded in crystal.

He was still listening to the flowers screaming when Ouima returned with a rescue party.

"Dr. Lance?" Ouima's voice, warm and gentle. She spoke in a whisper, because she knew how much the noise hurt his sensitized ears. "I brought you lunch."

He was in a room in the hospital, soundproofed, and the white silence felt safe now. Comforting. He flinched at every loud noise, and he'd had his earpods removed. He couldn't imagine listening to music again, not after...

Not after the crystal.

Ouima deposited a tray on a padded table. The slight sound of the plates and glasses jingling made him take in a sharp breath, but he smiled at her, grateful for the company. Ouima had come every day to see him. They played cards or had whispered conversations. She told him that the Company had wanted to recall him to Earth, but she'd fought for him to choose his own reassignment. He'd picked a water-farming planet, one with a barren, rocky landscape and little vegetation to speak of. It'd still be quiet, but he thought— he hoped—it would be a different kind of quiet.

"The flowers?" he asked.

"We did some analysis," she said. "They do vibrate, but it's on a wavelength we can't hear. It doesn't affect anything we use here, but it does appear that prolonged exposure to the sound waves can trigger a kind of anxiety and even paranoia in some people. Nothing that can't be treated, though."

"They'll change," he whispered. "They'll find a frequency that hurts us. We have to leave this place. Abandon the colony."

Ouima's eyes were gentle, and so was her smile, but he knew she didn't believe him. "Dr. Lance, I believe you that the crystal you found might have been some kind of recording device, but no one else has been able to hear or detect anything from it. Not me, not anyone else in the colony. Only you. So we only have your word about what you saw. Do you understand?"

"You think I'm crazy," he said. "Right?"

"I'm a geologist. I don't make those kinds of judgments."

"Set up scanners. Watch the flowers. If the frequencies start changing..."

"We'll be on the alert," she said. "I promise you that."

He knew it was an empty promise.

They talked for a while. He ate his lunch—soup and crisp hot bread—and afterward, they played cards. Lance won, for the fourth time in a row. Ouima invited him to leave the room and come for a walk, but he shook his head. He knew that she—and all of them— thought he was crazy. Thought the injury on the back of his head had done this to him.

But he felt them out there, tens of thousands of gently nodding flowers, searching for the right note to sing.

Always searching.

He gave it one last try as Ouima gathered up the tray to leave. "You have to come with me," he said. "You. All of them. Off this planet."

"Lance," Ouima sighed and shook her head. "I can't. Listen, the ship will be here in three days. I'll see you tomorrow, all right? We'll play some chess."

He didn't try to argue with her anymore. He wrote a letter to Administration, a formal notice of the danger they were facing. He copied it to the Company and sent it under his own personal frequency code, in hopes that something, anything would be done.

And three days later, he said goodbye to Ouima, his only real friend on Nelson's World. He boarded the *White Lady*, en route from Nelson's World to Harriman's Moon, and as soon as the ship lifted off he felt a tremendous sense of relief. Of release.

The Company sent him an acknowledgement of his warning, carefully worded to imply that he was, in fact, crazy, but they didn't hold that against him.

He'd been on Harriman's Moon for three weeks, treating coughs and colds and the occasional broken bone, when word hit the waves about Nelson's World. He downloaded video of the wreckage of The Town. The flowers covered it, shrieking on a frequency that had shorted out the sound system after a second or two of recording.

Ouima hadn't made it out. None of them had.

"Lucky you left, Doc," said his assistant, Geri, as they stood together watching the vid. "Hard to believe. Flowers! Who'd have worried about the flowers?"

"Nobody," he said. "Well, just me."

The Company sent a suit to tell him he was under seal of confidence about the warning he'd issued, and that he'd be fired if he talked to any reporters.

He put in a call to the vid service as soon as the suit left the building and told them everything, the whole story. The news that the Company had been warned about Nelson's World broke like a summer storm, sweeping across all the colonies. Dr. Paul Lance was a hero.

Dr. Paul Lance was out of a job in short order, but that didn't much matter to the colonists on Harriman's Moon. They paid his salary out of their own pocket, and for the first time he began to feel at home. He had friends, and one day, perhaps, he'd have family.

In his dreams, he still heard the sounds. He'd had his earpods put back in, but even playing the music as loud as he dared, it didn't drown out the hum of the trees, the chirp of the grass, the screaming song of the flowers.

And he knew it never, ever would.

On the day that the first flower appeared on Harriman's Moon, he knew he'd brought it there.

Zombrarians Attack
by Moe Biers

The lightning storm that sizzled the sky and shrouded the city of New Orleans in darkness last night did more than knock out electricity; it set in motion events rarely seen outside of a Stephen King novel.

Eye witnesses say "Zombrarians"—the reanimated corpses of former librarians—had taken over the medical library.

"There were about a dozen of them," said librarian Crystal Weary. "They staggered around like zombies tend to do, moaning 'braiiiinnnssss' and 'sssssshhhhhhhhh.'"

Weary stumbled upon the creatures after receiving a strange message from renowned New Orleans psychic Creola Dejean warning Weary that she would be in danger if she returned to the library.

"I was on my way to Aunt Tiki's to meet my housemate [Chesney Forbanter], when this woman stopped me in Jackson Square warning me not to go back to the library," Weary recalled.

Dejean, who had been receiving flashes of vision with each lightning strike, had been searching the square for the woman she knew she had to warn. When asked to share her visions, the thirty-year-old hid her face behind her long curly hair, saying it was "too horrendous to talk about."

Weary didn't put much stock into Dejean's prediction, but she said she wanted to calm the obviously concerned woman.

"So I called Kevin [O'Neal], who was still at the library, to make sure everything was okay," Weary said. "But when he answered the phone, there was nothing but people screaming and the sounds of books falling and then the lights went out across the city."

It was then that Weary raced to the bar to grab Forbanter before both headed toward the library.

Weary wasn't the only one to experience a disconcerting phone call. O'Neal's friend Alex Raclitson had also tried to reach him, only to hear a scream for help before the phone went dead.

"I didn't know what was going down, but I wanted to be there to help out," said Raclitson, who is a karate and kung fu master. "I know how to take care of myself and my friends."

University medical student Melody Alvar was the first to spot the Zombrarians.

"I was in the anatomy section of the library doing research for my autopsy class when I heard this dragging sound from the stacks," Alvar said. "It was then that I heard my lab partners Kirsten and Tara shouting."

Kirsten Holmes and Tara Elizabeth Norton, also first-year med students, were mapping out a drawing of the brain when the two say they were rudely pushed aside and onto the floor by what they at first thought were third-years they had "dissed the day before in class."

"It was something that Lance would do," said Norton.

"But then we got a look at their faces," said Holmes, whose own face was screwed up in a look of disgust. "There were pockets of rotting flesh and their eyes were milky—"

"It was obvious they were suffering from Torticollis," interrupted Norton.

"Yes! It was just like Dr. Quickbeam said!" agreed Holmes. "Look how that one's ear is nearly touching its shoulder."

"They obviously weren't very intelligent," continued Norton, once the excitement of the diagnosis wore off. "They were eating the pictures of the brains."

"Well, they were missing their own," allowed Holmes.

When asked if they were frightened, Norton reiterated, "Did you hear the part of about them eating *pictures?*"

"They were definitely more interested in books than in us," said Holmes.

The co-eds separated and raced through the stacks, alerting others to the presence of the creatures, who, according to several witnesses, seemed to be getting stronger, faster, and smarter with each book they ate.

Librarian Winn King, who is blind in one eye, was taken by surprise when one of the Zombrarians came at him from the side.

"At first, I was scared because, well, it was the living dead and all," he said. "But it just pushed me out of its way as it reached for the books behind me."

"It could have been a bloodbath," he continued. "But the only real victims were the poor books."

Once King and O'Neal and fellow librarians Jan Germaine and Lucy McFadden ushered all patrons out of the library, the four decided to take a stand and fight the creatures destroying their beloved library.

"Of course the people were our first concern," said McFadden. "But once they were safe, we couldn't stand to see the library get destroyed, not when we could do something about it."

"Once it was clear that the zombies weren't a threat to us personally, there was no reason not to fight them," added Germaine.

It was about this time that Weary, Forbranter, and Raclitson reached the library. The seven quickly devised a plan.

"We needed to get them away from the rare books section," said O'Neal.

"After a quick brainstorming session we decided the best thing to do was lure them to the basement and trap them there until we figured out what to do with them," said King.

Raclitson, at great risk to himself, played decoy by holding out some of the rarest books in an attempt to get the zombies to chase him. O'Neal, Germaine, and McFadden acted as herders, making sure the zombies followed Raclitson, while Weary, Forbanter, and King did a sweep of the entire library to make sure there were no other creatures lurking about.

"I almost had a heart attack when I opened what I thought was a janitor's closet and saw a woman there," confessed Forbanter. "I thought it was a Zombrarian."

It wasn't a Zombrarian, but head librarian Imani Hughes.

"I was nearly attacked in my office," said Hughes, who was un-aware at the time of what was happening on the other side of the building. "This blonde chick burst in wielding a broom and de-manding to know why I was here. Why shouldn't I be here? It's my office. This is practically my home."

Once King arrived and clarified the matter, Hughes joined in the fight to reclaim the library.

"It was much simpler than we expected to get them into the base-ment," said O'Neal. "We just kept waving books in front of their faces. Anatomy books with pictures of the human brain on the cover seemed to work best."

"We tried to get them to move by yelling 'Brains over here,' but all they did was moan 'Ssshhhhh,'" added King. "They must have been stern librarians when they were alive."

But the situation escalated when they reached the basement.

"When Alex opened the door, we found blood all over the room and candles and strange symbols on the floor," said O'Neal.

"But it was too late to change our plans. The zombies were getting agitated with our game of keep-away," said Germaine.

"We did the only thing we could, which was get them in the room as fast as we could and then get out," said King.

By the time the group had made it back to the main floor, the police and FBI agents had arrived, having been tipped off by the three med students.

"We're still not sure exactly what happened in that library," said Federal Bureau of Investigation representative Charles Dashiell, "but you can be sure we're looking into it."

When asked about the zombies in the basement, all Dashiell would say is "no comment."

The existence of the Zombrarians cannot be confirmed by anyone other than the eleven eyewitnesses.

"I'm telling you, they are in the basement," insists Forbanter.

O'Neal said he believes the federal government is executing a cover-up.

"They are going to deny that are zombies there. And that the witch brought them," he insists.

The "witch" in question is Grace Tulane.

While admitting to being in the library's basement the night of the storm, Tulane claims that, like Dejean, she had a vision of the atrocities about to happen.

"There was a strange energy in the air that night," she said. "I was reading my tarot cards when I saw what was about to happen. I knew that I had to be there, that they would need my help to survive."

When asked about the bloodied knife and the allegation that there was a circle of blood on the library floor, Tulane simply said, "How else was I supposed to cast the circle?"

Was Tulane trying to help, or was she the one behind the zombie uprising?

"If I had that kind of power, why would I raise an army of Zombrarians?" Tulane asked.

And so the questions remain: Did Zombrarians really attack the medical library? If so, where did they come from? Are they still trapped in the basement? And is the government trying to hide their existence?

You can be sure the *Bizarre Bazaar* will keep you updated as this story develops.

There You Are, Then You Go
by Emily Moreton

Hannah gets stopped twelve times making her deliveries. Mostly in standard patrol checks, which have doubled during the past month, but three times on the street as well.

"What are you looking for?" she asks the twelfth time, kicking her heavy boots against the curb and refastening the blue bandana in her short hair. "Maybe I can help you if you tell me."

The police officer carries on unpacking boxes from the freezer cart attached to her bicycle and pretends she can't hear Hannah. "Those will melt if you leave them out in the sun," Hannah tells her.

"Write to HQ for compensation," the police officer says. She's not much older than Hannah, young to be on solo foot patrol, too young to have learned to hide her worry. Hannah is no threat; everyone knows the delivery drivers never are, too visible, too easy for the police to target, and Hannah feels a cold trickle of fear down her spine despite the burning mid-summer heat.

She's the last one back to the factory they've been living in for the last six months, since they were evicted from their abandoned apartment block during a security sweep. Hannah's not wild about the factory—it's not easy to secure, and there are too many ways for people to get in and hide—but there are fifty of them now, and they need the space. People bonded together with anyone who'd have them at first, but nothing's stable these days.

Everyone's buzzing with the new security, the additional stops; most in Hannah's group are messengers like her.

"Jackson's refused the package," Frederick complains. "Security sweeps made me an hour and a half late."

Half a dozen people add their own complaints, a babble of irritation that makes Hannah's heat- and smog-induced headache worse. She locks her bike and wanders into the makeshift kitchen, where the fridge is actually working for once and filled with bottles of ice-cold tap water. The after-taste of boiling lingers in her throat when she swallows half of one without pausing for breath.

"What do you think the extra security's about?" John asks from his seat on the edge of the sink, a bowl of half-shelled pea pods between his knees.

Hannah shrugs. "Probably just getting paranoid again. Or the president's on another tour of the country." If he is, they'll need to work on fitting better locks to the factory, unless they want to start looking for a new home. She's sure they just took in someone who works at a hardware manufactory; maybe he can get them something.

John pops a couple of peas in his mouth. "Still, it's weird," he says, and Hannah sighs in agreement.

Hannah was eighteen at the time of the outbreak. She didn't understand how serious it was at first, even with wards being closed at the hospital for infection control and the number of people in her college classes dropping due to illness. Everyone was paranoid about any sign of sickness, wondering if they'd caught it every time they sneezed, but only in the way people always got when the news started talking about something health-related.

She was packing to go home for spring break when the radio news announced that the state borders were being closed, and all transportation stopped. She's never made it out of the state since. It's impossible without a high-level ID.

A week after that, the president declared martial law in the face of a stream of claims on online blogs that no one even knew what the illness was, that they couldn't find a cure, that people were dying clueless and screaming. Their bodies were being thrown into mass graves.

A week after that, people woke up to find that every communication system in the city was off-line: power failed; running water was cut out. People rioted, and Hannah got used to walking through police patrols to buy milk.

A year after that, people started saying that the progression of the virus had been stopped and that things would go back to the way they had been.

Hannah is twenty-six now, and she's still waiting.

"I'm going out," she tells John later that week, clipping her ID prominently to the front of her vest. The security patrols get trigger happy when they're nervous.

"Out where?" John asks. "Curfew's in less than an hour."

Hannah shrugs. "I won't miss it, don't worry." John raises an eyebrow at her. "Okay, I won't get caught by a patrol coming home, how's that?"

John waves her off, and she heads out into the late evening sun. It's still warm enough for people to be wandering around, like her, in shirt sleeves, and it could almost be a normal day, if it weren't for the extra police officers lounging in the entrances to side streets and eyeing everyone like they're about to set off a bomb or start proselytizing. Wouldn't be the first time, in either case.

The café is busy as Hannah makes her way between the tables and through the heavy drape curtaining off the back room.

Bradley looks up from the large center table as the curtain falls closed behind her, leaving the room only dimly lit by a handful of candles, the window still boarded up. "Hannah," he says. "I wasn't sure you'd be able to come."

Hannah takes an empty chair and looks round the group of familiar faces. "Me neither."

She's known Bradley since she was twenty-two, from a jail cell when she was caught somewhere she shouldn't have been after curfew. He ran a group, he told her, that gathered information and got people out of the city.

"Out?" Hannah asked, resting her head in her hands. There were twelve of them in a cell that obviously hadn't been designed to hold more than two or three, and the smell was getting to her.

"Out," Bradley said. "Back to their homes if they can go, or just—out. There are better places than this." He sat down next to her and leaned in, smelling of familiar sweet smoke. "Did you know Canada reopened the border last month? They still have *elections* up there, for free governments."

When they managed to talk (Bradley) and bribe (Hannah) their way out of a court hearing, Hannah had committed to running intelligence in the city, finding people who wanted to go, and putting them in touch with Bradley and his people.

"Perfect cover," Bradley would say, handing her a couple of innocuous-looking packages. "Delivery riders go everywhere. No one will even remember you've been there."

"Thanks," Hannah said dryly, but it was true. People with money had gotten out before the city was locked down, leaving behind the people without. With her mother's West Indian genes, she blended right in.

Toni hands her a cup of water, and Bradley nods for Angel to pick up where she left off when Hannah walked in. "They're getting wise to being tracked," Angel says with a shrug. It's not impossible to stay one step ahead of the police and the security forces, but it's getting harder. "But everything points to them gearing up for something major. They're not just setting up more sweeps so the president will think they're doing a good job; something's coming."

"But what?" Bradley asks. "And is it really something we'd be better off getting people away from?"

Angel shrugs again. "I can't tell yet. It sounds like an attack, but I don't know who by."

Toni looks away, and her voice is quiet when she says, "Maybe they're coming to rescue us."

Hannah can't sleep for thinking of it that night, lying perfectly still on her pallet, staring at the ceiling, too far away for her to see in the darkness, listening to fifty people breathing around her.

Maybe they're coming to rescue us.

John's been with her since the dean at college announced they were suspending classes indefinitely, a couple of weeks before the military took control of the city. Frederick brought six people when he knocked at their door asking for living space. Maria's got two children, and David's deaf brother Alex looks after them while everyone else works. They speak sign language better than English.

Maybe they're coming to rescue us.

Maybe, but what kind of rescue are they offering? She's not at all sure it's the kind she and her people will fit into.

When the military returns, a week later, she breathes a sigh of relief, like she's been waiting for it. The city's been officially under military control ever since the outbreak, but in reality, the police took it over years ago. Maria's kids are too young to recognize the rumble of tanks rolling down the streets, the rattle of barbed wire fences going up and the smell of cordite in the air.

"Come away from the window," Hannah tells them, hands on their shoulders to steady them as they stand on the back of the couch. Maria's on early shift at the hospital, and Hannah hopes she'll have managed to slip away and be on her way back. "Kids, come on."

"No!" Darren whines. "I want to watch the soldiers."

"I know you do." She looks over her shoulder at the dark interior of the factory, people sitting together pressed back into the shadows, like that will help them not be noticed. If the soldiers do a sweep, they'll have to run, and the rush of adrenaline is making her hands shake. "Maybe later, okay, but come down now."

"No," Darren says again. He pushes Hannah's hands away. "Mom would let us."

"I don't care." Hannah tugs him and Lucy a little harder than she probably should, and the three of them go backward off the couch, landing hard on the floor. Lucy starts crying instantly, the sound bouncing loud off the walls, and Hannah sees John wince at the volume. She claps her hand over Lucy's mouth and gets close in the little girl's face. "Shut up. Shut up or I'll give you to the soldiers."

Lucy's eyes go wide, her cries cut off like Hannah's flipped a switch. She scrambles away from Hannah, clutching at Darren's hand and scuttling across the floor to Alex.

Hannah takes a deep breath and goes to sit with John and the others. She won't be going out to work today, not until they know a bit more about what's going on. "I was just trying to keep her quiet," she says to John's frown.

"I think it worked," he says, looking away.

The soldiers divide up the city with barbed wire fences and security points held at gunpoint. A messenger ID isn't enough to get through them, and, apparently, neither is a hospital one. Maria doesn't come back, and Hannah is cut off from Bradley's group, the café in another sector.

"Why do you think they're here?" John asks, drinking tea in the early evening gloom. They don't dare turn on the lights after dark now—there's a patrol based two streets over, and the boards on the windows won't keep the light from showing.

"I don't know," Hannah says truthfully. She's not sure she wants to.

The next morning, worn down by Maria's kids' crying and the low-level tension curling through the factory, she slips out and hits the street.

There are more people there than usual, but they're drifting, standing in clumps on the sidewalk, going nowhere. Hardly anyone lives near where they work, and the sector checkpoints have rendered almost everyone unemployed in the space of a few days.

She's been out there for an hour, drinking takeout coffee and listening to speculation getting wilder and wilder, when something taps her on the shoulder and a voice hisses, "This way."

She tenses, ready to fight even though she knows it's a bad idea, but lets herself be pulled off the street and into the gap between two apartment buildings.

"Relax," the voice says. The hand on her arm loosens, allowing her to step back and look up.

"Grace."

"Where've you been?" Hannah asks, tucked in the back of a dark coffee shop. Grace is too tall, too dark-haired, too striking in her all-black outfit to ever blend in, but at least this way, she's a little hidden. "It's been months."

Grace smiles slightly and sips her tea. "Lots of people need me, not just here."

Hannah blinks. She still can't wrap her mind around Grace being here, now, just when they need her, like she's got a sixth sense for these things. "You were out of the city?"

"Yes." Grace reaches across to ruffle Hannah's hair, and Hannah grins. No one else gets away with that, but she owes Grace her life for rescuing her from a group of thieves who wanted one of her packages and weren't bothered about going a bit beyond theft to get it. She only remembers the snap of Grace's coat before she was on the floor, fighting not to lose consciousness, but Grace was there when she woke up, and the boys were gone. Grace even took the parcel for her, when she was too dizzy to walk in a straight line and terrified she'd be fired if she didn't make the delivery. "There's a whole world outside the city, you know."

"No, since I can't get out of it."

Grace smiles again, a slight lift at the corners of her mouth. "I think you're going to need to."

Everyone knows Grace, and walking through the city with her is a little like Hannah imagines it would have been to know a celebrity, back when celebrities were more than just memories. Half the people they pass say hello, and plenty of them come up to talk as well, to thank Grace for some tiny act of kindness she showed them, sometimes years ago. Hannah feels invisible next to her, watching the people who back into the shadows, avoiding Grace's eye, too shy to approach her. Not that she minds—the last thing she needs is for anyone to realize she's someone memorable.

"I have to go through the checkpoint," Grace says when the wire fence comes in sight. "There's a young woman who was born during the outbreak living there. I promised I'd bring the medication she needs."

"Oh," Hannah says, a little disappointed. Of course she's no one special to Grace, not when everyone loves her.

Grace laughs at her and gives her a brief hug. "I'd love to bring you with me, but it's too dangerous. I don't want to risk you, and you should talk to your group. We can meet again in a couple of days."

John shakes his head and sighs, the way he always does when Hannah mentions seeing Grace. "What?" Hannah asks, like she always does.

"Sorry," John says. He's holding Lucy in his lap, her face tear-stained where it's pressed into his shirt, but she's sleeping, finally. "I don't know why you're so much quicker to trust her than anyone else."

"Because I can," Hannah protests quietly. They've had this argument before, and she hates it but can't help having it again. "She's got medication for people in the next sector. She saved my life the first time I met her."

"I know." John looks down at Lucy and touches her hair gently.

Hannah flops onto the couch next to him and offers him her mug of tea. "Why don't you trust her?" It's not the first time she's asked this, but John guards his secrets close, and this one is no different.

John just shakes his head again and accepts her tea, and Hannah decides she'll wait to tell him the rest of what Grace said till they've met up again.

Everyone has a theory about why the military are back; it's all Hannah hears when she's out, all that her gang in the factory talks about when they're all there in the evenings. Even Lucy and Darren have stopped wanting to look at the soldiers. They haven't been out of the factory since the tanks rolled into town, and Hannah plans to keep it that way. She doesn't like the rumors she's hearing about the hospital staff, how they're being held there for something that the soldiers won't explain, and she doesn't want Lucy and Darren hearing it as well.

She's used to people talking, to the wild ideas that people come up with when they're frightened and confused, but it's different this time. There are still wild, out-there suggestions, of course, but it doesn't take long for most people to start saying the same thing: The military have come to clear out the city. They've thrown up the fences to make their job easier, and they're not going to stop until everyone's gone.

"What would they want with the city?" Frederick asks when the third person mentions it as they're gathering for the evening meal.

Hannah looks down at her plate, not willing to give an answer, so it's Nishma who says it: "Ready for another outbreak. They bring everyone who's infected here, and…" She glances at Lucy and doesn't finish, but Hannah sees Frederick's eyes flicker in acknowledgement of what she hasn't said.

"Do you think it's true?" she asks Grace when she finds her at the coffee shop the next morning. Grace's expression is troubled as she nods.

"I do. I think it's time for you and your people to think about getting out of the city before the military do it for you, because they're not going to stop at asking nicely."

Out of the city. No one Hannah knows has been out of the city in eight years. She has no idea what it's like out there, where they'd go or how, especially without Bradley and his people to help them. She finds people who want to leave, not places for them to go when they do. Not fifty of them, wanting to stay together, safety in numbers and familiarity…

Grace's hand closes over hers. "I can help you," she says.

Hannah's made plenty of decisions about what her group should do—leave, stay, get a new job, take up a trade that's not so legal, dump a girlfriend who's maybe not so safe, string along a boyfriend a bit longer for some good information—but she can't make this decision for them.

She puts it to a vote instead.

"Wow, like a democracy," David says with a grin. He was too young to vote when people still could, and no one's voted on anything for years.

"Just like," Hannah agrees, except that in a democracy, the majority vote would affect the actions of everyone, and in this case, it's really more like a show of hands to see who's going and who's staying. This is too serious for her to try to exert control over them when they have no idea what the soldiers will do to get people out. It's an ingrained fear from the first time—never, ever trust them, not even the ones who seem trustworthy, not unless you want to disappear and never come back.

In the end, it doesn't matter: Everyone votes to leave, even John, with a sigh of defeat after hearing that Grace is going to get them out.

"I'll need money to organize it," Grace says when Hannah tells her. "Identity cards for all of you won't be cheap, not when people know what's going on here."

Hannah shakes her head. She should have asked more questions, should never have raised their hopes. Even Grace can't make fifty people disappear just by waving her hand. "I haven't got any," she says. "We can't even get to work, not since the fences went up."

"It's all right," Grace says calmly. "You're trustworthy, aren't you? And your people? I'm sure we can work something out."

"Thank you," Hannah says. They've all got skills; they can raise whatever money Grace needs, just as long as they don't have to face the soldiers. She takes a deep breath and asks the question she's been trying to avoid since Darren curled up next to her one night, glancing over his shoulder to check on Lucy before whispering in her ear. "What about Maria?"

"Your friend who works at the hospital?" Grace asks. "I can probably do something about that as well."

They designate ten people to each group, one group going every week, Hannah and John in the last group. They're down to twenty people in the factory when Hannah's woken up by a thump of sound and vibrations running through the floor.

Over to the east, the stars are hidden by smoke, the dark night cut through with flames.

"Jesus," John breathes next to her. "They bombed it."

Grace doesn't show up when she's supposed to, nor the next day.

John shakes his head as Hannah bites at her fingernails. "Don't say anything," she tells him. "She must have been held up."

"Sure," John says, and goes to huddle with Frederick, trying to figure out how the last of them can get out. Rumor is the soldiers bombed the sector when the people living there didn't leave fast enough, then dusted off their hands and moved west. No one moves fast enough for the military when they've got a deadline, and they're great at big gestures to bring people into line.

They're all packed up, the last two groups; they agreed, after the bomb, that they'd rather risk capture by going out together. There's still no move by the soldiers in their section to do anything beyond eye them suspiciously and keep them where they are, but they're taking the city in sections; it's only a matter of time. Hannah tries not to think about the people they took before the bomb, or the ones who were still there when it detonated.

They give it a week, then John says, "This is ridiculous. She's not coming."

"She promised," Hannah says, but she can feel herself wavering. What if…? There are too many what ifs for her to pick one. "She was going to get Maria. What if she's just been held up coming across the city? It's probably harder now."

The look John gives her says he thinks she's naïve to keep hoping. "Please," she says. "One more day."

Chances are they won't make it anyway, without Grace. One more day can't do them any harm.

"Oh thank God," Grace's voice says in the pitch dark of early morning, and Hannah gasps, breathless with relief. "I was so worried you'd have tried to leave without me. Hannah, are you there?"

Hannah lights a candle with shaking hands. "Yes, I'm here. We're all here. We were going to leave today."

Grace crosses the room and gives her a quick hug. She doesn't look any different. Around them, the others are slowly waking up, muttering and rubbing their eyes. "It's gotten so much harder to get through the checkpoints. They wouldn't accept my ID in sector five; I thought I was never going to get back in time."

"Did you get Maria?" Frederick asks, looking behind her. They sent Alex with Maria's kids in the first group, just in case.

"Of course," Grace says, half-turning to look at him. "I got her out first, she's waiting for you all, with her children. Are you ready? Can you leave now? If we hurry, we can get out before daybreak."

The curfew's still in effect, won't lift for another couple of hours, and the empty city makes Hannah shiver. The only lights come from the guard points as they creep past them, all in black, moving on silent feet. Grace is out front, leading the way, and John is guarding the back of the line, but all Hannah's really aware of is the person in front of her, sliding round corners and through gaps in the wire fences until she's too turned around to know where they are. If they lose someone now, that's it, they're gone.

The sky's turning gray, freezing pre-dawn light when the person in front of her—Nishma, maybe, she's not sure—comes to a stop. "What's wrong?" Hannah asks, and Grace's voice answers, close to her, "We're here."

Hannah looks up, and she's right. There's one last fence between them and a wide, empty expanse of burned-out trees and sunken, twisted freeway, and Hannah's breath catches. They're going to make it, free and clear with lives that aren't constrained by the police and the soldiers and wherever they can find to live when they lose their place to a security sweep. She blinks to clear her eyes, blurry with tiredness and maybe a little with emotion.

Grace is pushing people through the fence, pointing them toward the tree line fifty feet away. "Go," she says, grabbing for Hannah's arm.

Hannah shakes her off. "The others first."

Grace doesn't argue, just pushes them forward. There's no light this far out of the city—she half-expects sweeping lights like in prison films, but of course there hasn't been that kind of power for years now, and so all she sees is patches of black moving against the darkness. And then...

She squints at the treeline as John brushes passed her. There's something there, something moving slowly toward them, the movement clear against the rapid flight of her people away from the city. "Do you—" she starts, meaning to ask if Grace has people there to receive them.

"Go," Grace says, pushing her, and she does, propelled by Grace's shove, the intense low rumble of her voice in the dark, stumbling in the grass as she starts to run without meaning to. Toward the light, except no one could have a light out here without raising suspicion, and that's not the steady beam of a flashlight; it's a flash, and she knows that flash.

She screams, still running, helpless, not even sure what she's screaming.

It doesn't matter. The flash comes again, and she knows she's far too late to do anything but keep going.

No Place Like Home

by Tamela J. Ritter

At the end of the Galaxy, Judy Garland had never looked better. In life, she had been a tragic figure that the studio system had chewed up and spit out, but in the Galaxy Diner in the French Quarter of New Orleans, she had her place of honor. She was positioned next to lesser names—so that she shone brightest—and right above the coffee urns so that it had become a tradition among the waitstaff, especially the starving-artist types, to say a little prayer to Ms. Garland as they brewed their third, fourth, and fifth pots of their shift.

Even Alex, the effeminate busboy who spent his nights as Lady Freya, the MC at the All Male Nude Revue—but dreamed of even more—said a prayer to Judy. To him, Judy Garland was like the Virgin Mary, as her daughter Liza was the Christ. And when he dreamed of becoming something with his art, instead of the sign of the cross, it was three clicks of his heels.

Tara prayed to Judy that, like the character that had made her a legend, she too would be swept away from her dreary black-and-white world and be spiraled to a colorful life of adventure with strange men: straw men, tin men, and lion men. Any man but the one she currently knew. Her husband, Kevin, was the most black-and-white, dust-bowl man she had ever met.

Her prayers had gone unanswered for so long that she was beginning to doubt the power of Alex's deity as much as she had her own God.

As the coffee sputtered its last drops, she checked that she wasn't being observed, leaned into the picture, and chanted quietly, "I wish for a Technicolor world."

"No, honey, you are doing it wrong," she heard from behind.

She panicked; her first thought was of the coffee and the boss's many loud declarations that if she couldn't master coffee-making that she was going to be "shit-canned."

"No, not that," Alex said, standing beside her with his hand on her shoulder, staring dreamily at Judy.

This was one of the many things Tara had been forced to get used to when she took Alex as her best friend. The touching. With Kevin, she would have to be falling down a stairwell before he would reach out to make any physical contact that didn't include the possibility of procreation. But Alex was truly a "hands-on" friend.

"You aren't asking right," Alex corrected. "You have to make your request three times while clicking your heels. Dontcha know nothin'?"

Tara put her palm to her forehead. "Of course." Then turning back to the signed photo, she whispered, "Please forgive me." She closed her eyes to imagine ruby slippers on her feet as she clicked them together. "I wish for a Technicolor world. I wish for a Technicolor world. I wish for a Technicolor world."

She opened her eyes, almost expecting to be transported to a musically enhanced world instead of the almost-deserted diner.

Nope, still on the farm, Toto.

"Forget that," Alex said, waving away the disappointment Tara tried to hide. "I'll show you a Technicolor world. Come to my performance tonight at Aunt Tiki's."

"You're finally ready to reveal your masterpiece to the general public?" Tara teased.

"No, but the bums at Auntie's don't count, do they?"

"Well, how can I miss that? I'll just have to see if Kevin has any plans for tonight; if not, then I will definitely be there."

"Honey, you tell that man that if you can't come out, then I will come and perform in your living room. He'll push you out the door."

"True," Tara said with a smile as she took the full coffee pot. "I'll see you tonight." She went to fill her lone customer's cup, but not before glaring at Judy. *Thanks for nothing.*

But what Tara had forgotten—and what she was soon going to be painfully aware of—was that before Dorothy got her Oz, she first had had to survive some pretty nasty weather.

Creola Dejean—and yes, that is her real name—hated the rain. It was bad for business, sure, but she also hated it for the same reasons that meteorologists hated it. Like people think weatherpersons should know the future to its last dew point, people expected the same from their fortune tellers. Never mind that weather was usually the last of most people's worries—the term fortune teller was an insult to what it was she did.

She didn't read a person's fortune; she read people. She saw who they were, what they wanted, needed, and had to have. The cards she used, merely tools; reading lines on palms was an excuse to make contact, to feel the energy behind their skin; runes spoke to her, but it was people's reactions she looked for.

So, if there was a bit of weather, a spot of rain, a speck of thunder, what did that matter to her? Except that no one came to Jackson Square in the rain. The busy walkways that bordered the park on most days were deserted, and the jazz bands, acrobats, and dance troupes that regularly mingled and rubbed against the dozens of others like herself were somewhere dry, because if there were no tourists, there were no coins thrown into their coffers.

Then why are you here? she thought to herself, running her hands over the silk cover of her small table. She couldn't really say. Just an inkling that she needed to be there. Sometimes, she even freaked herself out. And sometimes she thought she was full of shit. The problem was she never knew which one was true at any given time.

She checked her watch. Five more minutes and then she was going for a drink. Weather and lost souls be damned. She had just made that decision when a lost soul presented itself in the form of a drenched girl who was walking from table to table even though there were only a handful of people stupid enough to be trying to make a buck in this weather.

Creola watched and knew the girl would come to her, knew she was looking for something, and knew she would find it with Creola. She loved these types of clients, the ones who were tuned to the psychic vibrations that emanated from people. They were hard to find, because they had to feel a connection to you, but when they did, it wasn't about money or what color you happened to be wearing that day; it was a feeling they had that you were *the* person to be reading their cards.

The girl was what Creola's mama would have called a "Honey Child." One of those pasty-white, delicate flowers that were more than likely in their mid-thirties but would always look to be someone's child. Always look like they needed someone to protect them.

Creola waited patiently for the girl to come to her. She didn't call out to her but sat and patted her cards, starting her reading already. Creola knew one of the girl's needs before she even sat down. It wasn't her third eye that was telling her; it was the first two. The girl desperately needed an umbrella. Her long, dark curls were plastered to her face, and her silk-blend flowered dress stuck to her curves.

Finally the girl chose Creola and sat down. The first question Creola asked surprised them both: "Do you trust me?"

The girl seemed even more shocked by her own speedy answer: "Yes."

"Then come with me," Creola said, getting up and beginning to put away her table with the haste of a black market hawker when the cops come to patrol. The girl followed obediently, yet skittishly, as they made their way down the street. The wind was picking up and making it impossible to walk a straight line and keep their clothes where they belonged.

What they needed was a quiet place to get out of the storm. What they found was Aunt Tiki's.

"Grace, close the goddamned door would ya? We got enough of Mother Nature in here already," Brian scolded his wild-haired, tattooed barmaid from across the bar where he was sweeping up debris from the last time someone ventured in and brought the hammering wind with them.

The first set of customers to disturb the quiet of the bar was two women who found a quiet table in a corner. The older one, a black lady with an animal print turban over her long brown hair, Brian had seen at Jackson Square before, hawking fortunes. The younger one, who he had to card before serving, looked as if this might be her first time in a bar.

The new customers were Alex, a guy who had hit on Brian more than once, wearing all black and chalk white face paint for some odd reason, and the girl he brings in sometimes who always reminded Brian of Dorothy from *The Wizard of Oz*—something about the lost look in her eyes perhaps.

Grace, who usually worked only weekends because of the tips and her adversity to talking to people, thought the girl was more like Alice in *Alice's Adventures in Wonderland*, which had traumatized her as a child but not nearly as badly as *The Wizard of Oz*—flying monkeys for Chrissake! Who wasn't frightened of flying monkeys?

Having cleaned up the mess, Brian went back to what he was doing before: covering the windows with plywood. Growing up in Tornado Alley and spending his adulthood in the tropical climes of Florida and now New Orleans, he knew the signs. He was resigned to riding out the worst of it and preparing himself for all Mother Nature's possibilities.

Grace thought he was being a cautionary pussy.

"I can't believe no one is here," Alex pouted, his pancake makeup already looking well-used, and his single tear made with black eyeliner was smearing. "This was supposed to be my big night."

Tara, who was having trouble concentrating with the barman's pounding hammer and the violently whistling wind, tried to console him. "It's all right. You can practice on me and…" she looked around, "the four other people in the bar. Then after the storm, when people come out…or you know…another night, you will be that much more prepared."

Alex looked uplifted for a moment then looked at his surroundings. There was a woman wearing an African print dress and a matching turban in a corner dealing cards to a mouse of a girl, and there was the bartender bickering with his waitress. Not exactly the audience he was looking for. "Nah, I'm changing. Maybe we can still get to the Exile before that new, hot bartender leaves."

Tara was about to comment that all the bartenders at Exile were hot when a shock of thunder rattled the walls of the bar, and a half a breath later, lightning lit up the sky right outside the only two windows that had yet to be boarded up. She jumped out of her seat and found herself shaking under the table by the time the darkness came.

Alex watched this and then raised his hand in the air to alert the waitress. "We're going to need two shots of tequila over here."

"So, what's your name, child?" Creola asked as she removed her favorite set of cards from her bag.

"Kirsten," the client answered. "And you are?"

"Unimportant," Creola said, handing the cards to Kirsten. "Now shuffle those cards, and if there are specific questions you want the answers to, think of those while shuffling."

Separating the worn, damp deck into two piles, Kirsten looked hesitantly to Creola, not sure if she should shuffle them like she would her pinochle cards—and if so, would a bridge be totally inappropriate?—or if there was a special way. After that she worried that if she spent all her time while shuffling concerned about proper technique, she would have none left to concentrate on the questions she wanted answers to. If she didn't think hard about the questions, would she get the wrong answers? Would she know any more than she did right now and if not, what was the point? *And, oh, by the way,* she said to herself, completely disgusted, *what are the questions you want answered anyway?* There were too many swimming inside her head. Why did she come to New Orleans? To Jackson Square? The only question she could think right now was: Is it too late to run?

"Child, relax. The cards ain't going to hurt you, and neither will I," Creola said, reaching out and patting Kirsten on the hand. The girl flinched, but then smiled shakily. Suddenly there was a boom that sounded as if the air was being ripped apart, and they both flinched, Kirsten screamed.

They heard the call for shots from across the room. Creola echoed the request right before the power went out.

"Shit! Goddamned!" Grace cursed into the darkness.

"Well said," an effeminate voice from somewhere in the fringe of the blackness said. Another voice giggled nervously, and Brian's voice of reasoned calm soon filled the room.

"Everyone relax. We got plenty of candles; let me find the—" There was a spark of light and then the room was thrown into a haze that barely cast more than shadow. More candles were lit, and Grace walked around with shot glasses and tequila. Brian directed everyone to the center of the room as the walls continued to shake with even more force.

They lit candles all around them as they sat at a table in the middle of the room and tried hard to disregard the roaring wind beyond the walls and plywood windows.

"So, Marcel Marceau, you going to do something for us?" Grace asked Alex as she downed her shot, slamming the empty glass upside down.

Alex looked highly affronted at his art being disregarded, yet Tara's earlier comment reminded him that that was their reason for coming to Aunt Tiki's in the first place.

"I am not a trained monkey to prance around at your every whim. I am an artist!" Alex huffed.

Grace was unimpressed. "You know, for a mime, you talk a lot."

Alex did the only thing a mime can do while being heckled: He flipped her off.

"Well shit. If we don't got no entertainment, no music and no way out, what are we going to do to pass the time?" Grace asked.

They all looked around at each other and shrugged.

"Drinking games?" Brian finally suggested.

Grace and Alex's faces lit up. Creola looked maternally disapproving, and Kirsten looked terrified. Tara didn't like the idea of getting drunk with a bunch of strangers in the middle of a hurricane, but she didn't like any of her other choices, either.

"What kind of drinking game?" she asked hesitantly.

"Spin the Bottle?" Brian offered.

Grace looked around the group. "That's not a drinking game, and there is no one here I want to see with no clothes on."

"I don't know where you learned your Spin the Bottle, but where I'm from, it's a kissing game."

"Of course it is," Brian laughed. "But it could be a drinking game if we take shots instead of removing clothes."

"Where's the fun in that?" Grace asked. "Spinning a bottle and taking a drink. That's boring. How about," she tapped her chin with her index finger, "I Never?"

Tara, who had always been intimidated by the hostile bar maiden, was weary of this game from the title alone. "How's it played?"

"You say something you've never done, and then everyone who has done it has to take a shot," Creola answered. They all looked at her. "What? I went to college."

"For example," started Grace, filling the shot glasses, "I've never swum in the ocean." Most of them took a drink to that, Tara remembering her honeymoon in Miami Beach.

"I've never kissed a man," Brian said next.

The rest of them all took a drink.

"That is so not fair," said Tara. Then it was her turn. "I've never kissed a woman."

Again everyone drank, everyone but herself and Kirsten.

Creola was thinking back to college; she certainly had learned a lot at Tulane.

"Never kissed another woman?" Grace asked Tara. "You don't know what you are missing."

"You going to show her?" Brian said with a hopeful smile.

Tara gulped and Grace laughed. "Maybe later."

"Your turn, Kirsten," Creola said softly to the girl who looked like she wanted to crouch in a corner.

"Mine?" Kirsten whispered. "I don't...well...I've...I've never played this game before."

Grace was just about to retort when Brian cut across her. "Good one. Not many rookies pull that one out." He tipped his shot back; Creola, Grace, and Alex shortly followed.

Creola said, "I've never sung in public."

Again Tara and Kirsten did not take a drink.

"I never drank milk past its expiration," Alex said.

Everyone else had to stop laughing before they took their drinks. Alex looked disgusted.

"I've never puked in a public place," said Grace.

Again Tara and Kirsten did not take a drink; again Creola thought of Tulane.

"I've never gone down on a man," Brian said, beaming.

Once again, Tara and Kirsten did not drink; once again, Creola thought of Tulane; Alex thought of the night before.

"You never went down on Kevin?" Alex asked Tara. "No wonder that man is such a walking mood-killer."

Grace looked disgustedly from Tara to Kirsten. "Jesus, what *have* you guys done?"

Kirsten looked ashamed at her inexperience, but Tara was pissed. "I don't want to play this game anymore."

"What? Why?" Alex said.

"It's stupid. I don't want to share my experiences, or lack of them, with a bunch of strangers."

"Strangers are the best people to share your embarrassing lack of experience with," Brain said. "You'll never have to see us again. We won't mock you for the rest of your life."

"Yeah, only tonight," Grace said. "If we survive this storm, we'll never have to see each other again. So, ya wanna make out?"

Tara glared at her and then took a shot for no good reason other than she didn't have a retort.

"Whose turn is it?" Alex asked.

"Little Mousy," Grace said, pointing her finger at Kirsten, who gulped again.

"Um," Kirsten thought and then thought some more and a bit more for good measure. Grace began to tap her fingers aggravatingly on the table, which only flustered Kirsten more. "I've never snorted coke."

Grace and Tara took a shot.

They all looked at Tara.

"What? I had to be doing something when I wasn't servicing my husband, didn't I?"

"When did you snort coke?" Alex asked.

"You don't know me as well as you think you do. Before I met Kevin, I hung with a different crowd, a crowd that did coke, among other things."

"Is that when you worked at Harrah's?" Alex asked.

"Yeah."

"Alrighty, well if get-to-know Alice is over, can we continue with the game?" Grace asked.

"Alice?" Tara asked.

"Alice. Like *Alice in Wonderland*. You got 'looking for a way out' written all over you, honey. Even Fortune Teller over there could see that, couldn't ya?"

The looks shot at Grace by both Tara and Creola could have ignited another electrical storm. This all made Grace laugh as she pounded another tequila shot.

"Anyway," Alex said to ease tensions. "It's my turn. I've never slept outside under the stars."

Everyone else drank to that one, Kirsten coughing harshly with the first time she'd actually slammed a shot. Creola smacked her lightly on the back. Grace rolled her eyes and filled everyone up again.

Creola, who was beginning to flush from the amount of alcohol she had consumed, said, "I've never flashed my titties for beads."

Grace, Tara, Kirsten all took a drink. This time they all looked at Kirsten. She blushed, "I had come here for Mardi Gras on my twenty-first birthday. I think it was the last time I got drunk."

"Oh goody, so we'll have flashing to look forward to later?" asked Grace.

"Grace, were you beaten as a child?" Brian asked.

Grace laughed. "Oh, great defender of women and small animals, show me the error of my ways. Punish me for my transgressions and all that shit. Fuck you. You know I call 'em as I see 'em."

"And how do you see them?" Creola asked politely.

Grace beamed as if she had just received a rare gift, which she had. No one ever gave her license to say what she thought. She usually didn't need it, but to have it offered to her like that was too good to turn down. She looked at the sorry assembly about her and took a deep breath, as if to have enough air to get it all out before she was cut off.

"Let's see...Marcel over there wants people to look at him, to appreciate him and take him seriously—for once. This one over here, the Voodoo Empress, also wants to be taken seriously, and she wonders how she could still be in debt for a college education that got her fuckin' nowhere and prayin' 'Please, God, don't let anyone see that I'm making it up as I go.' Then there is these two," she said, pointing her index and middle fingers at Tara and Kirsten. "They want to be saved so bad you can smell the reek of it on their skin. She," pointing now to Kirsten, "wants her white knight to sweep her up and ride her out of town. She wants to be touched, to feel as good with someone else as she does by herself. Then this one, she wonders how it is that her knight in shining armor turned out to be such a disappointment, and is he the reason her life is in such a shitty mess? Is it his fault? Please say yes, because if not, if not, she's going to have to deal with the fact that it might actually be her own."

Suddenly the storm outside got louder; the wind rattled the boards violently against their nails, and the pelting rain on the rooftop sounded as if it were beating against the gates of hell. Or it could be that the room stilled and quieted as they all individually thought of ways to kill this woman and, simultaneously, and extremely begrudgingly, wondering how she had possibly figured them out. Creola was even half tempted to bequeath the evil wench her cards and runes upon her death.

"And you, Grace?" Brian asked after the silence roared on an uncomfortable amount of time.

"Me?" Grace asked, laughing then taking a swig directly from the almost empty bottle. "I'm just a bitch who takes out her own bad life choices on the innocent and the dumb."

"Hear, hear," Alex said, toasting and downing his drink with a flourish of jazz hands, again trying to lighten the mood. He was the only drag queen/mime he knew who didn't like the drama involved in a cat fight. He was also trying not to wonder which of those two he was: innocent or dumb.

Tara got up and walked to the boarded-up door. Hiding her tears and silent panic, she placed her hand on the wood, as if to gauge the storm and if there was any possible way to get out of there. She had felt the walls closing in on her, her breath harder to catch. But when she put her hand on that piece of wood, she felt the power that rocketed outside these walls. She wanted to be part of that, wanted this to be the answer to her prayer, this to swirl her to her own Technicolor world.

The wind knocked her back before she even realized that she had opened the door. It would be tough to determine whose scream had been louder, Kirsten's or Alex's.

"Jesus!" Alex screamed. "What are you doing?"

But Tara couldn't hear him. The eye of the storm that had been calling her out with its deceptive calm and eerie lack of movement was now over the bar and all of the lower French Quarter. For a brief, glorious moment, the streets were empty and the only sound she heard was the water dripping off the roofs above her and the glass from the smashed windows settling onto the ground.

Without a look back, she began walking slowly, as if in a trance, down Decatur. Others had discovered the phenomenon of being in the exact middle of their utter destruction and had begun cautiously opening doors and entering the street as if having just woken from death. She disregarded them, disregarded the wall of water and doom in the distance, and made her way toward home.

"Are you fucking crazy?" someone said behind her. It wasn't until she was grabbed forcibly around her middle from the back and tugged that she acknowledged someone had followed her.

"Alex, let me go!"

"Jesus, Tara! This is not Kansas, and you are not really Dorothy. This storm is not going to take you to Oz."

Struggling against him but growing weak because of the tears and the fight with herself to keep them from leaking out, she turned and began squirming to get free. But the beating she did on his chest was so light, it was like a forfeit.

He sensed her surrender and let her go. She reached into her pocket. "Do you know what this is?"

"Yeah, it's your cell phone. So what?"

"How many times have you seen me trying to call Kevin? How many times did I wonder aloud, or even to myself how he was? He could be dead, swept away to sea, and I found myself barely caring."

"Is that why you're out here? To get to him? To prove that the marriage is worth saving?"

"Don't you see? She's right. Everything she said is right. I'm the reason I'm miserable, not him, not my career, or lack of. I've got to change my own life."

"Of course she was, and of course you do, but not tonight and not right now."

"I've got to get to him. It's not fair to him."

"What the hell is your problem?" This was not Alex. This was Grace, and she looked pissed at both Tara and herself for being out at all.

"What the fuck do you care?" Tara asked. Just because Grace was the catalyst for change didn't mean Tara had to actually like her.

"I don't care. But for some reason, everyone else does and yet are too chickenshit to do anything about it. You see those clouds back there?" They all looked behind them at the swirl of precarious rain and loose rubble. "Now, you see that in front of us?"

Tara looked all around her and knew it was suicide to be out there, yet felt incapable of movement.

After a good two minutes of Grace watching the clouds get closer, feeling the air get wetter, and hearing the wind grow shriller as the pathetic lump in front of her just stood there looking lost, she took matters into her own hand—fist actually—and clocked the bitch.

Bits of cracked conversation, raised voices, and even fractured laughter drifted to Tara's unconscious mind. "Come on, Dorothy," she heard close to her ear and thought of a friend made of tin who only wanted the thing he'd always had. "You are missing a party. The storm has returned, and everyone is drowning their fear with booze and inappropriate behavior. Kirsten has gone straight past the flashin' titty drunk and is, right now as we speak, getting all kinds of nasty with Brian. And Grace? Grace is, swear to Judy in the sky, getting her cards read by Creola. The world has just gone and vomited a Technicolor explosion. You don't want to miss it, do you?"

Somewhere in the distance, she heard a cackle that she knew was Grace, but all she thought to herself was, *I'll get you, my sweet. And your little dog too.*

Yes, that's right, Tara thought to herself, slowly coming around. *If I'm Dorothy, then Grace is definitely the Wicked Witch.* But then, thinking even more as she blinked against the bare bulb above her, she surmised, *Well, yes, maybe the Wicked Witch but, perhaps, a bit of the Wizard as well.*

Ghosts
by Gwyneth Cooper

It feels strange to see a ghost in a place where she, herself, is a ghost. No one says it to her face, but Elizabeth hears some of the old women mutter it as they visually track her progress through the market. They take in the foreign whiteness of her hands as she chooses her rice and turns over mounds of green vegetables. If she ever buys from one of them, she can see a potent mixture of curiosity and revulsion shining in the seller's face.

The rice she chooses is smooth and long grained. The vegetables she buys are not readily identifiable and have yellow flowers. The seller assures her, using a mixture of simple Chinese phrases and exaggerated mime, that she can stir-fry them with garlic and asks her name. The Chinese version still sounds funny to her, but the seller pats her ghostly white hand and assures her she speaks very well. Elizabeth takes the vegetables and goes to find garlic.

The rice is rough under her fingers. Wash and rinse; wash and rinse, until the water runs clear and the rice is separate and the small stones have been picked out. Perfect. It will come out of the cooker in twenty minutes as a lovely, sticky, white mound of starch that Elizabeth can heap with vegetables and slowly work into her mouth.

An e-mail tells her Hannah from the recruitment agency is coming this weekend and wants to stay in her spare room. Perhaps Hannah can advise her on whether seeing ghosts is usual here. Perhaps she can tell her the name of that funny vegetable with the yellow flowers that turned out hot and mustardy on the rice. She might cook it for Hannah, who had been so helpful in her e-mails as Elizabeth worked through getting to this place.

Elizabeth remembers the days of waiting, the prodding and poking of medical examinations, and the endless, endless rounds of doc-

umentation: verifying, copying, faxing, signing, and posting till her head had spun. Hannah had always been calm and unflappable at the delays and the confusions. Mustardy greens with yellow flowers would be a small repayment.

Hannah is waiting at the gates of the school when Elizabeth gets the call to come and collect her. Despite skin that is even paler than Elizabeth's, Hannah manages to look much more a part of the life bustling around outside the gates. Elizabeth wonders how she manages to look less ostentatiously foreign. Perhaps it's the Chinese fashions she wears, or the angle of her arm waving. Maybe Elizabeth's foreignness is what has allowed the ghost to find her.

Hannah's smile is warm, and she chats about her bus ride. Elizabeth thinks that maybe Hannah's ability to fit in comes from her acceptance of live chickens in sacks under the seats and drivers who seem to have only the faintest grasp of braking. Elizabeth has seen those buses drive pass, juddering over the rough concrete, and is not sure she's relaxed enough to ride in one. Perhaps when she's been here a bit longer, she might be able to accept the presence of live poultry on buses. Maybe three months is not long enough to get used to that.

"It's not so bad when you get used to it," Hannah assures her, a hardened veteran of bus journeys, long and short. "It's all about the ride, isn't it?"

Elizabeth isn't so sure. Sometimes the ride isn't so nice, or the destination is the important part.

Crossing the playground toward the apartment buildings, Elizabeth spots the ghost again. She restrains herself from grabbing Hannah's arm and demanding that she look, look at this ghost that has pursued her across an ocean.

The mustardy greens are a few lonely leaves and soggy flowers in a plate when dinner is finished. Hannah cooked a dish with tofu, pineapple, and dark sesame paste that Elizabeth had eyed doubtfully, then wolfed down, enjoying the range of textures and tastes. The rice is as sticky and white as ever. Cradling her cup of tea, Elizabeth sinks down into her sofa. Hannah tucks her legs underneath herself and blows on her tea to cool it before taking a cautious sip.

"When I went home last year, I missed jasmine tea, but when I'm here, I think about tea as it's made at home. This is nice."

Elizabeth knows that Hannah has lived in China for five years. "What was it like when you went home?" she asks.

"Strange." Hannah shakes her head. "I had to remember that shop assistants can speak English and can, therefore, understand my complaining. I couldn't get my favorite noodles for breakfast. My family couldn't understand my fascination with the toaster. I hadn't eaten toast—real toast—for two years. The sky was bluer than I believed possible, but there were no splashes of red on the walls and doorways."

"I miss chocolate," Elizabeth admits, "and other things, too."

"When I was home, I stared like a tourist and ate far too many avocados."

"Avocados?"

"Have you seen any in the markets? They're impossible to find here." Hannah takes a sip of tea and continues, "I would see people in the street and think they were people I knew from here, then they would turn and not be."

Elizabeth looks at her quickly. "Mistaken identity?" she asks.

"Ghosts," Hannah smiles. "There are always ghosts when you change your place in the world. Let me tell you a story."

Ghosts? Perhaps they were a common affliction here after all, thinks Elizabeth. Slowly nodding her agreement, she gets comfortable on the couch.

"Once, long ago, the eldest son of a poor but worthy family in a border province took the Imperial examinations. He did well, and all factors pointed to his success as an official. At this time, all officials were appointed to positions far from their families for the emperor of the day wished to discourage nepotism. The boy worked hard, was modest, fair, orderly, and kept his counsel. He prospered. He sent a little of his wages, as much as he could spare, home to his parents each month, because they had another son to educate. With it went a letter that told the story of his journey from a humble assistant to a knowledgeable young man and worthy official. Only two things bothered him. Sometimes, when walking the streets to the market or sitting in the tea house, he would think he saw his brother, but when he turned to look, he was always gone. And he never received word or letter from his family.

"Several years passed, and the young man could finally travel home for Spring Festival. He journeyed for several days to reach his home town. With buoyant feet, he traced the familiar route to his family's home. The threshold was cleanly swept, and the door showed fresh red paint, but where was the sound of his father's song-birds, or the shuffle of his mother's broom over the bare floors?

"As he pondered this, the neighbor, an old woman by the name of Bai FeiXue, poked her head out her door. When she saw who it was, she rushed forward to greet him. After these were exchanged, he gestured to his home. 'Why do I find my home so silent, Auntie?' She sighed and moved to the door. Unlocking it, she ushered him in. He took in the sparkle of clean floors and the jewel-bright cushions on the furniture before he noticed stacks of envelopes on the table. Bai FeiXue ushered him to a seat and handed him one pile. He turned one over. 'These are mine,' he exclaimed in surprise. 'Auntie, what has happened here?'

"She sat next to him. 'About a month after you left, war swept over us from the west. People ran from their homes; there was fire, fear, and all kinds of disorderliness and looting. After it passed, people crept back to their homes. Some found only a charred shell. Some did not return. I came back, and by the great grace of the gods, found these houses standing. They were a mess. I did not want your parents to find the house in such a state, so I cleaned it for them. They did not return that day, but, I reasoned, who knew where they may have been forced to seek shelter? So I kept the house in a state of readiness, for whenever they may return.' The young man swallowed. 'And did they return?' Bai FeiXue looked grave. 'They have not yet,' she said.

"The young man turned the envelopes over in his hands. None had been opened. 'Why did you not write to me?' he asked. 'You know I cannot write, nephew. And to whom could I entrust this message?' The young man looked down at his hands. 'So that may have been my brother I have seen in the streets and at the tea house, always on the edge of my vision,' he said. She shook her head. 'I think more likely he was always with you in your heart, and sometimes your eyes saw him too.' The young man sighed and looked troubled.

"The old woman saw his sadness in his face. 'These I kept, for I knew they were yours,' she said. 'They were supposed to provide food for my parents and books for my brother,' he said. 'Instead,' she answered, 'they will provide a house for your bride and perhaps assist your promotion.' The young man smiled. 'You are so practical, Auntie,' he said. 'Someone must be practical,' she replied, 'for floors do not sweep themselves, and the promotion of officials relies on more than luck and diligence.'"

Hannah stops and takes a long gulp of her tea. "How does it end?" asks Elizabeth.

"End?" echoes Hannah. "It never ends."

Elizabeth drains her cup and sits it down on the table next to her. "But the young man—he'll never find out what happened to his parents and brother."

"No, but maybe he'll marry a nice girl and rise through the ranks of officialdom, and be content with that."

"What about the neighbor?"

"Oh, I daresay he will give her the house, thus making her very much better off than she was before and compensating her for all the trouble she took."

"That's a strange story."

"All stories are strange, I think."

"I'd still like to know what happened to the parents and brother."

Hannah smiles and shakes her head. Holding out her hand for Elizabeth's cup, she asks, "Can I make us some more tea?"

"That would be nice."

Hannah calls back from the kitchen, "You could write your own ending, couldn't you?"

"I'm no storyteller."

"You're a teacher, aren't you? You must be able to spin tales to amuse and fascinate."

"I think my students are more perplexed than fascinated."

"What about amused?"

That night, nothing more is said of ghosts or stories. But Elizabeth lies awake later, seeing bewildered young officials in the perfect shells of houses and families fleeing looters and invasion in a blur of patterned brocade.

Next morning, Hannah holds earnest discussions with school officials that cause Elizabeth to nervously cast her mind over her past three months of teaching. Had she done everything right? Were the books she'd toiled to carry in acceptable? She has the feeling the ghost might be watching from behind the flagpole. When Hannah rejoins her, she squeezes Elizabeth's arm gently and smiles. "They're really happy with your work and want to know if you'll stay for another year."

Elizabeth splutters in astonishment. "I've only been here three months!" Hannah's smile grows wider and she puts her arm around Elizabeth in a friendly hug.

"Chinese schools like to snaffle good teachers whenever they can find them. Let's go. I have something to show you."

Strolling through the streets, Hannah leads her toward the vegetable market before taking a turn down a narrow alley. "Where are we going?" asks Elizabeth in surprise.

"Here!" said Hannah, sounding satisfied. Elizabeth looks round. A number of shops and stalls sold bright red candles and huge bundles of incense, but the street held no clues for her. Following Hannah through an old, red door, Elizabeth coughs on a sudden mouthful of smoke. The smoke eddies away, and she can see a courtyard in front of her, with a few people bowing solemnly and lighting candles in the middle in front of a gaily painted building.

Hannah leads her discreetly around the central courtyard and out into a garden area. Trees shade the clean pavers, and sturdy, shiny tables and chairs cluster convivially. Rowdy groups of old men battle over chess and mah-jhong, while old women knit and talk, needles clicking like metronomes. "Lovely, isn't it?" asked Hannah. "Like a little oasis in the middle of the concrete and tile desert outside." She chooses a table and two chairs with scarlet and yellow cushions and smiles at the waitress as she orders.

"It is. How did you know it was here?"

"Oh, I asked the head of your department this morning."

Their tea arrives in a large, dull terra-cotta pot with two small cups, and they relax back in their chairs. Elizabeth watches a group of old men argue loudly over their chess, the dappled light playing over their lined faces. "Can anyone come here?" she asks, having no experience with temples of any kind.

"Yes," Hannah says, "and they serve several kinds of tea. I've ordered the eight treasure kind for us, but I can change it if you don't like it."

"What is it?"

"A special mixture of eight treasures, sure to invigorate your blood."

Sipping the tea doubtfully, Elizabeth is surprised by the subtle flavors. "It's delicious."

"I'm very fond of it," says Hannah. "You know, when I first came here, I stayed in contact with my best friends. We wrote and e-mailed. Then I got back home, eighteen months later, to find that, in that time, they had started a relationship, had a pregnancy scare, broken up, moved in as flatmates and moved out as flatmates, and neither had said a word to me in our correspondence."

"Really?"

"Oh, yes. And my parents separated, and no one told me for about six weeks, until my mum casually mentioned it in passing."

"Weird. Why are you telling me this?"

"Elizabeth, when we're here and see the ghosts, sometimes that's just us, seeing with our eyes what we always see with our hearts. And others see us as ghosts at home. That's why their letters are sometimes full of strange gaps, because to them, we're still there."

"Do I look like there might be gaps?"

"You seem a little unsettled. I've seen it before. Try to see the ghosts as part of your heart."

"But when I send letters, what if they go to a house that's empty?"

"Then you still send them, because maybe it's the writing that's important, not the audience."

"Maybe." Elizabeth gulps her tea. "Like your fondness for bus travel, I suppose."

"Oh, when catching buses, the journey's definitely the important thing, especially if you know what to expect at the destination."

"And the live chickens?"

"I only get creeped out by plastic bags of live fish now. Or goats."

"And did the young official ever find his family?"

"No one knows. Can you make your own ending to the story?"

Elizabeth looks round. Not a ghost in sight, but the tea was hot and fresh and bitter with the faintest hint of sweetness to come, and she drank it down as she thought that perhaps, just maybe, she might be able to make her own ending.

The Killer
by Donna Beltz

"The librarian?"

"Yep."

"Why?"

"I dunno. That's just the way it is."

The killer gazed across the wide, green expanse of the town square, passed the playground, the park benches, and neatly trimmed flower beds, to the library. He didn't have much experience with libraries.

"Be crowded in there," he commented. "Better to wait 'til later, maybe catch her on the way home."

"Nah, gotta be there. In the library."

The killer gave him an irritated glance. "What the hell for?"

"I dunno. That's just the way it is."

"Well, aren't you a fucking fountain of knowledge."

"Hey!" The tone was slightly wounded. "I'm trying to help out here!"

"Right. Sorry. I'll take care of it then."

"Okay. See ya around maybe."

"Maybe." He watched the other man walk away and then crossed the street toward the square, looking both ways automatically. Not that it was necessary in this small town. There were very few cars and even those slowed down to let a person cross, not at all like the big cities he was used to, full of cars and angry drivers honking horns.

He took the center path through the square. It was sunny and warm, not hot. One of those perfect days when you could feel the sun on your face, and it just felt good, wholesome somehow. Not that the killer had much experience of wholesome, either. He passed the small playground, dotted here and there with kids and their moms. Kids still too young for school. A blue ball rolled across the grass and onto the sidewalk just in front of him. He bent down and picked it up in one long-fingered hand, then looked around. A dark-eyed little girl stood a few feet away, eyeing him curiously.

"This yours?" he asked, keeping his gravelly voice low to avoid frightening her.

The child nodded and came a couple of steps closer, her hands held wide.

"Here you go." He gave it a gentle toss. The little girl caught it awkwardly in both arms, curling them around the blue sphere to hold it against her chest. She rewarded him with a brilliant smile, her small teeth white against a peaches-and-cream complexion.

"Molly!" a woman's voice called out, frightened and maybe a little angry—probably at him more than the girl. She ran over, grabbed her daughter, clutching her close, putting her body between him and the child with a suspicious glare.

Smart woman, he thought. She didn't have a reason to distrust him and yet she did—some instinct deep in her mother's heart. He wasn't offended. He'd never hurt a child, but she didn't know that—couldn't know that. He gave her a polite nod and continued through the square, crossing the street on the other side and stopping in front of the library.

It seemed bigger from here, standing right in front of it this way. More imposing. He sighed. *Why'd it have to be the librarian? All those damn books.* His life hadn't had many books in it, not when he was young and dodging his father's fists and certainly not since he'd taken to the streets at thirteen when his mother died. *Worn down more than died*, he thought. Dying was too simple.

He'd joined the army at seventeen to escape prison, and there, he'd finally found something he was good at. Killing. Made a damn decent living at it after the army, too. There were a lot of shady people out there willing to pay him a whole lot of money to off other shady people. He never did the personal stuff, the revenge killings, the husbands too cheap to pay off their ex-wives. The people he killed would have stuck a knife in his belly without thinking twice. Not that it justified what he did. He didn't pretend that, not even to himself.

But he was tired of the killing, tired of moving from place to place, never settling down, never having somewhere of his own. He wanted something different, something peaceful. He probably hadn't earned that peace, but he wanted it anyway. And he'd heard about this town, Sumner. *Magic*, they'd whispered. A place where you could build a new life, if you were willing.

And a witch with power enough to send you packing if she didn't like your looks. A witch who was also a librarian, it seemed.

He shook his shoulders loose and walked up the concrete stairs, feeling the chill settle in as he stepped under the small portico and left the sunshine behind.

The light was dim inside, the long lines of bookshelves disappearing into shadow, hanging lamps shedding bright circles of light over the rows of wooden tables and chairs. It was quiet, the way libraries are. That sense of imminent noise held silent, as if at any moment, someone might burst into bright laughter quickly squelched by the power of all those words hanging overhead. He drew a deep breath and smelled the old dust one could never completely erase in a room full of books.

He'd been wrong about the crowds. There were only a couple of people inside. Too nice outside probably. He didn't mind that. Privacy was better for what he needed to do. He heard a footstep and turned to see a woman emerge from the stacks, a pile of books clutched to her shapely chest. She was about his age, neatly dressed—fluttery, mid-calf skirt around slim legs and a lavender, old-fashioned sweater set, sleeves pushed up above her elbows. It brought out the unusual color of her eyes. And why the hell was he noticing that?

Those eyes flicked up and over him, doing a quick head-to-toe inventory before she walked on over behind the tall counter to a holding shelf and proceeded to slide her books in among those already standing there. She turned and made a small circuit of the desk area, touching everything, straightening corners, brushing away invisible dirt before finally giving him an inquiring glance. "Is there something I can help you with?" Her voice was almost melodic, just short of singing the simple words.

He blinked and nodded uncomfortably. "Yes, ma'am. I'd uh..." He took a deep breath, let it out slowly. "That is, I'm told you're the one to see about..."

She smiled, just a small smile. Amused. "You're thinking about settling here in Sumner?"

He felt himself deflate with relief. "Yes, ma'am. I would like to."

"Well." She did another inventory of him, but her eyes never left his face. It was his soul she was examining this time, not his appearance. It made no sense, but somehow he knew it was true. Just like he knew what she'd find there.

"Well," she said again. "We'll see. You're staying here in town, Robert?"

It was an effort not to show his shock when she said his name. His real name. Not the one he'd used when he rented a room at the small guest house that was the only hotel in town. Not the one anyone who might want to hire him would know. But his real name. The one he hadn't spoken out loud in more than two decades. The one his mother had given him on the day he was born. *Witch*, he thought.

He studied her for a long minute then nodded. "Yes, ma'am, I am. The guest house."

"Natalie's place," she nodded. "Lovely rooms. Don't skip breakfast; her cranberry orange muffins are delicious."

The killer just stared at her. This was unreal, or maybe surreal, like one of those paintings where everything was melting and nothing made sense.

He waited for the librarian to say something else, but she just studied him with a patient look in those purple eyes of hers. "So..." He drew another deep breath. "That is...what now?"

"Well, now you just go about your business, be yourself, and we'll see," she said pleasantly.

"That's it?"

"Pretty much," she agreed, turning away to straighten the blank squares of notepaper in their neat box on the counter, shuffling the number two pencils in their tall, ceramic glass. Casting her eye over the tables, she spied a jumbled stack of books someone had left behind and hurried around the counter. She gathered them up with a disapproving little click of her tongue and dashed away among the shelves, already rearranging the books into a neat stack in her arms.

The killer watched her go, feeling forgotten, dismissed. It wasn't a feeling he was used to. He shrugged, spun on one thick-booted heel, and walked back out into the sunshine.

The killer sat on the porch of Natalie's guest house, rocking gently in the old bentwood chair. He'd been right about this town. It was a good place, good people—almost too good, unnatural. Especially for someone like him. But then it *was* unnatural, wasn't it? He hadn't seen the witch much, just the occasional glimpse across the square or walking down the street. And he hadn't figured out yet just

why she would let someone like him stay in her town.

He'd made a few friends in the two weeks he'd been staying at Natalie's. Or, if not friends, then certainly friendly acquaintances. And that was unusual enough in his life. The eponymous Natalie was welcoming and polite without being nosy about how he spent his time. She cooked up her muffins every morning without fail, leaving a basket on the tabletop in the downstairs kitchen, right in front of the big picture window that was never shuttered as far as he'd seen. Sun came through that window and filled the kitchen every morning, making it warm and comfortable as he sat and enjoyed the coffee and fresh juice that were always waiting for him alongside the muffins.

There was one other item waiting for him every morning. It was a book. The first one had appeared the day after his talk with the librarian. A children's book about a spider and a pig. He wasn't much of a reader, but he'd picked it up and read it dutifully while having his coffee and muffins.

The next morning, a different book had appeared in the same place. It had taken him a couple of days to get through that one, but when he finished, a new book showed up right on schedule.

There didn't seem to be any order to the selections—fiction, history, science. The only constant was their perfectly timed appearance next to his coffee.

Most days, he ended his morning sitting on the porch like he was now, watching the town wake up, go to school, each to his own routine. Twice a week, the local paper showed up on the front porch, filled with what would be called gossip almost anywhere else. There was no mention of the world outside their small town, no international crisis, no war of the week. Just births and weddings and the occasional fund-raising pancake breakfast or school play. He wasn't sure how many people actually lived here, but based on what he saw as he sat on the front porch and what he read in the paper, it couldn't be many more than a few thousand.

Sumner was the kind of place most kids couldn't wait to escape from after high school, the kind of place people came back to when the world was too much or they were ready to retire. A quiet place, a safe place. A place where one could put aside the burdens and sins of a lifetime and live in peace. Or so he hoped.

He stood up, stretching toward the worn wood of the covered porch. It was just about time for a more substantial breakfast and a second cup of coffee. Time to amble down the quiet street to the local café and sit amongst the citizens, listening more than talking.

The café was doing its usual weekday morning business. Not crowded, but full enough that the small room buzzed with conversation over the clank of dishes and silverware. The proprietress and lone waitress, Janet Pedroza, weaved a rapid dance among the tightly packed tables, her hands always busy as she moved from place to place, pouring coffee, writing orders, delivering food, and taking away plates. She and her husband, Samuel, ran the place. Sam was the cook. Sam was also the former Shelby Dutton, mob accountant and money launderer. He'd disappeared a few years back, and everyone had assumed he turned state's evidence. When no indictments followed his disappearance, the speculation had turned, instead, to people like the killer. He raised his hand and gave Sam a wave through the service window to the kitchen.

Sam waved back, seeing only another customer come for breakfast. He didn't see the killer. There were only one or two people in the world who could make the killer for who he was, and Sam wasn't one of them. But seeing the former mob accountant behind that counter gave the killer hope. If a man like Sam could make it here, maybe he could, too.

He sat at the counter as he always did. No sense in taking up one of the few tables just for himself. Besides, he liked the comings and goings. People always stopped by on the way to have a word with the counter patrons. It was as if by sitting at the counter, you announced you were open for talk, didn't matter who.

Janet dropped a plain mug in front of him and filled it with coffee, sliding the cream and sugar closer. "Ham or bacon this morning?" she asked, pencil poised.

"Bacon, I think."

"Extra crispy. You got it." And she spun away.

She knew his preferences by now. He was a man of habit—in this at least. After a lifetime of avoiding patterns as a matter of self-preservation, he took particular pleasure in the commonplace of having a waitress who knew his tastes.

He doctored his coffee, adding sugar and cream. That too was different. He'd always taken it straight and black, a hard jolt of caffeine quickly poured down his throat. But now he sipped, enjoying the warm balm of the cream, the sweetness of the sugar on his tongue. Yes, Sumner was proving to be everything he expected. If only he knew what the librarian wanted.

He stepped outside, the café door swinging shut behind him, bells jingling as the steady hum of conversation faded. He stood on the clean-swept sidewalk and gazed over the town. A piercing trill sounded in the distance, followed by the sudden eruption of children's voices as the elementary school released its charges to the playground for their noon recess. The little buggers had already eaten their lunches and were now free to run about, working off all that energy before the afternoon's classroom captivity. The high school next door would follow soon; their schedules were staggered a bit so the little kids had the equipment to themselves before the teenagers took over.

His glance moved from the school grounds to the nearby stores and on to the town square. There were no pretty, little girls with their mommas out there today. The summer flowers were fading; their graceful stalks wilted curls of brown as they drooped toward the bare ground. The trees had begun to turn; their leaves littering the grass and walks. A cold wind gusted across the open square, carrying the sound of raucous laughter. He frowned, his attention drawn to a discordant cluster of noise near the empty swings.

There were five of them. Men too big to be on the children's equipment, too loud, too boisterous for the town square. They wore stereotypical leather and chains, their hair long and uncombed, or shaved flat to their skulls with the glint of an earring. Tattoos were plentiful, the color flashing through the opened zipper of a jacket or sported on biceps bulging from beneath a leather vest.

"A shame, isn't it?"

The killer turned to find Casey Grendle, local pharmacist and busybody. He'd quickly learned that anything said to Casey would be all over town within an hour.

He gave Casey a friendly nod and turned back to study the troublemakers. "There must be someone who takes care of that sort of thing," he said absently.

"There was," Casey agreed. "Herb Emerson handled it for years. He died just a month ago. Only 77, still a young man."

The killer just grunted, his mind automatically sizing up the men, calculating the odds, the angles. He sighed deeply. He'd really hoped to get away from this sort of thing. Movement drew his eye to the library.

The librarian was standing at the top of the stairs, the wind swirling a dark skirt around her pretty legs as she watched the loud group near the swings. A lock of hair blew across her face and she reached up to brush it behind one ear. Her gaze met his across the square.

The killer froze under the impact of that lavender regard. He sighed again, then gave a small nod, raising one hand to his forehead in a kind of salute. The librarian's lips curved in a bare smile of satisfaction. She glanced once more at the troublemakers then turned and disappeared beneath the stone façade.

He stood alone, aware that Casey had bid him a good day and gone back to his store. He was pretty sure he'd mumbled something polite in return, but he wouldn't have put money on it. His eyes narrowed against the chill wind as he eyed the five troublemakers once again before he spun around and headed back to the guest house. He was no longer wondering why a man like him had been welcomed to Sumner.

The killer gathered the last of his shirts, laying them carefully in his duffle bag on top of the rest of his belongings. He'd just picked the shirts up at the laundry yesterday. They were folded and neat, collars starched just the way he liked them. He was going to miss the Sumner Fluff and Fold. And so much else. He drew a deep breath, blowing it out in a rush of emotion. It didn't do anything to relieve the pressure on his chest, the heavy sadness that made his movements sluggish, his thoughts unfocused. He'd really thought Sumner would be his home. Finally somewhere he could settle down and watch the years pass by in a slow, boring routine of days. But it was not to be. And maybe he'd never deserved it anyway.

His gaze swept the small, cheerful guestroom, falling finally on the gun resting on top of the antique bureau, incongruous against the lacy doily. The heavy metal fit his hand comfortably, nestling into his palm like an old friend. He checked automatically to see if it was loaded, though he'd pulled the magazine himself after cleaning the weapon completely late last night. Even if he never planned to use it again, it was a discipline of too many years for him to put a gun away dirty. But then, he'd never thought to use it again after he arrived in Sumner either.

That thought brought back the sorrowful weight of loss he'd been feeling all morning and he scoffed at himself. *Sentimental fool.* Had the years taught him nothing? He zipped the duffle in a single long movement, lifting it easily in one hand and pulling the door open with the other.

The smell of Natalie's muffins rushed into the room as if it had been hovering outside the door, waiting for him. He lowered his head for a moment, then hefted the duffle over his shoulder with a determined jerk and went on down the stairs, careful to tread softly lest Natalie hear his departure.

The Librarian was waiting for him outside the house, standing down on the sidewalk. She didn't see him at first, occupied with the flower boxes along Natalie's white picket fence, plucking the fading blossoms and shaking her head, lips moving in a silent conversation with herself. He almost stepped back and closed the door, but then she turned and saw him. She smiled. He squared his shoulders and walked out onto the porch, shutting the door quietly behind him. The bentwood rocker moved gently as he walked by.

She looked up at him. "Robert," she said in greeting. Her head tilted curiously and her hands stilled over the flowers. "You're leaving Natalie's?"

That's what she said, but he heard the real question. *"You're leaving us? Leaving Sumner?"*

He stared at her. "Yes, ma'am," he said finally.

"I see." She studied him a moment longer then smiled and resumed her plucking. "Tell me, Robert. Did you happen to notice those young men who were hanging about the playground yesterday?"

He glanced at the town square almost unwillingly. The children were back on the swings, their high-pitched shouts of joy drifting on the breeze, their mommas lingering nearby, laughing and talking among themselves. Sumner was once again as it should be. He was struck by a yearning so deep it brought tears to his eyes, and he slapped sunglasses onto his face, feeling naked beneath her penetrating gaze.

"I saw them," he said grudgingly.

"And would you know where they are now?" she inquired pleasantly.

He frowned, eyes downcast behind the dark lenses, feeling his shoulders slump in dejection. He dropped the heavy duffle to the ground with a thud and drew himself up straight. "I couldn't do it. I'm sorry, ma'am. This is a wonderful town you've got here, but...I couldn't do it. Not anymore. That's not why I came here."

Her smile grew and she came closer, brushing her hands off to lay slender fingers on his thick arm. "And why did you come here, Robert?"

"To find peace, a home of my own. I'd heard this place was different, that a man like me, a man who..." He couldn't go on, couldn't read the litany of his sins under the warm morning sun.

"And did you? Did you find a home here?"

"Yes," he whispered, then jerked back. "Or, I thought so. But I couldn't do what you wanted. You need someone to protect this town, that's natural, but...I'm not your man. Not anymore."

"Why would you think this town needs protecting?" She crinkled her face in puzzlement.

"Casey said...er, that is, I heard Mr. Emerson had passed away, that he'd taken care of such things."

The librarian laughed a lovely sound as she tilted her head back and let her enjoyment flow. He flushed, wondering what he'd said that was so damn funny.

As if she'd heard his thought, her laughter died. "I apologize, Robert. It was kind of you to hurry those boys on their way, but they would have gone anyway. This town...well, it's mine, and I don't tolerate their kind in my town. I thought you understood that, understood about this town, about me. You do, don't you?" It seemed important to her that he understand.

"But how..." he began, then realized he didn't really want to know. "I guess I do. And Mr. Emerson?"

"Herb Emerson was the town landscaper," she said, her eyes glinting with humor beneath long lashes. "Casey was no doubt bemoaning the state of the flower beds on the town square. He's quite the fuss budget when it comes to the gardens, not that he'd move his chubby little bottom to do anything about it," she added in a mutter. She looked up, her cheeks blushing with delicate color at her own words.

A lovely woman, he thought, then shook himself slightly and looked at her in confusion. "But why me? Why would you let a killer—"

"I believe in our first conversation I said you should just be yourself."

"Yes, ma'am, you did."

"And is that who you are, Robert? Are you a killer?"

"No, ma'am," he said with a rush of relief. "Not anymore."

"Well, then, that answers your question, wouldn't you say?"

He blew out a breath that felt like it had been pent up for days, letting the weight of sadness fall away. "Yes, ma'am, I guess it does."

She tilted her head again and gave him a lopsided smile. "I understand George Peabody's selling his house. He and the widow Brown are finally going to tie the knot; they'll live in her place. It has that nice view of the river, perfect for the two of them. A second chance if you will. We believe in second chances here in Sumner." She shifted her gaze to meet his eyes directly. "Do you believe in second chances, Robert?"

"Yes, ma'am, I guess I do."

The librarian stepped even closer and gave him a wicked look. "I believe you should call me Grace, Robert."

And Robert, who had once been a killer, smiled.

Puss in Boots
by Tanya Bentham

The trouble with spaceports, Ben thought dejectedly, especially the ones that misguidedly style themselves as intergalactic pleasure hubs, is that you get some right fucking weirdos hanging about in them. He watched suspiciously as a golden being that he thought might be female approached another creature, obviously selling the lithe, asexual body its clothing so advantageously displayed. After some haggling, the transaction was apparently agreed upon, and the two disappeared into the warmth of one of the adjacent domes to conduct their business.

Ben shivered as he watched them with a hint of jealousy, his stomach rumbling loudly in the thin night air; any real atmosphere this place owned was confined within the large geodesic domes that housed the nightclubs, hotels, and brothels. Outside there was only the cold and the woebegone dregs of sentient life whose ranks he had recently joined. He tried not to think about how many days it was since he'd eaten; in the time since his arrival on the hub, he'd been turned down for job after job, but he was still too proud to beg. The cramps in his gut were so bad now that he could think of little else, and he feared that soon he might be forced to swallow his pride, or something far worse.

"How much for an hour?" asked a soft, liltingly feminine voice at his back.

Ben turned sharply, startled by the presence of another being so close without his knowledge, and wondered how friendly his stealthy companion would turn out to be. His first instinct was to snap that he was intent upon finding honest employment, not selling his body, but a quiet voice at the back of his mind told him that perhaps he should take the opportunity while he still had the strength and the merchandise to negotiate a fair price. There were so many species continually passing through the Hub that Ben, who until recently had worked as an astro on a quiet local run between solar systems, was hard pushed to name many of them, but this one he knew: Felidae. No one knew the origins of the cat people, since they admitted to no home world, and though they were rare indeed, traveling alone, they invariably insinuating themselves into the most luxurious and pleasure-loving of worlds, so it should have been no surprise to find one here.

He must have hesitated for a moment too long in answering, because she asked again, face twisted into an enigmatic feline smile. "I asked how much?"

"It depends," he replied, desperate not to let his nerves show in his voice and knowing that his performance in the art of cool was far surpassed by hers.

Amber eyes traveled up and down his body, making Ben silently curse the shabbiness of his aged work clothes and wonder if she would believe his appearance was a gimmick, a costume designed to appeal to the female who wanted a bit of rough. She opened her mouth, but not to speak, tasting the air like the household kitty she so deceptively resembled. "Not much, by the scent of you. I'd say it's been days since you last had a decent meal. Right now, I bet you'd sell your soul for a bowl of kibble." She stepped closer, almost but not quite brushing against him, and let her tongue flicker out to taste the sweat that had appeared on his cheek before smugly announcing: "Human, and pureblood at that. There aren't many of your kind left these days. I think you'd better come along with your aunt Felicity before some big bad wolfie snaps up such a tasty, tender, young morsel."

When he made no coherent reply, she smirked, and turning her back, she gestured that he should follow with a flick of her long, white tail as she prowled noiselessly away.

Ben hesitated for a moment, watching as her silver-white furred body seemed to float in the gloom, her black patent leather thigh boots almost invisible, before he realized he had little choice but to follow; to hesitate was to starve.

Never once did she look back at him; perhaps she didn't care or perhaps the famed instinct of her kind allowed her an awareness of his presence that would have been beyond the means of a more mundane being. Creatures of every shape and size cleared a way for her, even the most dangerous-looking stepping meekly out of her way, overawed by her predatory, hypnotic grace. Only once did she casually flash razor-sharp claws at a big thug who hesitated for a split second too long before clearing her path. Ben studied her intently; although tiny diamonds dripped from the end of each long whisker and her ears were pierced with golden hoops, the boots were the only clothing she wore, presumably because her unadorned fur was more luxurious than any of the silks this galaxy could offer. Ben shivered again, but not from the cold this time, as he wondered what Felicity intended to do with those carefully polished claws of hers once they reached their destination, yet for all his trepidation, he followed obediently, excitement and apprehension running a relay down his spine.

She led him to one of the smaller, more exclusive domes on the far edge of town, the kind that his short experience of the Hub had taught him belonged almost exclusively to the wealthiest shipping magnates, drug dealers, and pimps. The door hissed softly open to reveal two waiting servants draped in gauzy black silk, one a blue-eyed Kareelian male, the other a human, or mostly human at least, a female of quite exquisite loveliness—perhaps Felicity had a taste for his kind. Both wore red leather collars in ironic imitation of those worn by domestic pets, whose silver bells tinkled as the two bowed deeply, the male quietly murmuring, "Welcome home, Mistress Felicity."

Felicity barely acknowledged them, saying only, "This is Ben. Take him away and clean him up; he smells bad."

That there was no contesting the veracity of her statement made it sound no less insulting, but Felicity was gone so quickly that Ben had no chance to retort. He turned at once to the female and asked her name, but she simply smiled shyly before slipping away though a side door.

"Venga doesn't speak," the big Kareelian said softly, his deep voice more vibration than sound.

"Why not?"

"Felicity found her in the slave market on Xocalo, but the pirates had already cut out her tongue; who knows why."

"Are you Felicity's slave, too?"

He shook his head. "No slaves here; we stay by choice. Come this way."

Ben followed the Kareelian down another corridor, panting to keep up with the other's long stride. "I'm Ben."

"I know."

"Custom would have it that you tell me your name in return," he pointed out as he followed him into a large tiled bathroom.

"Ahkshay," the Kareelian smiled as he shut the door, leaving Ben all alone. He assumed Ahkshay was a name rather than a sneeze or some weird Kareelian insult.

Half an hour later, having taken his time to revel in the rare luxury of a real shower, Ben was clean, dry, and dressed in a silk bathrobe similar to the garments worn by Venga and Ahkshay that had mysteriously replaced his own tattered clothes whilst he was in the shower. Just as he began to feel slightly foolish, wondering what you were meant to do in such a situation, Ahkshay re-entered the room without knocking. "Come."

Another corridor led to a softly lit room littered with even softer cushions. At first, Ben thought that some soft hypnotic music was playing, but then as he looked around, he realized that the sound came from Felicity herself, who was stretched out on the cushions, rolling in abandon and purring loudly as Venga rubbed her ears. As soon as Venga realized he had entered the room, she ceased her ministrations, causing Felicity to spit angrily as she narrowed her eyes at Ben. "Go," she hissed abruptly at the girl, who scurried quickly to obey. Felicity next turned her attention to Ben, nodding to the cushion by her feet. "Sit," she said as peremptorily as though she spoke to no more than a dog.

Ben grudgingly obeyed, feeling so weak from hunger that he suspected defiance might have seen him collapse from fatigue anyway. No sooner had he sat than Ahkshay reappeared bearing a tray of hot stew and potatoes.

Manners dictated that he shouldn't eat without his hostess' permission, and instinct told him that Felicity would not take kindly to any form of discourtesy. She stared silently at him for what seemed like forever, and Ben knew she was toying with him, languidly exercising her power. His back stiffened with determination, and he sat as straight as the cushions would allow, only stubbornness preventing him from either fainting or falling on the plate like a wild dog.

When he feared he might finally break, taunted by the rich smell of the food, Felicity idly said, "Eat. Ahkshay gets cranky if his cooking gets cold."

With a supreme effort of will, Ben forced himself to remember his best table manners and eat slowly. His hands shook as he lifted the food to his mouth, so that despite his best efforts, he slopped some of the delicious gravy on the borrowed silk robe, and before he could check himself, he'd wiped it up with his fingers and licked them clean, causing his hostess to comment, "My, my, I can see we'll have to work on your table manners."

He reddened, fury and embarrassment warring openly over his cheeks, but he kept slowly chewing as Felicity smirked. The meal was a small one, all too soon consumed in spite of his self-imposed sloth, and he was left knowing that he could have eaten the whole thing over again and still had room for dessert, but his pride prevented him from asking for more even though he practically licked the dish clean.

Felicity seemed to read his mind, whispering, "More would only make you sick after so long a fast."

He nodded silently, aware of the truth and discomforted by her apparent concern. It was she who pressed on with the conversation. "Why are you here?"

Ben looked up sharply, his consternation betrayed on his face before he could school his reaction. "You hired me."

Felicity smiled, displaying petite yet razor-sharp fangs. "Actually, I did no such thing. I merely inquired as to how much you charged, and then you followed me home. Luckily for you, you caught me on an evening when I was feeling charitably disposed toward the feeding of strays."

Ben wondered if it was the way of all cat people to bend the truth to suit themselves or if he had simply found a particularly obtuse specimen. "I thought you wanted me to follow, Aunt Felicity."

She growled a soft warning in the back of her throat. "In my own home, it would be wise to refer to me as Mistress Felicity."

"And will I be expected to wear one of your pretty red collars?"

"Perhaps; I haven't decided yet. Tell me, Ben, would you have followed me home so eagerly if I had been male?" Her voice was musical, cool, and cruel like a symphony played in blue ice.

"Perhaps." His eyes drifted with intense interest to the tassels on the cushion he occupied, wondering why gender preference remained an issue at all when there were so many species at large on the Hub.

"Don't be evasive; I can smell it. Your ambiguous sexuality is even more fragrant now that you no longer smell like a dirty little ape."

He looked up again, but before he could speak, she smirked and said, "Clean monkeys are so much easier to read, I always find."

"How convenient for you," he said dryly.

"It might be," she commented enigmatically. "You are certainly attractive enough for my purposes."

"I'm flattered," he replied with an insincerity to match her own. "Perhaps we should just settle upon a price for my services so that I can earn my meal and get back to my life?"

Felicity stretched languidly, doubling the length of her body with a lithe ripple of perfectly toned feline muscle. "Oh, I'm not interested in sex; I'm only interested in power."

"Aren't they one and the same thing in most instances?" He eyed her black leather boots with suspicion; he'd never liked being dominated, but right now, he was prepared to do whatever it took to keep himself from starvation.

She made a sound in the back of her throat that was halfway between a purr and a chuckle. "I knew you were smarter than the average astro. But one thing at a time, Ben. You didn't answer my question; what brings my pretty monkey to my quiet corner of the galaxy?"

Back on the colony that he'd once called home, before life had fallen apart and forced him out into the cold, unwelcoming expanse of space to earn his keep, Ben had once read in the newspaper that prostitutes often had clients who wanted to talk more than they wanted sex, but he'd never expected himself to experience the phenomenon first-hand. Then again, if it kept him at a safe distance from those claws and those boots, who was he to argue? If she wanted to feed him and hear a story that she could have heard for the price of a synthetic beer in any cheap bar in any cheap solar system, far be it from him to stand in her way. "I was born on a backwater agricultural colony called Arcadia 3—"

"A farmboy!" Felicity purred as she snuggled down into her cushion. "How delightful. There's nothing quite like a little bit of rustic charm, is there?"

The comment rankled more than a little with Ben, who didn't like to be thought of as an ignorant hick and was therefore quick to point out, "My parents owned the planet."

Felicity made no effort to hide her amusement, giving him the impression that his parents would have had to own an entire galaxy to impress her with their financial prowess. "Even better! But now I'm intrigued, how does the princeling of Arcadia 3 end up as a down-and-out astro selling his body on the streets of my little pleasure Hub, I wonder?"

"Simple really," Ben said bitterly. "I was nineteen and away at university when the colony was targeted by pirates. They murdered everyone when my father refused to pay protection money and then nuked the planet. The money was all gone, and I had no choice but to find work where I could. So for the last four years, I've been part of the crew of a small cargo vessel, *The Seraph*, but last week, my jackass of a captain lost the ship in a game of poker, and the new owner prefers to use a slave crew because pirate activity has made the insurance premiums prohibitive to the employment of free entities."

"Poor, poor, Ben," Felicity purred nonchalantly as she cleaned her claws, not even sparing him a glance in her insincerity. "Life has been unkind to you, hasn't it?"

He shrugged, hating to admit defeat. "Life's what you make it; today is a glitch, nothing more."

Felicity sheathed her claws so abruptly that Ben almost heard them snap back into her short fingers and turned her head slowly toward him, subjecting him to the full and unnerving intensity of her gaze. "That's more like it," she whispered as she padded toward him on all fours. There was nothing of the domestic cat in her demeanor anymore; she was all predator now. He felt the prickle of her whiskers against his neck as she sniffed him eagerly, her hot, slightly tuna-scented breath searing his face. "I knew there was a backbone in there."

Ben had the sneaking suspicion as she pushed him none too gently down onto the cushion and straddled him that Felicity was more than capable of ripping said backbone right out through his chest if she so desired. As she opened the front of the silk bathrobe to run her sheathed claws down the firm muscle of his chest, purring with satisfaction, he whispered, "I thought you said you weren't interested in sex?"

"It's not my main focus of interest," Felicity admitted with another enigmatic little smile, "but one should never turn down fringe benefits."

"I'm not sure I like being referred to as a fringe benefit," he grouched.

Felicity laughed softly, sitting back up on her haunches to peer imperiously down at him. "The eternal fragility of the male ego, no matter what the species, never fails to amuse me, but you're right of course—business before pleasure."

Ben wasn't quite sure if he was relieved or disappointed when she sprang away from him with a somersault of breathtaking agility and landed back on her own cushion, continuing her conversation as blithely as if they'd done no more than shake hands. "Tell me, Ben, what do you want?"

Right now, he wanted to get this over with and get some sleep, but something told him it would be unwise to admit as much to his unpredictable companion. He shrugged noncommittally. "What do you mean?"

"You are both intelligent and attractive—for a monkey, at least—do you really expect me to believe that you would be content to do nothing more with your life than work as an astro on backwater cargo runs?"

"I have plans." Had would be more accurate.

"I can see that," she said sarcastically.

He realized that he might as well admit the truth; it could do him no harm anymore. "I had money saved up, another year or so, and I could have bought my own cruiser, but I wasn't allowed back onboard *The Seraph* to collect my possessions."

"Impressive—I wasn't aware that working as an astro paid so well."

He almost laughed at that. "It doesn't; I had a sideline trading various small, hard-to-come-by items."

"Smuggling, you mean?"

"That depends entirely upon your viewpoint."

"Of course it does; how enterprising of you."

He looked directly into those searing amber eyes. "It must take a certain amount of enterprise to maintain a place like this."

She grinned as widely as the proverbial Cheshire tabby. "Touche! Which is where I'm hoping you can help me."

He narrowed his eyes. "Tonight is a one-off; I don't need a pimp, or a madame, or whatever you care to call yourself."

Felicity chose to ignore the challenge, skirting around the verbal fight as skillfully as any alley cat. "I had nothing so gauche in mind, my dear. I would never lower myself to the level of a common pimp."

Ben began to take an interest, wondering what she had in mind, and if he could use her to his advantage. "But an uncommon one?"

The grin made its reappearance, unfeasibly wider this time. "Clever, clever, monkey."

* * *

For all the seeming indolence of cats, Felicity turned out to be fast worker, as well as a smooth operator. It had taken her a mere month after their initial meeting to polish Ben into the refined young gentleman she required for her purposes, although what that purpose might be, she refused to tell. He had been groomed, pampered, and manicured to perfection. His table manners had been whipped into shape and his conversational skills honed by endless debates on current affairs. Then she had dressed him in a wardrobe that she, herself, had chosen, subtly designed to show his looks and body to their greatest advantage whilst retaining the illusion of sophistication, and he had begun to escort her to parties almost every night.

It was at one such affair that Ben had met Brandon and Bethany, both many years his senior. Brandon was Arcturan, ridiculously handsome, and even more ridiculously rich. Bethany was his wife, as beautiful as her husband, and with the same pure human blood in her veins as Ben himself. By some quirk of good fortune, both had fallen in love with him, and both had proposed. No doubt their affections had been spurred on by Felicity's eloquent recitation of his pureblood human pedigree. That she had spoken of him in terms of breeding had excited his two potential lovers, because neither Brandon nor Bethany made any secret of their interest in propagating the human race in its purest, least scientifically altered form. Old-fashioned, left to the grace of mother nature was the latest fad with those who could afford any luxury money could buy; they found the genetic lottery an amusing gamble when the hoi polloi were routinely bankrupting themselves to ensure perfect offspring.

Not that Ben believed in any of that neo-fascist crap about the purity of species, he just didn't believe in starving for his ideals either. Which was how, one year after nearly starving to death on an obscure, second-rate pleasure hub at the edge of the galaxy, Ben found himself soaking up the sun at a waterside café on the exclusive beach planet Aegeas 4, the second wife of one of the richest beings in the universe.

Occasionally, just occasionally, in the deepest, darkest moments of the night, it would occur to Ben that sooner or later a certain Felicity was going to require payment for her services as matchmaker, and that he had no idea what payment would be demanded of him. On the whole, it was safer to his mental health not to think about it at all, so he didn't.

He had just ordered another obscenely expensive cocktail from the pretty waitress whose name he couldn't remember but whom he had every intention of being unfaithful with later on when a lithe, jewel-bedecked white form in black patent leather boots draped herself over the lounger to his side. "My, my, my, if I ever saw a human who looked thoroughly shagged, he's sitting next to me!"

He peered over the top of his designer shades and said with a sense of resignation that he made no attempt to conceal, "Hello, Felicity."

"All alone?" she quirked one sardonic brow. "Surely the lovely Brandon and Bethany haven't got bored with you already?"

"I'm not their new toy."

"No, my dear, you're their pretty, little pet."

There was really no point in denying the honest truth, no matter how much it might chafe his dignity. Ben was now a kept man, and the fact that he rather enjoyed being kept made his reply no less grumpy. "The pet has the weekend off, for a bit of rest and relaxation."

"A little bird told me you're being rewarded for getting the lovely Bethany pregnant with the pureblood human child Brandon has wanted for many a year," Felicity commented idly, leaving Ben in no doubt that talkative canary in question had ended up as an appetizer.

"So...?"

"So it seems to me," she purred so deeply that Ben could swear he felt the vibration of her voice cross the gap between them, "that you ought to be thanking your aunt Felicity for introducing you to your perfect mates."

"Are you claiming to be my fairy godmother now?"

Felicity chuckled darkly. "Do you really believe me to be so foolishly altruistic?"

"Not for one moment. What do you want, Felicity?"

"I seem to remember I asked you the same question barely a year ago. Do you have what you want now?" Her voice was cool.

"Yes, but I get the impression you do not yet have what you want."

"Such a clever monkey."

"Why should I pay you?"

"It would be a terrible shame if Brandon found out that I'd neglected to mention a few shadier branches of your family tree."

"They were all human," he countered.

"Yes, they were, weren't they, even the pirates. Just think of the scandal in the media if they found out that Brandon and Bethany's boy toy wasn't quite the stud they thought they were buying. Pure-blood is what it is, but your little friends thought they were getting an aristocrat, not a common mongrel."

"How much do you want?" He failed to hide the tremor in his voice. He could get money, but it wouldn't be easy.

Felicity laughed, causing the jewels on her whiskers to tinkle lightly. "Silly monkey! I don't want money—well, not the pitiful amount you can lay your hands on, anyway. I told you before, I want power, real power, and real power takes real money."

"Then I'm no use to you, am I—you said yourself that I'm just the pet. Pets have no power."

"They have eyes though, and ears. Pets can spy on their masters and pass knowledge of their masters' business dealings along to their dear, old friends."

"And knowledge is power?"

"Clever monkey!"

Otherworldly Conversations
by Caitlin Young

"So, just out of curiosity, if I told you I was from another world, you'd think I was crazy, right?"

Jan paused with her sandwich halfway to her mouth, blinking.

"Um. Depends. Are you going to?"

Zee, who hadn't even looked up from her own lunch, gave a little half-shrug.

"I may be giving it some thought."

It was a fairly common belief among the employees at the library that Zee was a little bit crazy. A good kind of crazy—eccentric, imaginative, and just maybe kind of a genius—but a coworker who casually dropped questions like the one she'd just asked Jan into everyday conversation had to be either crazy or joking, and Zee never seemed to be joking.

Case in point: "Are we talking, like, from another planet via spaceship, or from a magical land via common household objects?" Jan asked. She was still vaguely hoping, even though it was Zee, that Zee would laugh and they would end up talking about sci-fi tropes versus fantasy tropes until they both had to go back to work.

But it was Zee, which meant that she paused for a moment, then said thoughtfully, "Both, actually. Sort of. It's another planet, but it's so far away that the most practical way to bridge the distance is with a portal. And something like a wardrobe or a mirror *would* make an excellent one, now that you mention it."

When Zee got like this, you could change the subject, and she'd usually go with it, or ignore her, and she'd usually be content to let it drop. Or you could play along, and the ensuing conversation would be probably surreal, but never boring.

"So it's like...folding space or tessering or something? Traveling a huge distance really quickly?" Jan asked before taking a few more quick bites of her sandwich. Lunchtime was running short.

Zee nodded. "Not *quite* like either of those, but they're probably the closest comparisons."

"Okay," Jan said, smiling a little in spite of herself. "Let's say you're from another world that you get here from by something that's sort of but not quite like tessering and might involve a wardrobe."

"All of which I have neither confirmed nor denied at this point," Zee pointed out, still with every appearance of sincerity.

"Right, you're hypothetically from this hypothetical other world. So how is it you end up here, working in a library?"

"It's what I was sent here for," Zee said simply, crumpling the trash from her lunch into a neat, compact ball. Before Jan could say anything else, Zee stood up, flashing her a quick smile. "I ought to get back to work. I'll see you."

Jan waited to see if Zee would bring the whole thing up again, but for the next three days, all Zee talked about during lunch—when she talked at all—was work. There was a lot to talk about there; the main branch of the library had been reopened three months and wasn't yet back to what it was before Hurricane Katrina, even considering that it stood up to the storm pretty well.

They were both fairly recent employees at the library, and both had a hand in the restoration. Jan was in acquisitions, working to rebuild the library's collection to what it was before Katrina, and Zee was a preservationist working in the archives, doing what she could to restore books that weren't completely destroyed. Unlike Jan, Zee was new to the city as well as the library. Zee was easygoing, friendly, and prone to either long periods of quiet or intelligent but bizarre conversation. Jan tended to be both shy and high-strung, but the two of them got along well from the start, bonding over similar tastes in books and music, and eating lunch together most days.

It was Jan who brought their conversation from a few days ago up again, while they were eating in the park across the street from the library.

"Hey, remember the part where you might or might not be an alien?"

"Only an alien from an Earth native's point of view," Zee pointed out. "But yes?"

"Well you said you'd been sent here," Jan reminded her. "But nothing about why or by who."

"Sent to help, by the people I work for," Zee replied simply. "We're...a sort of volunteer organization, I suppose you could say."

Jan's eyebrows went up slightly. "An intergalactic volunteer organization? That sent you to restore books in a New Orleans library? Great."

"Everyone works according to their talents," Zee said, and it had the air of an often-repeated mantra. "There are others in the city—a carpenter working in the Ninth Ward, a doctor at a free clinic—and that's to say nothing of the ones who were here just after the storm."

Jan looked at her, frowning a little now. "Okay, you're losing me. I mean, you've got a group of people who can go to different worlds, and out of, like, the whole universe and whatever's out there, they come here?"

"Oh, not just New Orleans," Zee clarified. "There are agents in a lot of places, in this world or others. The organization goes where it's needed."

"You're really serious about all of this, aren't you?" Jan wasn't sure what made her so certain of that all of a sudden—Zee hadn't seemed any *less* serious up to that point—but it was like something clicked, and Jan couldn't treat it like a joke anymore.

Zee ducked her head, smiling very faintly. "I suppose I haven't been doing so well at keeping things in hypothetical terms. Yes, I'm serious."

Jan just sat still and looked at Zee until the silence stretched out enough that Jan felt like one of them ought to say *something*.

"Huh," was all she managed though.

"Are you..." Zee paused, as if searching for the right words, "weirded out?"

"I'm not really sure *how* I feel about it," Jan said after a moment's consideration. She knew how she *ought* to feel, but...Zee came off as pretty crazy, all right, but she'd never struck Jan as seriously, out-of-touch-with-reality crazy. "It's a hell of a thing to just ask someone to start thinking un-hypothetically about, Zee."

"I know," Zee agreed. "But I needed to tell someone, and I thought you seemed like the person I'd be most likely to convince."

"Why?" Jan asked. "I mean, why'd you have to tell someone?" Why Zee picked her didn't take a genius to figure out—they were each other's closest friends at work, and Zee knew that Jan was into fantasy and science fiction, considering how many times they'd talk-ed about books and movies.

Zee shrugged a little, still with that faint smile. "I think we should wait and see if you decide I'm crazy or lying before we get into that. Think about it, all right?"

It wasn't, Jan decided a few days later, that she was prepared to just believe all of this. But she wasn't about to do anything like stop talking to Zee or report her to anyone, either. Even if Zee *was* crazy, she was Jan's friend and had always seemed like a good person. If it started seeming like she might be a danger to herself or anyone else, it might be a different matter, but as it was, Jan was willing to indulge her and to at least talk to her about it a bit more.

"You're a skeptic," Zee told her when Jan said all of that to her, seeming pleased. "In the philosophical sense, I mean. It's a good way to be when dealing with this sort of thing for the first time. And that you're still willing to listen is all I could ask for."

Jan drew her knee up on the park bench they were sharing, rest-ing her chin on it. "Okay, so talk to me."

Zee had the crumbs from her sandwich in a paper towel on her lap; she scattered them on the ground as she spoke, her voice low.

"I learned of the organization when they came to my world when I was younger—the equivalent of a teenager, by Earth's standards. Where I lived was all farmland, and we'd had a bad famine that year, so the organization sent agents to help us recover. And one day, one of them—a young man who'd hired on at my family's farm, who seemed able to coax crops out of the ground as if by magic—began to talk to me, the same way I've been talking to you."

Jan blinked. "Is that what this is? Are you trying to recruit me, or something?"

"If not you, then I'll have to find someone else," Zee said. "It's how we work. The organization started with a very small group of friends, on a world that had discovered the method of traveling by portal. They decided that what they wanted to use that ability for ways to help people. Some of those they helped, they told, and some of those that were told joined them."

"You keep just saying 'the organization,'" Jan pointed out. "Has it not got a name?"

Zee shrugged. "It's never really needed one. As far as I know, it's the only one of its kind."

She scattered the last of her crumbs and balled up the paper towel, glancing at her watch. "We should get back." Glancing at Jan, she added, hopefully, "Same time tomorrow?"

Jan only hesitated a moment before nodding.

"But, see, here's the thing," Jan said. Lunch that day was a smoothie, and she was stirring it with her straw as she spoke, agitatedly. "If you want me to believe that there's this group of people from all over the universe, with the kind of technology that lets them do something like that, and all they do with it is travel around helping people out..."

"Yes?" Zee had a way of looking when she was listening, a quiet sort of focus in her expression that left no doubt she was really *listening*.

"Well, I mean—look at the city," Jan went on, her brow furrowing. "Look at how bad things were after Katrina, how bad some things still are all this time after. Look at the rest of the world. You said you had agents in other places. If we've got *people from other worlds* coming here just to help us—"

"It seems like things should be better?" Zee finished gently. "Like it should be making more of a difference?"

"Yes!" Jan said, thumping her smoothie cup against her knee for emphasis.

Zee nodded, with a small, wry smile. "I felt the same way when I found all this out. The organization helped us, certainly, but we still suffered, and our road to recovery was still long. I had the same questions."

"Did anyone ever answer them?" Jan asked.

Zee shrugged. "Imagine what this world would look like to someone unfamiliar with it. The things you can create, the progress you've made—travel by portal might be a dream on this world, but travel by spacecraft hasn't even been dreamt of on many—yet millions still suffer what you call inhumanities, and millions who could help them don't. One might ask why the human race even requires help from other worlds."

"One might," Jan agreed, looking at Zee steadily. "That doesn't really answer my question."

Zee sighed. "All right. There are many natives of your world who *do* dedicate themselves to helping others, and have great resources at their disposal—but it only goes so far, only makes so much of a difference. The organization does what it can, but we're not many, and the technology we have doesn't make us all-powerful."

Unsure what to say to all that, Jan took a long pull on her straw, getting mostly air and slurping noises. "It's just...sort of a letdown, you know? The idea of it not making more of a difference."

It was also, she thought but didn't say out loud, *convenient if you were trying to claim that something existed even though there was no apparent evidence of it.*

Zee nodded. "I know. But it's better than nothing."

If Jan thought about it, really thought about it—*am I really spending my lunch talking about portals from other worlds? Really?*—it was still pretty damn weird and surreal.

What made it less bizarre, made it something she could deal with, was treating it as though it were just another story they were talking about. It was definitely made harder by the fact that she couldn't pretend Zee wasn't taking it seriously, meaning every word of it, but Jan had to keep some sort of detachment from it in her mind somehow.

If it were a story, Jan thought, it would have to end eventually. And there were only two ends Jan could think of to this: Either what Zee had been telling her wasn't true—which had to be it, Jan kept telling herself, it was the only answer that made sense—or, somehow, it was true.

What Jan had never told anyone, even Zee, is that when she was younger, she would have had no trouble believing any of it. When Jan was younger, she believed in everything. And not only had she been sure that other worlds existed, she'd been sure she could find them if she just kept trying, kept believing.

It never happened. The back of her closet was only ever a closet, the mirror in her room stayed solid no matter how hard she pressed her fingers against it, and beaming Morse code messages up into the sky with a flashlight only ever led to needing new batteries. And as much as she had wanted to keep believing, every disappointment, every year when nothing happened but that she got another year older, had killed a little bit of that belief.

And now, when she was being asked to believe again, Jan didn't know if she still had it in her.

* * *

They'd been sort of circling around the question of belief, carrying on their discussions without either of them bringing it up again.

It was Zee who finally did, near the end of a lunch that had been spent mostly in silence.

"So, am I winning you over at all, or just convincing you that I'm crazy?"

Jan ducked her head a bit, an uncertain look on her face.

"The thing is," she said eventually, "except for, you know, what you're talking about, you don't *sound* crazy talking about any of this. Like, you're talking about crazy things in a totally sane way, if that makes any sense."

Zee smiled a little but didn't say anything, just kept giving Jan that look of focused listening.

"And...all right," Jan went on, pushing down the anxiety that welled up at the thought of admitting it, "I'd like to believe you. I would. I just...don't think I can without some kind of proof."

Zee nodded. "I thought it might come down to that."

"Well?" Jan prompted when Zee didn't say anything else.

"I *can* give you proof," Zee said, smiling wryly, "but not right now."

Jan raised an eyebrow, not bothering to conceal her skepticism. "Oh really?"

Zee gave a small sigh. "I realize how that sounds. But when we're assigned to a world, we don't bring anything that's not of that world. The only material proof I could show you would be a portal."

"And why can't you show me a portal, then?"

"Because I have no way of opening one from this side. One was opened for me when I came here, and another will be when my time here is over. Which won't be for some time yet."

Jan looked at her for a moment, seeing the same solemn earnestness Zee had shown the entire time. "You realize an excuse like that is only going to buy you so much time?"

"You've been willing to listen this far," Zee replied. "Now I just need you to be patient awhile longer."

The knock on the door came unexpectedly, in the middle of the night. Jan stumbled out of bed and kept the chain lock on as she opened the door. Zee was standing there, wearing a light coat over her pajamas.

"I know it's late, and I'm sorry, but can you come with me?" she asked.

Jan blinked a few times, her vision still fuzzy with sleepiness, and then pulled back to undo the lock and open the door all the way. "Zee. What the hell?"

"I need to go," Zee said urgently. "I got a message, and I need to go back to my home world. There'll be a portal, I can show you, but it has to be now."

"Whoa, okay, slow down," Jan protested, holding her hands up. "It's the middle of the night, Zee, I don't know if I can deal with this right now."

Zee made a low, frustrated noise. That was weird in and of itself; Zee always had the patience of a saint. "Jan, my father's been sick. He was sick even before I left, but he's getting worse, and they don't know how long he has. I *need* to go home." She paused, raking her loose hair back with her hand, and then said, "Look me in the eyes and tell me what I'm talking about isn't real."

Looking at Zee as she stood there, it was impossible to doubt that what she was talking about was real to *her*, at least, which still left Jan with a running mental picture of several scenarios involving Zee finally having gone off the deep end.

If Zee was crazy, that was. If everything Zee had been talking about all this time actually was real...

"Just come with me," Zee said, a note of pleading in her voice. "Just trust me, this one time. Please."

Jan looked at her for a long moment, biting her lip uncertainly.

What trusting Zee on this came down to, as it had with deciding to listen to her, was whether Jan felt that Zee, crazy or not, was at all dangerous. Jan hadn't thought so at the beginning of all this, and, she realized, she didn't think so now.

But *going* with Zee, going to see a portal to another world—it was going back to what Jan had done as a kid, all the times she'd gone looking for something just like this and never found it. It was setting herself up for a disappointment she thought she'd never face again.

Only maybe—just maybe—she *wouldn't* be disappointed this time.

"Give me five minutes to get dressed?" The voice sounded like it was coming from far off, but it was hers, and Zee was giving her a small, hopeful smile.

"You'll come with me?" she asked, and Jan nodded, not giving herself time to hesitate.

"Yeah—yeah. I'll come."

And In the Folly of My Mind
by Theresa Rogers

She rubs her forehead where it collided with his and sits up. Her waist-length red hair shoots white and gold sparks in the dying sun. It curtains her face.

"Quickbeam sent you." She looks up, and he gets lost in gold eyes. Not brown, not gold*en,* but *gold.* Her pupils are slitted like a cat's.

"Yes." He is staring at her. He offers his hand, but she ignores it and stands.

Something large shifts in the woods that surround them. In the next heartbeat, they are back to back, he with his dagger drawn. He tries not to notice how warm she is.

A unicorn points its head around a tree. She moves toward it. *"Jan!* Where have you *been?"* The unicorn enters the clearing. The man sucks in his breath. The last sunlight glints off her beautiful white back and down her...wings. He frowns. Her horn points at his chest.

"I'd put away the dagger, if I were you." The woman nods her head at his blade.

He sheaths it, and the unicorn comes closer to her. She drapes an arm over its withers, and there is a whispered conference. He stands taller, shifting from foot to foot.

"Name?"

He starts. "What?"

"What is your *name?"*

"Rogerson Jarbridge."

"We get all the freaks."

He thinks she is talking to him until he sees the unicorn nod its head. He blinks and frowns again. "Just what the hell is going on here? Who the hell are *you?"*

"Not important for the moment. How did you get here?"

He pushes his black hair out of his face. "Well..." She rolls her eyes.

He scowls. "I was standing in front of Quickbeam; he handed me this message"—he looks down at the piece of paper in his hand—"then I was here, in this clearing...on top of you..." He turns crimson. "He has a message."

She turns back to the unicorn, which hides its head from him. "He always does." She puts her hands on the unicorn's flanks, fingers spread. "Why doesn't Quickbeam come himself?" Rogerson can barely hear her.

"*I* don't know." Rogerson shakes the paper. "Quickbeam says, *'Tell her please to bring it back.'*"

She pales. "He does, does he?" Her voice is muffled. She turns completely toward him. Her clothes are dirty and ripped in some places. Rogerson looks down and then away. Some *interesting* places.

"You know," he swallows, stuffing the note in his pocket. "I've been friends with him for years, and he's a nice guy..."

She laughs, but it isn't the sound he's used to hearing. It sounds like a wolf howling.

"He had to write that down? You couldn't remember it?" She puts her hand out toward him, and he backs up. "No, fool, come *here.*"

He stays put. He crosses his arms and glares down at her.

She waves her hand and holds it out to him again.

He doesn't move. Jan spreads a wing.

When he comes to, he is slung face-down over the unicorn's rump. Blood pounds in his head. The jerky gait is not making anything in his life easier.

He shoves himself off the unicorn, but his muscles don't work right yet, and he crumples to the ground.

The hooves stop.

"I said you were a fool."

He flops over onto his back. "Do you have *any* friends?"

Hands pull on his shoulders, and he is sitting. He takes in the dirt track, the trees surrounding them. Her hair floats around him. Tiny gold sparks fly through the air. One lands on his hand. "Ouch!" He sucks his skin.

She pulls her hair back and ties it in a knot at the base of her skull. "Yeah. Sorry 'bout that."

He looks around, but he can't for the life of him find the fire. "About knocking me out? You should be."

"Yeah, that. Better?"

He stands. "Um."

"Better." She walks away.

"So..."

"If you can walk now, we can keep going."

"I'm not going anywhere with you. I'm just the messenger." He stops, looking around. "In fact, if you can tell me where—"

"There isn't one."

"You don't even know what I'm going to ask for!"

"City, town, village, crossroads, hut, transpoint, whatever it is, there isn't one."

"Well, surely—"

"Nope."

"There's a transpoint *somewhere*. Otherwise, how did I get here?"

She stops walking and turns to him. "Were you standing on a transpoint when Quickbeam sent you to me?"

He nearly runs into her and dances around to keep his balance. "I must have been. There's no other way to travel such great distances so quickly."

"So you know where you are?" She narrows her eyes.

He waves around him. "Quickbeam lives in the center of Alderwom. Alderwom is a big city. This isn't Alderwom. Ergo, I have traveled a great distance in an instant."

She turns and walks off. He looks backward at the path, then forward to where she is walking. He walks after her.

Night falls. They are seated, leaning against some rocks, Jan grazing a few feet away. Millions of stars burn themselves up above them. He doesn't recognize any of the constellations and something twists deep within him. He rubs his face. "Where am I?"

"Oh, not so far from where you *dropped in.*"

"No, I mean, where..."

"I know what you mean. I can't tell you."

He looks at her, his mouth a thin line. "You can tell me. I can handle it."

"I'm sure you could. I just don't *know.*"

He stands up. "Okay, I've had enough. Enough of this," he spreads his arms, "enough of *you.*" He walks toward a path. It's a stream. He turns right, following it. "I'll find my own way out."

She sighs and leans back against the rock. "Suit yourself."

He walks. He walks. He walks some more. The stream never seems to get any bigger or smaller. He stumbles over small rocks and is relieved when a clearing opens up in front of him. He steps into it.

She is leaning forward from the rock, her eyes anxious. When she sees him, she leans back. "Fool."

He sprints back to the stream, turning left. He falls over rocks and tumbles into the water. He splashes up the center to be sure he is not turning or looping back. He sees a clearing up ahead.

She is leaning against the rocks. "Do you know the definition of insanity?"

He sinks to his knees, panting. "Being anywhere near you?"

"Trying the same thing over and over, hoping for a different result."

His hands close into fists. His eyes fly around the clearing. "This is impossible! Impossible! We walked farther to get here than I just walked!"

She picks a blade of grass and puts it between her teeth. "It only does that if you try to leave."

"And if you *don't?*"

"Then you can go anywhere you like."

He shakes his head. "You've been here your whole life?"

"No. Of course not. Just...awhile."

"Who *are* you?"

"If I was somebody, don't you think I could get out of here?"

"Just give me your *name*. Polite people go about it like this: 'Hello, I'm Rogerson Jarbridge.' 'Oh. Nice to meet you, Mr. Jarbridge. My name...'"

"With a name like yours, I wouldn't be introducing myself to many people."

"'*My name is...*' and you fill in the blank." He glares at her.

She sighs. "You can call me Atur."

"Adder?"

"Close enough."

"What an apt name for you."

"Okay, Barbridge."

"*Jar*bridge."

"Sorry." She chews the grass and doesn't lower her eyes.

* * *

The stars wheel about them, and she is asleep, slumped against the unicorn, but he hasn't shut his eyes once.

He presses his lips together. Quickbeam is a writer. He has never, in all the time they have been friends, mentioned anything like what is currently happening to him. Quickbeam is a nice, normal man who has an amazing house with amazing antique...things...and he makes piles of money. End of story. One second Rogerson is talking to him; the next, Quickbeam hands him a message, and then here he is, wherever here is, on top of someone soft...he shakes himself... someone strange. In the woods.

He squints his eyes at the stars. *Maybe I'm in the Southern hemisphere?* But no, even down there he would see The Guardian in the upper part of the sky. *And that creek...*he shudders.

He stands up and ambles over to the creek. *Pay no mind, just going for a walk...*He ambles some more. To the left, to the right, amble, amble, amble. And there is the clearing again. And there she is again.

Damn.

The sky is pinking when she wakes. She isn't one of those slow stretchers. She wakes up and stands in the same instant, eyes flying about the clearing. Sparks fly from her hair like stars, and she looks like a pyrotechnics display. She settles on him and the embers fade.

He is leaning against a tree, his arms crossed. "I could swear I just saw sparks fly out of your hair. But that's impossible, so maybe I'm just going crazy. Who's here besides us?"

Now she stretches. "No one." She walks to the stream and kneels down, tying her hair carefully behind her and tucking it down her shirt.

He walks to her. "You're lying. Who's here besides us?"

She puts her hands above the water but doesn't touch it. "Why do you think there are others here?"

"Because nobody wakes up like that unless they're expecting something."

"I'm a nervous sleeper. Always have been." She moves her hands rhythmically over the surface, still not touching it.

"Yeah. And when I first met you, and we heard a sound, you drew up to my back."

"I'm a nervous person in general."

"I don't believe you."

She stands and moves back into the clearing.

"If you're here alone, why are you so dirty, and why are your clothes torn? You look like you've been in a fight."

She stands in front of him, her hands on her hips. "If *you* were somewhere alone, and *you* had no one to bug you every blessed second of the day, *you* might just let a few things go, too."

"Like my fear."

She shoves past him. He grabs her arm and turns her back around, again noticing how warm her skin is. *Hot* would be a better word. "Now listen..."

Something jabs his spine, and he sucks air though his teeth.

"Unless you want to be skewered, I'd suggest you let me go." Her voice is quiet but her eyes throw daggers into him. Jan presses her horn just a bit more forcefully.

He stands still for a moment longer and then allows his grip to slacken just enough for her to pull free. "Quite a little guardian animal you have there, in this place where there is *only you.*"

She is at him in two paces, and his own dagger is at his throat. It is the final ignominy. He grabs her arm and twists it behind her, pressing her wrist at the same time. She yelps and drops the dagger. He turns her to face the unicorn, which moves its horn away. He holds her close to him, her back against his chest, breathing the hot air between them.

She relaxes. "Well, thank the Guardians of the Hearth. Maybe you're not such a fool after all."

She flexes, and her skin glows white. With a roar, he releases her. He looks at his hands. They are red and raw. *"What* the *hell..."*

"Just put them on Jan." She points to the unicorn, who looks sideways at him, but does not point its horn at him. He presses his burned hands to its flank. Ice flows just under his skin, and when he pulls away, he is completely healed.

She walks toward the edge of the clearing. He crosses his arms. "Give me your weapon, or I don't walk another foot."

Once again, the horn is directed at him. "One thing, Jarbrain. Whatever weapon I do or do not have, it's none of your business."

"Jar*bridge.*"

"Whatever." Atur walks ahead. Jan lowers her horn and he follows.

"It very much is my business if you're going to use it on me." She stops, and he runs into her. "Will you *please...*"

She reaches back and covers his mouth with her hand.

He peers through the trees but sees nothing. He brings his hand up to pull her away, and she grabs it and holds it still.

"Don't. Move." She is talking out of the side of her mouth.

A breeze kicks up and the leaves shudder and twist above them. He remembers his burned hands and tries to pull himself free, but she clamps her fingers around his hand, and he stops.

The forest is empty, and then it is not. He blinks, but it isn't his imagination. Wisps of cloud are moving toward them. Their outlines aren't fixed, and it's as if steam has developed volition and decided to take a stroll. She drops his hand.

One stops directly in front of her. "Aturdokht."

Rogerson backs up and runs into Jan. Jan swishes her tail and tucks a wing around him. He can feel her heart beating. The unicorn is trembling. He clenches his hands into fists.

Atur bows her head. "Tishtar."

"We have spoken with Air."

"Yes."

The thing in front of her holds out a hand, palm out. She does the same. They do not touch but a hissing issues forth and, as Rogerson watches, her hand begins to smoke and the water being's hand begins to dissipate.

She begins to moan and twist, but she does not remove her hand. The thing in front of her shimmers, and now he can see through it.

"Enough!" The water being lowers its hand. "It will take more." She falls to her knees, and her hair tumbles loose from its knot, spilling around her shoulders and touching the grass, which curls and turns black.

Rogerson steps forward, his hand on his dagger.

The water beings move together, crowding around Aturdokht. She pales.

"Dust has made its attempt?"

"Yes." She points to a tear in her shirt.

One of the water beings reaches out, touches Aturdokht's hair. She jerks as if burned. Another reaches out, then another, and another, until he can hardly make her out in their midst. She is shaking now, her whole body vibrating from head to foot, and then they cover her.

"Use your weapon!" He is to them before he realizes it, his dagger drawn, his eyes fierce, but the movement of the blade is through water. He feels them wet and freezing against his body as he runs through them. They jerk away from him, and he sees her writhing on the ground. He crouches at her side and takes her hand in his. It is no longer warm—it is cold, ice, and he chafes it between his own. "Atur! *Atur!*" He pulls her to him.

Tishtar alone of the water beings stands with them now. He feels whiskers on the back of his neck and turns to find Jan. He moves aside but does not let go of Atur's hand. Jan reaches down, presses her nose to Aturdokht's chest, pushes hard. Aturdokht chokes and water flows from her mouth. She rolls to her side and vomits, but what comes up is clear, cold water.

He brings her upright and holds her to him. Her arms find their way around his chest, and she clings to him. She is so pale he can almost see through her.

"What have you done to her?" His eyes focus on the being next to him.

"It was an attempt. It is beyond our doing."

"Is she going to die?"

"Fire does not die. It is here, and it is there. But she is only here."

"She is fire?"

"She is the daughter of fire."

"Where the hell am I?"

Tishtar turns. "He is a human?"

Jan nods her head, her mane flying.

"What does that mean?"

"It means you are what I said you are—a fool." Atur twists to face Tishtar.

Tishtar bows low. Aturdokht nods her head.

They walk beneath a canopy of leaves. Atur is a bit ahead of him. Jan is ambling behind. Rogerson's brow is furrowed. "So these other beings who aren't here are also not trying to kill you."

She slows. "No, they are not trying to kill me."

"It looked a hell of a lot like it from where I was."

She sighs. "Don't go down paths you don't understand."

"I understand that you were *afraid*. I understand that you *needed* me."

"I didn't *need* you. I would have been fine even without your idiotic heroics."

He stops. "Didn't feel so 'not needed' when your arms were around me tight enough to keep me from breathing."

She stops but does not turn around. "Yes. Well. I felt sick."

"Call it what you will."

She begins walking again.

He follows. "And what was all that...being of fire? Who...or *what*...are you?"

"That's what I am."

He looks at his hands. "You're...fire?"

"I'm a fire *being*. It's different."

"Ah, yes, back in primary school, we went over the difference. I had just forgotten."

She turns. "Fire, Air, Water, Dust." She ticks them off on her fingers. "Who do you think governs your world?"

"What about Dark and L..."

She smashes her hands over his mouth. *"Don't say that."* Her hair lights up, millions of tiny sparks dancing among the strands. She is burning him.

"Mphm *mmmp.*"

She takes her hands down and runs them through her hair. Embers fly out like a meteor shower, igniting a small twig. She stamps on the twig. "Don't." She stamps on it again. "Ever." And again. "Say that." She is stamping the twig to within an inch of its life. She turns away but not before he sees the tears glinting on her lower lashes.

He grabs her hand. "I won't. I promise." He reaches out to touch her hair, but she slaps his hand away. He points to her head. "That's how you burned me."

"I didn't mean to."

He stands still for a moment. "Why can't I say L...that word?"

"That's what k-killed the others."

"The other *what?*"

"The other humans. That Quickbeam sent."

"Others have been here before me?"

"How do you think I got the other messages?"

"And they *died?*"

"Yes! They said...that word...and then they were *gone!*"

The tension in his shoulders dissipates. *"Gone.* But maybe not *dead."*

"What's the difference?"

"Rather a lot."

"R-Rogerson," she presses her face into her hands. "I have to get... something...to Quickbeam, but I don't...I don't know *how!*" She sobs, her whole body trembling, and he moves to her.

"I can help."

"You can't *help!* No one can *help!*" She pulls away from him.

He walks to her again but doesn't touch her. "Aturdokht, how do you know Quickbeam?"

She raises her head, tears streaming down her face. "He...I...I watched him for so long, and he...one day he saw me, there, in the fire...and I saw him...and we...I learned how to pull myself from the fire...but I..." She sinks to the ground, pointing to the burned twig.

"Did you love him?"

Her head falls forward and hair covers her face. "Yes."

Rogerson stands for a long time. She does not move from the ground. He crosses his arms over his chest. "What did you take?"

They are astride Jan, who is now flying. Jan dives, and Rogerson clutches Aturdokht with all his strength, digging his knees into Jan, who shivers her skin as if he were a fly.

They land in front of a fissure in a rock wall. They dismount, and Aturkokht disappears. Rogerson draws his dagger and follows.

He is engulfed in cool air, and he has to stop to allow his eyes to adjust. Then there is light, golden and soft, and he looks up to see that Aturdokht is glowing. Her hair has turned bright orange and her outline flickers, as if tiny flames were burning on the surface of her skin. When he gets closer, he realizes that's exactly what is happening.

"Don't touch me."

He rolls his eyes. "I think I've got that one down."

She points to a smaller crack in the solid rock of the cave. He looks in and something fiery jumps and twists. He scoots back. "What is it?"

"You have to get it. I can't touch it right now or...well, you have to reach in there."

"I'm not reaching in to get something that's going to burn me."

"It won't; it's not on fire. It's just...sparkly."

"*Sparkly?*" He bends down and reaches in, encountering something smooth and cool. He brings it out. In his hand is a dark leather book embossed with golden flames. "*This* is what you stole?" He turns it in his hands. "Well, no wonder," he mutters. "Guardian help us."

* * *

They land back in the same cursed clearing with the creek running next to it. He jumps from Jan's back. Aturdokht is close behind.

He sits on the ground and opens the book to the back. Several pages are torn out. He takes the message from his pocket and unfolds it, lining it up with the shreds. He lets out a whoop. *"This* is how I got here!" He holds the paper in front of her. "He bought this book at an ancient market in Tirkaresh. It's encoded to return to its owner so it can never be lost. The paper must be encoded to return to the book itself. Because Quickbeam handed me the note, it had to take me with it."

She stands very still, looking at the book. Her eyes travel to the note. "Why didn't it bring Quickbeam *himself?"*

Rogerson frowns. "Why *wouldn't* it...he held the paper before I did..." He flips the pages, reading. He gets up and moves about the clearing, book open in his hands, flipping pages, turning from one spot to another, muttering to himself.

She puts her arms on her hips, and her eyes narrow. "Have you lost your mind, then?"

"So if *I...* " He stops, frowning at the book. "No *pen."*

"He has." Aturdokht moves to Jan.

"That will work." He strides to Jan and his puts hand on her wing, his fingers separating one feather and pulling. Jan jumps back and nickers, her teeth bared.

Aturdokht bats him away. "What are you *doing?"*

"I need a quill."

"A quill."

"Something to write with!" He snatches at Jan's wing again. Jan prances away.

"I'll do it." Aturdokht moves to Jan, who stills. She reaches in and when she comes away, there is a feather in her fingers. Jan licks her wing, her eyes on Rogerson.

He swipes the feather from her and unsheathes his dagger, stripping the last two inches of the quill and sharpening the point. "No ink." He turns the point and slashes his arm.

Aturdokht is to him in two steps. *"What are you doing?"* She grabs his arm and pulls him toward Jan.

"Watch!" He dips the quill in his blood and scribbles on a page. A sword explodes into existence and falls to the ground. Her eyes wide, Aturdokht stares at it. "Do you see?" He turns the book to her.

She reads out loud. "A sword." She looks at the sword, its tip buried in the ground.

"Quickbeam writes his ideas in this journal. Quickbeam *created* this world! With his writing! Didn't you ever *read* this?"

"*No!* I just...wanted something. Of his." She looks down.

"Well, when you stole his book, the *act* of stealing trapped you in his world! The book has its own protection system!" He is laughing now. "Because he owns the book, he can't go into it...he couldn't *write* in it if, when he touched it, he went into it. *That's* why the paper didn't bring him." His eyes are sparkling; blood is dripping down his forearm. "You're a prisoner in his book!"

"It's...I'm in..." She looks at the word he wrote, his arm, and the sword.

"*Yes!* And that's why the note didn't go to the book—that's why it came to you." He points to the note. "'Her.' The word told the paper where to come. If he had handed me a blank sheet, I would have gone directly to the cave." He flips backward through the pages. "Read *this!*"

She lowers her head, her hair a curtain, sparks floating from the ends. He jerks the book away. "Don't set it on fire. This is how we'll get out of here!"

The sparks are brighter.

"Okay, stand over there. I'll read it to you. 'In the clearing stood a white horse with wings with a horn in the center of its forehead. Human intelligence. Must be able to heal.' Do you see?" He points to Jan.

"That doesn't make any sense."

"*With wings* is crossed out! He didn't mean a horse with wings, he changed his mind to a *unicorn*, but..." He lowers his head, frowning. "Why did it keep the wings..." He turns to the page with *A sword*. He crosses it out. The sword remains. He draws an *X* through the word. Nothing. He circles it and draws a line through it. It remains. He growls and scribbles the word entirely out. The sword disappears. "*Aha!* The pages don't know the difference if it's crossed out! It only knows what is legible!"

"Um."

"She's not *supposed* to have both a horn and wings, but she does!" He bends over the book, writing again. Jan turns blue and whickers, prancing, her eyes white-rimmed. He crosses something out and she turns white. "See?" He holds the book out.

*"The unicorn is...*you crossed that word out so much I can't read it."

"It says *blue.* That's the only way to make it unreal—to cross it out so much the paper can't read it! Quickbeam only used one line to cross things out!" He flips backward. "Read *this!"*

She tilts her head toward the book, holding her hair back. *"Light will bring you home."*

"They didn't die! When they said that word, they got pulled back!"

"Well, it doesn't work so well, then. *Light, light, light, light.* You'll notice I'm still here."

He rolls his eyes. "You stole the book. It isn't going to let you go that easily. If *I* said it, I *would* disappear." He flips to the front, where the pages are filled with writing. "'Escape is circular—you can't run away from anything; you always end up in the same place.' I remember when he said that. This is a philosophical musing, but the book doesn't know that. This is why I couldn't get away from the clearing." He jabs a finger at the page. "And that's why you can't get out. It hasn't been *written* yet!"

"So you're saying that if I just write something in that book..."

"If *I* write something. I didn't steal it."

"So if *you* write that we're in Quickbeam's house..."

"We'll *be* in Quickbeam's house!" He frowns, turning through the pages. "One thing, though...he never wrote anything about water beings, or dust beings..."

"They are from...my world. We thought if I could change into one of the other elements, I could get out, too." She presses her lips together.

But Rogerson is writing again, his head bent over the book, the quill flying. The trees dissolve, replaced by a room with dark wood paneling, leather furniture, a tray with cut crystal glasses, and a bottle. Rogerson looks up and lets out a yell.

Aturdokht sinks to the floor.

Rogerson throws the book aside and sweeps her into his arms. "You're free."

He twines his fingers in her hair and pulls her lips to his. There is soft, then wet, and warm, and then *hot,* but he holds on to her, tighter than before. Her hair turns orange, then blue, then white hot and still he holds her, kissing her. She finally pushes him away, her body dissolving, the edges white-hot flames. Her eyes burn into him.

"Thank you, Rogerson Jarbridge." Her voice curls around his name like a cat.

Before he can say anything, she is gone.

He turns as Quickbeam opens the door.

"Why didn't you tell me?"

Quickbeam looks at the smoke curling up from the floor. "Couldn't, if I wanted it to work. I could only give you enough to figure it out on your own."

"That's not what I mean."

"I know." They stand, looking at the smoldering spot.

Quickbeam points to Rogerson's fingers. "You'll have a scar."

"Yes." His eyes are still on the floor. "I will."

Bindings of the Dead
by Pasquale J. Morrone

Dr. Angus Waterbee wiped his brow as he continued to work on the body that lay before him. His office was in shambles after Katrina, but even Doctor Frankenstein continued working long after his castle was in ruins. This was no different.

He opened the skull and carefully checked the brain one last time. It was then that one of his colleagues, Dr. Thomas Morley, came into the room. Morley was not amused at what was being done. "You are creating something that is ungodly. This poor creature is no different than Victor Frankenstein's monster."

Waterbee looked up at his friend. "In the story, Frankenstein deserted his creation. I will not do the same. I have used the brain of a very prominent librarian who died of complications due to hyperthermia. The brain was removed just as death knocked on her awaiting door. She will be an asset to our library when it is whole again. Have faith."

"Faith?" Morley looked down at the woman who was boasting a light green complexion. "The brain is dead. The brain has no oxygen. You were at my wife's bedside when she passed on. As a doctor, you should know that it is simply an organ that will take up space in the skull—nothing more. Even if she did show signs of life, she will simply sit around and drool. Would anyone really care to share a reading space with this...this repulsive mimic of a woman?"

Waterbee shook his head. "She will work after hours. In time, we will simply treat her as one who is sickly and nothing more. In time, she will walk among the patrons as though she was meant to be there. And she will be."

Morley walked over to the smoked-glass window. "And what will you call her?"

Waterbee laughed openly now. "She isn't just a creation like that of Victor Frankenstein, Thomas. She is a zombie. There will be no electrodes or water to bring life into my dear lady. I will be here to say her name over and over again. I will be here when she opens her eyes for the first time in her new life. Just as I was instructed to do, I will say her name over and over again."

Morley shook his head. "And that is?"

"Zombrarian."

"What? Good god, man. That's not a name."

"It's the name that was chosen for her. It's the name that will bring about her new life in the new city of New Orleans."

The opening of the library was a complete success. Below the library was the new medical school that trained young aspiring physicians in the art of surgery and autopsies. It was not uncommon to have both renowned and infamous characters lying on the stainless steel tables in silence.

Publishers from all over the country banded together, matching one another's donations of books and magazines. There was a reading room, a small café, and generous rows of hardcovers and paperbacks of all genres. The smell of paper and bindings filled the air along with the freshly brewed coffee and baked goods at the café.

Deep into the rows of books, there was Zombrarian. At 145 pounds, she stood a good six foot two. Covering her face was a small opaque veil of bluish green. She slowly wandered about the prose and poetry section, placing a new piece here, straightening up another there. Each book she touched flashed in her mind like a streak of lightning. It spoke to her in words that others could never hear. She knew each of the authors' works as well as she knew her own name.

She was close to the reading section now. Two men were arguing a bit too loud about one of the Saints football games.

"Ssssshhhhhrrrrrrrsshhhh!"

They quickly stopped squabbling and turned their heads. She stood straight and tall halfway down the aisle. It almost seemed as though the darkness followed her. The darkness actually became her, part of her. Anyone in her exact vicinity, in her aura of darkness, became engulfed in it. They would disappear, momentarily, until either they or she moved away. The two men eyeballed one another and went back to talking about the game but, this time, in a reasonable tone.

Morley carefully stepped up behind her. "Zombrarian."

The woman didn't turn. She stood her ground, motionless and aware. She knew the voice all too well. It was the voice of he whom she did not trust.

"Why are you up here at this time of day? It is not yet your time. The others here do not understand who or what you are. They are not ready for someone such as you."

"Braaaaaaiiinsssssssss." The word slid from her lips like the tongue of the most powerful asp.

Although Morley heard it as clear as any bell from a church steeple, he backed up slightly and tried to reposition himself at her side. "What did you say?"

"Sssshhhhrrrrrrsshhhh!"

She turned and moved passed him, unabated. The strength of her aura sent chills up the doctor's back as he pressed himself against the shelving. Looking into the veil, he could see her eyes for what they were. All white, with the exception of two black pupils, each the size of a BB. Without turning her head, the tiny black orbs slid over to stare at him as she passed.

Later that day, Zombrarian lurked in the dim light of the morgue. She silently wandered about the occupied tables and lifted the sheets to peer at the discolored faces of the dead. A tall man lay silent under one of the sheets in the back of the room. On a scale beside the table was the man's brain, the digital meter was still registering 3.5 pounds.

"Braaaaaaiiinsssssssss." Zombrarian bent slowly forward until her face was only inches from the severed organ. The smell of blood and tissue drifted up her nostrils. The man was not only a former librarian, but one of the library's patrons for more than fifty years. His knowledge of every book, every index card's entry, made her lips want to smack in literary hunger. What a waste it would be to sit in the skull of a dead former librarian.

Twenty minutes later, Dr. Thomas Morley shook his head. "I don't know what happened to it," he said. It was on the scale when I stepped out to use the restroom. Who would want to steal a brain?"

The school's director of physician's studies shook his head. "This is terrible. We must keep this quiet for the time being. If word ever gets out that we have some...some mad person running around steal-

ing body parts..." He looked down and closed his eyes, once again shaking his head. "This is insanity, just total insanity."

Angus Waterbee kept to himself but listened intently to the conversation from the other side of the room. This wasn't the first time something like this happened. Several times he closed up a human skull minus a brain. All of them were patrons of the library so many years ago. Why? He tried to answer the silent question, but nothing came to mind.

"Dr. Waterbee." The director walked to where the doctor was standing. "I'm puzzled by this. Is there anything or anyone you can think of who might have done this heinous deed?" He stopped short of the table and glanced down at the dead woman Waterbee had just closed up. "A college prank perhaps? Maybe it was one of those fraternity things?"

Waterbee shrugged. "We don't have that kind of thing here. This is a small school, and what is taught here is to be taken very seriously. We have no room here for childish pranks, especially something of that nature."

The director nodded. "Yes...yes I agree. I know you were working very late a few months ago. I didn't see any worksheets from you though, doctor. Is it something personal you're trying to work out? Perhaps something keeping you awake? You know, my office is always an open door policy, Dr. Waterbee."

Waterbee cleared his throat. "No, nothing like that. I just wanted to make sure there were fresh cadavers for our students, and those we had no further use for...well, that they were given a proper burial," he lied.

"Yes. Good man." The director turned and left him to his work. He suddenly stopped and turned once again. "That woman, the librarian you hired, doctor."

Waterbee nodded. "Yes, what about her?"

"Kind of quiet and shy. I don't see her very often, but she's quite efficient. What's her name?"

Waterbee knew this day was coming. "Her name is Zonba. Zonba Undade. I think she's some kind of Indian or something." He laughed for a second at the scrambled letters of the last name before looking up at the director. "We call her Zombrarian. Not to her face of course, but just because...well, just like you say. She's kind of mysterious and shy all at once."

"Yes. Absolutely. Well, carry on, doctor. Nice talking to you.

We'll get to the bottom of this mess sooner or later. We may have to install cameras. I would find great pleasure in showing the culprits some home movies of themselves."

He watched the director leave the room. The director was right though. This had to stop. Perhaps it was some sort of collegiate-type prank. But it was only the brain.

Waterbee finished up what he had to do. He showered, and made his way to the library in time to see his creation doing what she did best. "You're doing an excellent job here, Zombrarian. The horror and sci-fi section." He smiled slightly. "Right up our alley, isn't it?"

"Luvvvvvvcrraaaaaaaffft. Poooooooooeeeeeee. Kiiiiiiinnng. Koooo-nnnttzz."

Waterbee stepped back in amazement. He hadn't expected this. She was actually forming words. "You're becoming very proficient both in your job and your English. I'm very impressed. Have you been studying in some way?"

Zombrarian's eyes drifted over to him through her veil. Those white eyes with the small black dots for pupils ogled him in a way that made his skin crawl. She took a short raspy breath. "Braaaaaaaiiinssssssss."

He was aware that she said the word quite often. What was the association? He thought. The names of four horror writers. They were and are intelligent people. Brains. Yes, that was it, it had to be it. Intellectuals. Those who used their minds for writing. Her brain was that of...yes, that had to be it. The brain of a librarian. That brain would definitely be attracted to those minds with extreme intelligence.

She was in the dark place come nighttime. The secret room hidden by a small door just off from the morgue itself. Her bed was made of stainless steel and covered only by a thick black body bag, which she lay upon rather than climbed into. No one came into the room except Dr. Waterbee. Not even Dr. Morley would step foot into her own private mausoleum. Her eyes were always open. Staring into the darkness, she would recite to herself what she had learned from the last brain. It was becoming easier now.

Zombrarian let her mind drift off to places she had read in books, various places in fictitious works, authored by the likes of Poe and King. From the walls of these ungodly places, she would see tentacles rising from the floorboards, young people communicating with the dead. But she needed to have more. The knowl-

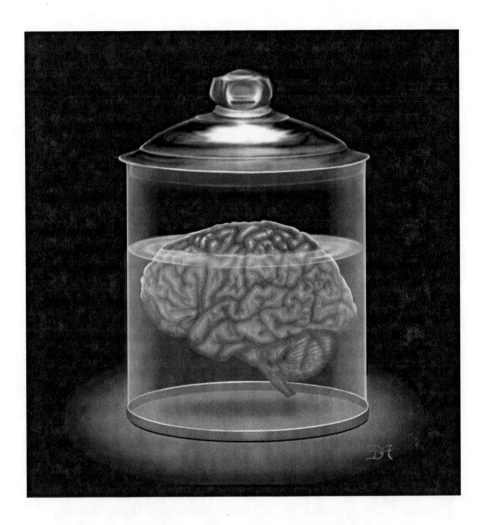

edge was now close to becoming an addiction. Her borrowed brain burned and screamed in a silent rage for more of the same.

"Braaaaaaiiinssssssss."

Waterbee's eyes snapped open from a deep sleep. That word. It was as clear as a bell once again, but his creation was nowhere around. He quickly showered and dressed. After breakfast, he walked into the room just as the director was throwing up his hands in total disbelief. "What do you mean it just showed up?"

Doctor Morley suddenly ripped off his surgical gloves and threw them down onto the steel gurney. "Sir, I do not need to be yelled at. I am a grown man, a physician in this institution...and a damned good one. I came in here this morning after breakfast, and there it was, right where you see it, soaking in a preservative, in," he pointed his finger closely to the container, "that jar."

The director nodded. "All right, Doctor Morley. I apologize for my outburst. You're absolutely right. I have no right to speak to you in that manner. I'm simply confounded by this whole matter of stealing body parts. What on earth are they doing with them?"

"It appears that whoever put the brain back had the intelligence and common sense to contain it where it would be preserved for the time being," Waterbee said, putting his two cents in whether it was wanted or not.

The director shook his finger in thought. "We should have a talk with Zo...whatever her name is. You know, ask her if she'd seen anyone suspicious. Well, maybe not actually suspicious, but someone who doesn't come around here often."

Waterbee slipped his lab jacket on and shook his head. "She does not know anything about this; you can be assured of that."

When the director left the room, Morley turned to his colleague. "How can you be so sure she has nothing to do with this? No one else comes down here. You have her set up in that room in the back, Angus. She's right here among the dead. Can you, in all honesty, say that she has not been parading around in here in the middle of the night?"

Waterbee leaned on the edge of one of the tables. "And do what with it? It's obvious that she did not eat the damned thing."

Morley poured himself a cup of coffee and walked toward the door. "There is something terribly wrong here, doctor. I have to be up front and honest with you. If I find that Zombrarian is behind this nasty business and, if it means my job here at the center, I will have to come clean and tell what I know."

Waterbee nodded. "I understand. We do what we have to do, Doctor Morley. If it comes to that, you will not have to speak up. I will do that for you."

Zombrarian's tasks were getting much easier. Some of the patrons would watch her work from afar. King before Koontz. She would squint her eyes and groan in disgust at the way some people put the books back in place. They weren't supposed to. That was her job and hers alone.

"Can you help me find a book?"

Zombrarian stopped what she was doing immediately. Her eyes slid over and down to find a little girl no taller than four feet standing beside her. No one had been this close to her in weeks. Slowly, she turned her head and looked down at the child.

"I want to find a book 'bout a little girl who gets lost in the woods. My friend said it was very very good. Somethin' 'bout baseball and..." The girl put her tiny hand up to her forehead. "I can't 'member the rest."

Zombrarian's long finger pointed downward. The little child was in the right section at least. The K's. "Kiiiiiiiinnnnnng."

Pulling the slender book from the shelf, the girl read the cover as though she weren't sure it was the right one. Then a smile spread across her tiny face. "That's the one. Oh, yes, that's the one all right. *The Girl Who Loved...*" Her little eyes squinted in thought.

"*Tommmm Gorrrrrrrrdooooonnn.*"

Once again the child smiled. "The baseball player. Yep. Thank you very much for helping me, lady."

"Sarah." A woman entered the aisle and shook her head. "Now you know that your friend is a few years older than you are. How do you expect to read that book?" She smiled as she looked up at the strange woman. "I hope you didn't have to look all over the—"

Zombrarian's slender fingers reached down suddenly and touched the little girl's head. "Smaaaarrrrt braaaaaaiiin."

The woman slowly took her daughter by the arm and led her away. Zombrarian turned her veiled features away from them. The child wasn't afraid, or didn't understand who or what she was talking to, but the woman did. Surely she would tell the little girl not to talk to her again. But Zombrarian's mind was opening up more and more. Something was whispering to her someplace deep into her brain. A name perhaps. She wished she could hear the voice more clearly. She was sure it was a name, her name.

In the dim light of the morgue, Zombrarian moved silently among the dead. Along the wall on shelving of galvanized steel, she inspected the organs preserved for the medical classes. In larger containers, there were lungs and stomach linings. In the smaller jars, there were eyes, hearts, and even a few tongues and ears. Zombrarian frowned as she walked past the last of the displays. There were absolutely no brains. *How could they expect to teach anatomy if there were no brains?* she thought.

On her way out of the room, she stopped and stared once again at the rows of containers. A smile crossed her lips. How could she have missed it? There in one of the bigger containers, but in the back of another jar, there was, indeed, a brain. She leaned forward and studied it carefully. There were no vibes coming from it. It wasn't a powerful brain. It wasn't the brain of someone she could... Zombrarian stopped all thought processes and turned her attention to the door. Someone was working the cipher lock.

Dr. Thomas Morley opened the door and stepped inside the room. He was in sweats and looked comfortable, except for the troubled look on his face. He slowly made a circle around the room, examining each of the bodies as he passed by. These were fresh cadavers for the first surgery examination of the year. Each of their heads was shaven clean. Zombrarian peered through the small glass in the center of her door, the lights turned off on the other side.

"I know you are watching me," Morley said. "I am not a stupid man. I know that in some way, you have something to do with this stealing business. Why not tell me why you take these things. I can keep a secret. If there is something you are looking for, perhaps I can help in some way. Dr. Waterbee does not have to know anything of what we shall speak of after I leave this room."

Morley's ears discerned a low squeaking sound. He slowly turned to face the door where Waterbee's creature stayed. Her tall, lean figure was always intimidating to look at when alone with her. Morley put himself between a stainless-steel table and the strange-looking being.

"Kaaaatriiiiinaaaaaaa."

Morley shook his head. "You mean the hurricane? What about it?"

Zombrarian repeated the name as she stepped into the room. This time the veil was no longer in place. Her face seemed to be familiar in some way. Even the expression she now showed him began to change.

Morley felt the blood drain from his face. Never in all his years as a medical examiner did he look upon the dead with so much vigilance. He quickly made his way to the exit and didn't stop until he was out of the building. Hanging onto the metal railing just outside the front doors, he tried to catch his breath. That face. Something in the eyes. Something in the voice. Everything. It was all as if...

Morley stopped the thought process and turned to the parking lot. His car was in the normal spot, the executive portion, where all the metal signs announced that they were indeed reserved. He wanted to go to it, step inside, and start the engine.

"Thomas."

Morley turned with a start. Angus Waterbee held the doors open for a moment before stepping outside and leaning on the rail beside him.

"You look as though you have seen a ghost. Are you all right?"

Morley took deep breaths before speaking. "Who is she?"

"She?"

"You know damn well whom I speak of, Angus. That...that beast of a woman you have created. Every single day, she seems to grow more aware of her surroundings. Her vocabulary, although minute, has picked up tremendously. Where did you get the brain?"

Waterbee walked to the other side of his colleague, eyeing him considerably before pressing his back against the cool metal of the rail. "From this institution, Thomas. Yes, I know it may be slightly on the unethical side, but—"

"Unethical!" Morley moved to the other side as well. "Unethical, you say? What you have done can lead to your dismissal." Morley shook his head. "I saw something in there. I saw something in her that brought back a memory. She said a name. Katrina."

"The hurricane?"

"I heard it as plain as day. It is more than the hurricane. Katrina was my wife's name, and you know that. I saw the look in her eyes. Suddenly, it was a look of intelligence. It was a look of something that jolted a memory. It was as though she knew me."

Waterbee shrugged. "Of course she knows you, Thomas. You work here and have seen her for...how long has it been now?"

"Do not patronize me in that manner, Angus. I have warned you before about my career and my efforts to keep a clean record. I see no big secret here. I see no reason why you could not divulge any information about where you got the brain."

Waterbee stepped to the middle of the aisle, facing his friend. "I told you where I got it, Thomas. Whose it is will remain with me for all time. There is nothing you need to worry about, Thomas. Nothing! There is absolutely nothing wrong with what I have done. She has not caused difficulties in any way. If worse comes to worse, I will take the blame. I will not implicate you in any way. You can be sure of that."

In the night, Thomas Morley pulled the blankets up under his chin. He suddenly felt a cold chill. Slowly opening his eyes, he turned his body slightly to face the doorway. In the diffused glow of the night-light, he caught her image blocking the entire area. Morley bolted upright in a cold sweat. There was nothing there.

Sleep eluded him. He made his way into his library. It was built the same way his wife had set it up before the killer storm. It was just as impressive as the original she had painstakingly put in alphabetical order by author. He smiled for a moment. Most people would probably put them in order according to the title, but not Katrina. She knew each author's works as well as she knew her ABC's. The volumes seemed to stare out at him.

He passed slowly by some of her favorite authors. Louisa May Alcott, Philip K. Dick, and Jonathan Lethem. At a separation in the shelving where she placed special artifacts from her past, he stared into the faces of William Powell and Myrna Loy. *The Thin Man.* The thought was so pronounced that it made him turn to see if it was actually a thought and not someone describing the portraits. Above the characters Nick and Nora Charles was the dashing figure of Dashiell Hammett standing next to a passenger train. Above Hammett were the smiling faces of Peter Lorre and Humphrey Bogart from *The Maltese Falcon*, another creation of Hammett's.

Morley's eyes began to burn as he touched a thin plaque above the pictures. Just above the plaque was the handsome portrait of Thomas Paine in a rust-colored suit. Morley once again ran his fingers over the plaque, slowly passing the tips over the wording.

"We have it in our power to begin the world over again."

This time there was a voice. Morley spun on his heels. "Katrina."

She smiled at him and slowly made her way to where he stood. "What's wrong? You look as though you've seen a ghost."

Déjà vu, he thought. "I love you. Did I tell you that before we went to bed?"

Katrina's fingers brushed away the tears that slid down his cheeks. "You have never failed to tell me in thirty-five years. Now, will you tell me what's wrong?"

"Nothing," he said, smiling. "There is nothing wrong at all. But Paine was right in what he said. We do have the power to change things, to start the world over again. I want to take your idea to the board. I want to get authors from all over the world to help build our city, to help build the library you loved and cared for so much."

Katrina's lips touched his ever-so-softly. "I'll start the paperwork. I love you, Thomas Morley."

Morley walked to the site where the library and medical center were well under construction. Even as he stood there watching, people were flocking into the partially built library. He went through the doors and immediately walked up to Angus Waterbee. The warm smile he received only reinforced the idea that it was only a bad dream. After sharing a cup of coffee, Morley stood in the rows of books to be slotted and alphabetized.

A young woman was busy reading the spines and placing them where they were supposed to be. He smiled and shook his head. "What does it take to be a good librarian?" he asked.

Even though he could see only her profile, he could see her blush as she smiled.

"Braaaaaiiiinnnns," she said.

A Jumbled Shelf
by Jennifer Racek

The wide stone steps of the St. Simon's Parish Library sprang up out of the sidewalk like a succession of broken teeth. Cracks had formed over most of their length, and scraggly, rust-green weeds surged through, attempting to reclaim the broken areas.

The weeds snatched at Lucy's ankles as she mounted the steps, barbed leaves catching on the ragged edges of her jeans. She'd once seen a picture of one of those big fancy libraries like they had in New York and Chicago. At libraries like that, stone lions guarded the entrance as though they'd leap down and maul anyone daring to bring a book back late.

St. Simon's boasted only a blazing red swirl of graffiti that sat beneath the building's modest nameplate like a large pimple. The city had sent a team out to scrub the wall clean twice, but they gave up after the third time the graffiti reappeared.

Lucy's mom, Amy LaRue, had been working at St. Simon's for three years. She had made her way up from a part-time stint at the circulation desk to a position as the catalog librarian. Lucy had been spending her after-school hours at the library for just as long. The face of the library never changed. The steps grew more cracked, the stone walls dingier, but overall, the only thing to mark the passing time was Lucy's own face reflected back in the smudged glass door as she pushed it open each day.

The library belched out an air-conditioned breath, and Lucy pulled the door closed behind her quickly. The stale air felt lovely and cool after the damp, sweltering heat outside. Summer strangled New Orleans in its stifling grip and refused to give way to fall, no matter what the calendar said.

"Hiya, Luce," Belinda called from behind the circulation desk.

Lucy didn't bother to reply. Belinda was as temporary as the flyers on the pockmarked corkboard by St. Simon's front door. The flyers would give way to new advertisements or pleas for lost pets, or fabulous weight loss and job opportunities, just as Belinda would be replaced by another fresh-faced, eager college student. Each one imagined herself a modern-day Hypatia, only to be chased from the library by the reality of shrinking budgets, moldering books, and a lack of upward job mobility.

"Lucy!" Amy's excited face popped above one of the low bookcases.

"Hi, Mom," Lucy muttered. She shoved her midterm report farther into her pocket and adjusted the backpack on her shoulder.

"You're just in time," Amy said, waving Lucy over as though directing air traffic. "I need an extra set of hands. It'll only take a minute."

Lucy sighed. "What are we reshelving this time?"

"A bit of this and that. I've had the most wonderful idea!"

Amy's white teeth flashed, emphasizing the espresso bean skin and high cheekbones that Lucy wished she'd inherited. Instead, Lucy more closely resembled her grandmother, with kinky hair that struggled to escape her braids and the same long, thin face. There was nothing elegant or beautiful about her.

"You can put your backpack under my desk while we work," Amy directed—as though Lucy hadn't done the same thing for time on end.

"Sure, whatever," Lucy said. She shambled over to Amy's desk, a lopsided pile of wood that was held together in equal parts by silver duct tape and sheer stubbornness. The sad wreck was perched at the back corner of the library, framed on one side by shelves of poetry and old plays and on the other by fat history texts that swelled with their own importance.

Mr. Hall, the library manager, occupied the only proper office in the entire place. The other employees made do with whatever space they could eke out amid the books.

"Hurry up, Miss Molasses," Amy called.

Lucy stashed her bag, raking the side against a piece of tape that had begun to peel back. She walked with steps as slow and ponderous as a sloth. Other girls were at the mall with friends or playing hoops; *she* was stuck shelving books. The injustice was unbearable.

"You've got the sullens today, don't you?" Amy observed. She sat cross-legged on the floor, flanked on one side by the bookshelves and Lucy on the other. Amy looked Lucy up and down. "It's that clothing. You need something bright and pretty. What about that pink shirt I got you last week?"

"The one with the kittens?" Lucy asked, tugging at her black T-shirt so the corners pulled down like a scowl.

"Yes." Amy laughed. "That'd be cheerful. Brighten you right up,"

"I'm not three," Lucy snapped. "Besides, black is *in*."

"Oh," Amy said with a shrug. "I hadn't realized. Well, we can't sit here and discuss your wardrobe all day; there's work to be done." She rubbed her hands together, then snatched a book from the shelf in front of her. "Look at this!"

Lucy frowned, reading the title. "*Peaches?*"

"Yes! Just got it in today, Mrs. Moore said little Alice is done with it and on to a new book series. So, we're welcome to it."

"Little Alice" was sixteen and one of the more popular girls at the senior high school. Lucy looked at the book with interest. Many of St.

Simon's books had come to the library that way, cast offs looking for a new home. Much like Amy and herself.

"It's perfect for my new shelf," Amy said, as though she'd been given an original Gutenberg Bible rather than a dog-eared teen novel.

Ah. So that was it: a new shelf. With a serious lack of new material, there really wasn't much for a cataloguing librarian to do. Amy, however, had made it her mission to reorganize every book in St. Simon's. She had to be on her third or fourth run by now. What would it be today? Moving the knitting books from the left side of the library to the right? Or perhaps they'd be changing the children's books from alphabetical to subject-based again. Lucy sighed.

"Well," Amy burst out, "aren't you going to ask what my wonderful idea is?"

Lucy merely plopped down beside her mother, chin in hand, and waited for the wondrous plan to unfold.

"What are people looking for when they come into the library?" Amy asked.

"Books?" Lucy said once it became obvious this wasn't a rhetorical question.

"Exactly!" Amy exclaimed. "They want books! But they don't always know what they want. A thriller? A romance? A treatise on fourteenth-century art? It could be anything. But they usually get stuck in one section and never even notice all the other books just waiting to be read. We are going to change all that."

"What, you're going to switch their Harry Potter for a Harry Houdini guide to magic on checkout?" Lucy asked, shaking her head. Her mom was so weird sometimes.

"Of course not! But if old Houdini was sitting on a shelf right next to Mr. Potter, someone might give it a second glance and consider picking the thing up."

Amy paused, and when Lucy didn't fall into raptures of delight at this profound thought, Amy huffed out a breath. "Well, I think it's a good idea."

Lucy shrugged. Shelving books in order or at random, it was still shelving. "Just tell me what we're supposed to be doing, so we can get it over with. Okay?"

"Fine. We have a lot to do anyway, I suppose." Amy sighed. "I want you to go into the stacks and just pull books at random. Try to get a lot of different subject areas. Pick the majors but go for some of the lesser gems as well."

Lucy looked at her dubiously. "Just take any book I feel like and bring it back here?"

"That's the idea," Amy said. She shoved up into a standing position, using the low bookshelf as leverage. "You start in the fiction stacks, and I'll go for nonfiction. Don't come back until your arms are full!"

Before Lucy could get to her feet, Amy was gone in a whirl of skirts. Amy tore through the library like a bright tornado, snatching books and then putting them down again. Pointless. And stupid. How were they supposed to organize a bunch of random books?

An hour later, there were two piles of books beside the shelf Amy had designated. Together Lucy and Amy sat, as they had earlier, though this time Amy faced away from Lucy and frequently twisted around to request another book or make a comment. Time continued to crawl by as slow as the city bus on a hot day.

At last they were finished. Amy sat back with a satisfied smile, stretching out her legs and wiggling her bare toes. She'd discarded her shoes long before as she normally did late in the afternoon.

"Isn't it perfect?" Amy breathed, taking in the hodgepodge of books wedged together like little buildings in a crowded downtown scene.

"Sure," Lucy said. "Perfect."

"Lucy," Amy said. "Pick a book."

"What! I've picked plenty of books already!" Lucy's voice rose in irritated protest.

"To take home," Amy added patiently, smile never wavering.

Lucy stared blankly at the rows of books. God, where to start? There was no rhyme or reason to it. How was anyone supposed to find anything? She tried scanning the titles but they were packed so tightly together it was difficult. Where was that *Peaches* book? After several long minutes, she located the pale cover wedged between a book about fertilizer techniques and a gaudy red-spined paperback thriller. Removing the slender book took as much effort as Arthur yanking his sword from the fabled stone.

"I think you have them packed in too tightly," Lucy said, slapping the book against her thigh.

Amy eyed the shelf critically, nudging the small bookcase around so it faced St. Simon's front door. "Nonsense! There's just a lot of variety, that's all."

Lucy shrugged and glanced at the round, white clock hanging on the back wall. Her mother's shift would be over in a few minutes, and then it would be time to head home. Thank goodness.

* * *

Amy's unique approach to shelving went unremarked for several days. On the third day, Lucy straggled into the library as usual. She was sweaty from the short walk and grumpy because Aaron Josephs had started calling her Loser Lucy after she'd failed to hit even one of the dozen softball pitches sent her way in gym class that afternoon.

"It's working perfectly," Amy exclaimed before Lucy had even had a chance to set her backpack down. "Mrs. Prentice came in for an Agatha Christie novel, and she left with two of them plus a history of the Orient Express."

"Great," Lucy growled, dropping her bag with a heavy thump. She perched on the edge of her mother's desk. "Just wonderful."

Over the coming days, there were more success stories. People discovered books that interested them and left the library with piles stacked higher than they had intended. However, there were also one or two complaints from patrons frustrated at not finding the books they wanted in logical places.

By Saturday, Lucy had finished the *Peaches* book and brought it back, a bit more dog-eared but triumphant. It was a real library book now, having been checked out and returned. Lucy placed the book back on the jumbled shelf with a smile, letting her hand linger on the spine. It was the first in a series and she wanted to read the sequel. Alice Moore, however, had not been obliging enough to discard the second book, and it was too new for St. Simon's to have acquired it.

Lucy ran her hand over the books on the jumbled shelf and searched for something else to read. She was reluctant to admit it, but the mix of titles and colors, of fat and thin books, was intriguing. She might discover anything on that shelf, and the quest took on a gamelike quality. What would she find next? Lucy was still searching when an older woman stormed up to Amy's desk. Glancing over, Lucy recognized Mrs. Crabtree, one of the library board members.

Lucy had only met the board members once or twice when their meetings overlapped her mother's work schedule, but they always made her feel grubby and small, as though she were five and might leave sticky fingerprints in all the books.

"I want to see Mr. Hall immediately!" Mrs. Crabtree bleated, not bothering to lower her voice. The noise carried through the library like a siren. Several people looked up, scowling at the disturbance.

Lucy pivoted, still balanced on the balls of her feet, with one hand extended toward the books like a supplicant. Mrs. Crabtree stood just a few feet away, body quivering with outrage and wearing the most hideous puke green dress Lucy had ever seen. It looked as though Mrs. Crabtree had wrapped herself with wilting cabbage leaves, and Lucy had to stifle a laugh. There was nothing comical, however, in the woman's red, angry face.

"Good morning, Edith," Amy said with a calm smile. "Tell me what's wrong, and I'll see if I can't help."

"You can't," Mrs. Crabtree spat the words like drops of acid onto Amy's scarred desk.

"Very well," Amy said, still conciliatory though the words sounded flat and thin. "Can I at least tell Mr. Hall what this is about?"

"Your shelving practices," Mrs. Crabtree snapped, "And the filth you're placing on those shelves."

Amy's eyebrows arched high, but she got to her feet and moved stiffly toward Mr. Hall's office. Mrs. Crabtree dogged Amy's heels. Through it all, Lucy sat unmoving and watched. Amy reached the office door, rapped sharply on it, and waited. Mrs. Crabtree bumped to a halt behind Amy. It was only luck that kept Mrs. Crabtree from knocking Amy into a wall with her bulk.

After a long moment, the door creaked open to reveal Mr. Hall's scowling face, with his round glasses perched lopsided on his snub, little nose. It was his usual look, slightly flustered, with wispy brown hair sticking out on the sides and bald pate shining in the glare of the overhead lights. The top of Mr. Hall's head reached only to Amy's shoulder. He tugged the lapels of his striped suit into place and straightened his spine, attempting to stare Amy down by tilting his head back so that his nose stuck into the air.

"Is there a problem, Amy?" Mr. Hall asked, like a petulant child pulled away from his blocks.

Lucy hunched lower, hoping he wouldn't notice her. Her constant presence at the library after school had been the cause for several lectures from Mr. Hall. He'd told Amy only yesterday, with Lucy standing red-faced beside her mother, that the library was not a daycare. As though Lucy was some snot-faced kid and not eleven, practically a teenager. Amy had just smiled and nodded. Mr. Hall had gone back to his office, the door snapping closed behind him so that its familiar brown face stared out on the library. Lucy liked him much better that way, with a solid chunk of wood between them.

"There certainly is!" Mrs. Crabtree boomed, making Mr. Hall totter on his loafer heels with the force of her voice. "Do you know what is on your shelves?"

Mr. Hall rocked forward, color flooding his cheeks. For the first time, he noticed Mrs. Crabtree lurking behind Amy. "Good afternoon, Edith," he said slowly. "I know every book in this library. I have read most of them."

Mrs. Crabtree scowled and jutted her chin out. "Then I am appalled at you, Edmond Hall! Allowing such muck into this library. And worse, promoting it! You should be ashamed."

Mr. Hall glanced at Amy and then back at Mrs. Crabtree, shaking his head as though he had sand in his ears. "I'm sorry, what?" he asked.

Mrs. Crabtree swelled out her chest and spun on her heel, charging forward so quickly that Lucy was forced to jump to her feet and scuttle away from the bookshelf. Mrs. Crabtree snatched a book off the end of the shelf and turned back, waving it in the air like a banner. "This," Mrs. Crabtree snarled, "this is the point! Filth! Racist, disgusting smut. I was so shocked when I saw it. I wasn't going to say anything, but I cannot stand idly by while this book sits on a shelf in plain view—and next to the holy Bible, no less!"

Mrs. Crabtree turned and pointed a long-nailed finger at Lucy. "Just look at how close to disaster you were! This little girl might have picked the thing up."

In danger of being speared by one of Mrs. Crabtree's talons, Lucy backed up, bumping into a nearby bookcase and sending several books tumbling. She quickly stooped to pick them up, glad for the excuse to look away from Mrs. Crabtree. Little girl! Lucy glanced surreptitiously at the book Mrs. Crabtree was waving, but she couldn't make out the title.

Amy stepped forward and gently plucked the book out of Mrs. Crabtree's clutches. She smoothed a hand over the cover, as though trying to wipe away Mrs. Crabtree's touch. Amy's mouth tightened as she read the book's title, and she tucked the book close to her side. *"I Know Why The Caged Bird Sings*? Really, Edith? I hardly see what's objectionable in that. It's the autobiography of one of the most celebrated poets of the twentieth century!"

"That," Mrs. Crabtree snapped, "is a matter for debate. It's a racist treatise filled with sex, violence, and malcontent, and it is not fit to sit on these shelves. If I'd known my pension money was going to fund books like *that,* I never would have volunteered for the library board!"

At the words "library board" Mr. Hall stiffened, and his face went blank. A soft thump broke the uncomfortable silence as Lucy shoved the last book into place. Three sets of eyes swiveled onto her. She stood up, making her back straight as a yardstick.

Mr. Hall frowned, he glanced from Lucy to the shelf where Mrs. Crabtree had snatched up the book, and slowly his forehead began to wrinkle, adding new lines every few seconds like a human Etch a Sketch.

"Amy," Mr. Hall said softly. "Why are those books not shelved properly?"

Lucy's eyes widened. Surely Amy had spoken with Mr. Hall about her reshelving adventures? No one did anything at St. Simon's without talking to Mr. Hall.

Amy smiled brightly, clutching the book in her hands as though it were a talisman against the devil. "It's an experiment to promote variety in our patrons' reading choices and to encourage cross-readership. It's been quite successful," she added, lifting her chin a little.

Mrs. Crabtree made an angry sound under her breath. "I don't care how you shelve the books. It's what is in them that is the issue here. I want that book pulled from this library, or so help me, Edmond, I will remove my patronage. Others will follow me, I assure you."

"We don't censor books," Amy snapped. She looked as though she'd like to say a lot more and was biting back the words.

"Then it's time you started," Mrs. Crabtree growled. "That drivel will infect the minds of our children and lead them astray. It fills their minds with dangerous images, puts words in their mouths. It might even incite them to violence!"

Amy mouthed silently, and then, quite out of the blue, she began to laugh. It wasn't the quiet, polite laugh that she normally used in the library but a deep belly laugh that bent her body in two. Lucy and the other two grownups looked on with equally shocked expressions. By now, the disagreement had drawn attention, and several people sidled closer to hear what was going on.

Mr. Hall glanced nervously at the onlookers and frowned. Amy regained control of herself and the laughs subsided to half-hysterical giggles, with tears leaking from the corners of her eyes.

"I will not be laughed at," Mrs. Crabtree said, glaring at Amy. "Do something, Edmond!"

"Amy," Mr. Hall snapped and the giggles disappeared completely. Amy's face paled. "I want that book placed in my office, and you are to reshelve all of these books," he gestured at the low bookcase, "in their proper places."

"But w-we can't," Amy stuttered. "We can't start yanking books from the stacks just because someone objects to them. Pretty soon there wouldn't be any books left."

"This is not a debate," Mr. Hall said, glowering. His expression relaxed into a conciliatory smile as he turned to Mrs. Crabtree. "Let us finish this discussion in my office."

Looking pleased, Mrs. Crabtree nodded and moved toward the open door of Mr. Hall's office. They disappeared inside. Amy stood still as a statue, her mouth slightly open and the book still clutched in one hand. When nothing else dramatic happened, the onlookers dispersed. Several people moved quickly to the circulation counter, while others moved back among the high shelves.

"Mom?" Lucy asked tentatively.

Amy jumped a little, looking at Lucy as though surprised to see her standing so close. "This is just so ridiculous," Amy muttered.

Lucy nodded, although she wasn't entirely sure what she was agreeing to. Amy sighed and moved forward, patting Lucy on the shoulder as she walked past her to the shelf.

"Come on," Amy said. "There are a lot of books to be moved."

Mr. Hall and Mrs. Crabtree stayed in his office for half an hour. Lucy and Amy had barely made a dent in their reshelving efforts by the time Mr. Hall was beside them again, clearing his throat fussily.

"Amy," Mr. Hall said, "I think it is best if you take a leave of absence for the next week. We will discuss your duties and place in this library when you return."

Amy stood up slowly, setting the books she'd gathered from the bottom shelf on top of the bookcase. "Are you going to let her do this?" Amy asked. The words carried no heat, though Lucy felt the accusation in them.

Mr. Hall grimaced. "Edith Crabtree is one of our largest donors, Amy. She is also a woman of some influence. Without her support and her fund-raising efforts, St. Simon's would be a lot worse off. There would be less money for new books, for games in the children's area, author visits, or other special programs. There might not even be enough to maintain our current staff," he added pointedly. "We cannot afford to alienate our patrons."

"Which is a very fancy way of saying because she's rich, she can censor whatever she wants, and you won't do a thing to stop her."

"It is one book," Mr. Hall said in a quiet voice. "Without our donors, people like Mrs. Crabtree, there might not be any books at all. Sometimes you must think of larger things, Amy."

"I am thinking of larger things," Amy snapped. "I am thinking of all the words that children like Lucy may never hear, may never read, because women like Mrs. Crabtree don't think they're appropriate."

"You are exaggerating. *I Know Why the Caged Bird Sings* is hardly a seminal work. I dare say Lucy will be just fine without it."

"I don't care what book Edith Crabtree is demanding we take away; it could be *Mein Kampf,* and it'd still be wrong."

Mr. Hall wearily shook his head. "I appreciate your fervor, and I don't like this any better than you do. But I have little choice. The book goes, Amy. Be thankful it isn't your job."

"I'm not certain I want a job at a library that is so willing to violate the First Amendment," Amy said in a low voice, hard as stone.

"You are angry and upset right now. A week off will be good for you. It will give you time to think the thing through. If you still want to resign after that, well, I am sure there are other librarians who want a job. Belinda has been hinting she'd like a permanent position."

Amy stiffened, but she raised her chin and stared at Mr. Hall with an icy look that was uncomfortably close to the one Mrs. Crabtree had worn earlier. "I don't need a week," she snapped. In one motion, Amy reached down and scooped up the contested book from where she'd set it on top of the bookcase. "Lucy, get your backpack. Grab my name plate and your picture off the desk while you're at it."

Lucy moved quickly. She was back at her mother's side in less than a minute. She felt shaky and adrift. The world was shifting all around her, and while she could feel the change, she was helpless to understand it or stop it. She clamped her lips shut on the stream of incoherent words that wanted to tumble from her lips and clutched the strap of her backpack tighter.

Amy nodded her approval and led the way out of the library with Mr. Hall standing behind them, looking as though a beloved pet had turned on him unexpectedly. The shock and disbelief on his face were almost comical. Lucy tried to memorize the patched and blotchy walls, the rows of uneven shelves, and the way the copy machine sat with its front paper compartment open, a stack of legal-size paper lolling over the end like a tongue.

The click of the library's glass door closing behind them was loud as a slap. It had rained while they were inside. The brief cloudburst had left raindrops sparkling on the ends of rusty brown-green leaves, and the bent handlebars of the three bikes waiting patiently outside St. Simon's for their owners to return. Where the sidewalk dipped lower in its drunken meander up the street, small puddles had formed. Lucy thought of younger days when she had jumped gleefully in mud puddles with Amy beside her doing the same. It seemed a very long time ago.

From the corner of her eye, Lucy saw a flash of brown. Looking down, she realized her mother was still barefoot, having left her shoes behind. The contrast of Amy's dignified march away from the library and those brown toes flashing like a child's grin made a bubble of laughter catch in Lucy's throat. She nearly choked on it. Amy paused, glancing at Lucy with concern.

"It'll be all right, Lucy. I'll find another job. There are plenty of other libraries in the world."

"Are you sure?" Lucy asked. From the corner of her eye, she could still see St. Simon's looming behind them.

"Yes," Amy said, and her voice was hard as the sidewalk beneath their feet. "I am very, very sure. What Mr. Hall and Mrs. Crabtree want to do is wrong."

Looking up at her mother's beautiful, set face, Lucy thought she looked like an Amazon warrior marching off to war.

"You understand, don't you, sweetie?" The faintest note of pleading had entered Amy's voice.

Lucy glanced at the book in her mother's hands and said slowly, "Why is that book so important? Is it really good?"

"It is," Amy said with a smile. "It's an excellent book. But that's not the reason we're leaving. No one should have the right to tell us what we can and can't read. The law says they can't. People like Mrs.

Crabtree try anyway. It's up to you and me, and everyone else with a bit of sense, to say something and tell her no."

Lucy nodded. "Can I read that?" she asked, gesturing at the book.

Amy smiled and passed the book to Lucy. It felt solid and real. The fragile cover still carried the warmth from Amy's hands. Amy looped her arm through Lucy's and gently tugged her forward. They fell back into step, and Lucy didn't look back at St. Simon's again.

The New Job
by Tanya Bentham

J an hovered nervously by the old-fashioned cake trolley, eyeing the scones as if they were incendiary devices liable to explode at any moment unless properly diffused. Since she wasn't in possession of the correct instruction manual, or even a certificate verifying her recent completion of a baked goods diffusing course, she decided that on the whole it was best to steer clear of the cake trolley.

She'd been waiting there for almost an hour—or at least it certainly felt like an hour, but she had recently become aware of the notorious elasticity of fictional time, so it might only have been a mere five minutes or so. Not for the first time, she felt herself on the verge of a panic attack and wondered frantically if there were any brown paper bags handy. Not that a panic attack required the paper bag to be brown per se, but she'd always found the anonymity of a generic brown bag to be infinitely comforting in times of crisis.

For all the air of insouciant comfort projected by battered leather armchairs, subtle fog of cigar smoke, and soft firelight, the Cynics Club seemed specifically designed to make her feel ill at ease. It didn't help hat the entire club exuded a kind of ingrained masculinity that made her idly speculate that someone somewhere must be burning testosterone incense. Naturally, Jan had heard of the famed Cynics Club before today, for the watering hole of the great detective Arthur Pyecroft was known to every lesser sleuth, gentleman spy, sidekick, flunky, arch-villain, or evil henchman on Fictionworld, but she'd never expected to see the inside of its hallowed halls or breathe the sacred air therein because the place remained stubbornly men only, snubbing its nose at political correctness. Her innate sense of shyness made Jan feel even more exposed than usual among so many men, even if most of them looked so venerable that they'd probably been around since Brother Cadfael had been a mere novice.

When she finally realized that the stout and rather tweedily dressed individual by the bar was not the man that she'd originally assumed, but none other than the famed Miss Marple, Jan actually began to relax a little and take a proper look around at the other occupants of the stuffy drawing room. What she saw was almost a roll call of the good, bad, and scarily ugly of the detective district: Hercule Poirot was animatedly discussing something with Miss Marple; Blowfled, Tin Tin, and James Bond were swapping notes with Inspector Gadget, and, on the far side of the room, a gangly, stubble-faced man whom she was certain she recognized from somewhere was apologizing profusely to a white-coated member of staff because his Great Dane had just consumed an entire buffet, table and all.

Jan had just noticed Charlie Chan and Fu-Manchu practising their tai chi together in the next room when someone made her jump halfway into her next incarnation by tapping her gently on the shoulder.

"Sorry, old girl," beamed the avuncular, bewhiskered man at her back, "I didn't mean to startle you. I suppose this old place must be quite fascinating if you've never been here before."

"My bad." She grinned guiltily back at him, ashamed to have her twitchiness publicly exposed. "No need to apologize."

Her companion looked somewhat taken aback. "Are you?"

"Am I what?"

"Bad? I was under the impression that you were one of what you Americans call the Good Guys?"

Jan suddenly realized her mistake; she really shouldn't have expected a crusty old duffer like Dr. Johnson to be fluent in any kind of slang, let alone the current patois of what he no doubt still regarded as the colonies. She flushed with embarrassment. "I'm sorry. It's just a saying; it means *my mistake.*"

"Does it really?" he exclaimed, sporting a look of utter bewilderment. "Do you know I simply cannot keep track of all the funny little sayings you young people keep coming up with; the flexibility of your language use simply boggles my mind. I must say, you had me quite worried for a moment there; I thought you'd got the wrong branch of the Sidekicks and Associated Evil Henchman's Union, you see."

Dealing with actual villains had always been her least-favorite aspect of being a sidekick. Actually, anything involving real danger had been low on her list of agreeable aspects of her job because she pretty much preferred researching things in the privacy of her boss' secret hideout whilst wearing fluffy slippers, sipping at a nice cup of hot cocoa, and generally not going anywhere near anyone or anything even remotely sinister. "Right branch," she whimpered, uncomfortably aware that Blowfeld and Bond had begun to eye her with considerable interest.

"Just the wrong end of the proverbial stick," Johnson filled in with a jovial wink. "No need to worry, my dear, but you'll have to forgive me; we old duffers tend to be a bit slow on the old uptake, you know. You shouldn't have any such problems with the chap I want you to meet today though, since he doesn't exactly speak the Queen's English himself. The two of you ought to get along quite handsomely."

Jan didn't have time to express her alarm at having apparently been set up on some kind of blind date because Johnson ushered her through to a cosy private parlor that lay off the main salon.

"Miss Janine Biblios, may I cordially introduce Mr. Samuel Jackson Mattock?"

At Johnson's rather formal announcement, a handsome, well-dressed man with sandy hair rose from one of the deep winged chairs by the crackling fire and shook her hand, an expression of bewilderment to match her own gracing his features. "Delighted to meet you, Ma'am."

Momentarily thrown by the existence of another American accent in such a crusty British establishment, Jan could do no more than gape somewhat stupidly at her new companion. She suddenly didn't feel quite so resentful toward the good doctor for setting her up, since it appeared he had damned fine taste in men. Sam gaped at her too, although she wasn't sure his expression was one of approval, causing her to silently curse her choice of outfit that morning; perhaps a shorter skirt and a less fluffy, less pink jumper would have been a better choice. They both jumped when Johnson brightly offered, "Tea? They do serve a rather spiffing Earl Grey here, don't you know?"

Once they were both ensconced on their respective armchairs with cups of steaming tea balanced precariously on their laps, Jan and Sam spoke almost simultaneously. "Why am I here, Johnson?"

They stared guiltily at one another whilst Johnson smirked, seemingly expecting them to get along simply by virtue of sharing a nationality. Eventually Sam hissed to Johnson, "You know I'm already seeing someone, Johnson. What's this all about?"

"Don't be a bloody fool, Sam old chap! I'm only too well aware of the current state of your love life." Johnson added in an aside for Jan's benefit, "He's seeing someone over in the Fairytale District, if you can believe it!"

Jan's eyes widened and she instantly forgot her disappointment that her uncalled-for blind date wasn't interested in her. She'd heard of the Fairytale District, of course—who hadn't—but she'd never found the courage to venture beyond the narrow confines of her own genre and see it for herself. "Do they really have dragons there?" she stammered in awe, intrigued by the mere existence of such an exotic animal.

"Unfortunately," Sam muttered darkly.

Johnson snorted into his tea. "You should know, old man—you're courting one!"

Sam scowled at Johnson and was about to speak when Jan blurted, "Really?"

Sam rolled his eyes. "He means metaphorically, not literally. My, erm...my lady friend has a formidable reputation."

"I'll say!" Johnson cheerfully exclaimed. "He's braver than he looks, is our Sam."

Obviously irritated, Sam demanded, "Is there any chance you're going to get to the point sometime soon? I'm quite busy these days, you know."

Johnson gave Sam a smirk so evil that it made Jan suspect that perhaps he was the one in the wrong branch of the union. "I know. I've been trying to get hold of you all week, but that Peaseblossom person on the reception desk kept telling me that you were a bit *tied up*. Whatever could she have meant, I wonder?"

Sam went crimson, and as he reflexively pulled down the cuffs of his shirt, Jan couldn't help but notice that his wrists seemed to be sore, as if something had rubbed them quite raw. "Erm. Yes, well, I have been a bit distracted of late, I must admit."

Johnson winked conspiratorially at Jan, who, although just as confused as ever, was at least intrigued. "Love's young dream, eh?"

"Oh cut the crap, Johnson!" Sam snarled. "And tell me why I dragged my ass out of bed?"

Johnson straightened up and announced, "As I'm sure you are aware, Sam, I am vice chairman of the Sidekicks and Associated Evil Henchman's Union."

"Are you?" Sam blinked.

"Yes, I am. I was sure I'd mentioned it before now?"

"I wasn't even aware that such a union even existed," Sam frowned. "Is there a Detectives' Union? I would hate to think I was missing out on retirement benefits."

"Oh yes—the Federation of Gentlemen Sleuths, Superheroes and Other Do-Gooders—I hear they have an excellent health plan—rebuilt the Bionic Man after his nasty accident, don't you know." Johnson told Sam, "You should see Miss Marple on your way out; she's their membership secretary."

"Okay," Sam nodded, making a note in the regulation detectives notebook he'd pulled from the inside pocket of his non-regulation bespoke suit.

Fearing they were in danger of becoming sidetracked once more, Jan asked timidly, "Why are we here?"

"Oh yes," Johnson seemed somewhat flustered. "Business, of course!"

"Sounds ominous," Sam muttered darkly, although he winked at Jan as he spoke.

"Well, Sam," Johnson continued briskly, "as you know, it can be very difficult for a fictional character to survive once their author dies or once their readership falls by the wayside, so the S.A.E.H.U. has recently started up a program to help neglected fictional characters build new lives for themselves. The idea is that characters who've lost the plot, so to speak, should receive sponsorship from others in the union who have either moved beyond the narrow confines into which they were written or who belong to works of fiction so enduringly popular as to be almost immortal.

"But I'm not a member of your union," Sam protested. "I don't qualify as a sidekick, or even a henchman, I'm a..." he swallowed awkwardly as if choking on the words before forcing out a pained whimper, "I'm a hero."

"Are you?" Jan asked, her natural curiosity getting the better of her shyness.

Sam made a face that was more grimace than smile, but nodded all the same.

"What's wrong with being a hero?" she asked kindly.

"It just sounds so freaking pretentious," Sam admitted, "which simply isn't me, honest."

Jan nodded understandingly. She felt such sympathy for Sam's display of reticence that she gave in to her normally suppressed tendency to act like a walking thesaurus and suggested, "You could call yourself a leading protagonist instead."

Sam considered this for a moment before asking, "Isn't that even more pretentious?"

Johnson patted Sam kindly on the knee. "No, no, my dear chap, it's not the slightest bit pretentious. In fact, I think it sounds quite dignified on you. I like it."

Sam blushed rather charmingly, but protested, "Still, surely I can't be Jan's sponsor—no offense intended, Jan—I'm simply not qualified, on account of not being a sidekick and all?"

"You misunderstand me, Sam; I am Jan's sponsor."

"Are you?" Sam was looking ever more bewildered. It seemed to Jan that bewildered was an expression that came a little too naturally to Sam's clean-cut face, and it made her wonder if he'd ever been any use at all as a detective. Then again, maybe that was the reason that she'd never heard of any of his adventures.

Jan decided it was time for her to offer some information, even though she had no more idea of the conversation's intended direction than Sam did. "Yes, Doctor Johnson here was kind enough to help me through my recent troubles. He's been there for me through thick and thin, letting me call him up at all hours of the day and night whenever I needed someone to talk things through with. There isn't anything he doesn't know about being a sidekick. He's been wonderful, absolutely wonderful."

Johnson blushed, his face as red as the strawberry jam he was ladling onto his third scone. "Steady on, old girl!"

Sam ignored Johnson, choosing instead to cock his head and interrogate Jan. "Troubles?"

Jan blushed this time. "My boss disappeared."

"What do you mean, exactly, by disappeared?"

Jan glanced anxiously at Johnson, but her sponsor leaned back into his chair and simply motioned with a wave of his hand that she should answer Sam's questions. She swallowed hard, but pressed on. "He just sort of faded away. He got paler and paler; one day I could see right through him like a ghost, and the next day, he wasn't there at all. I could feel it starting to happen to me too, and I was scared."

To her surprise, Sam nodded understandingly, not seeming to find this phenomenon in the slightest bit peculiar. "I take it no one was reading the books anymore, and without public interest, your respective characters began to lose their purpose in fiction?"

She blushed, shrugging, "To be honest, I don't think anyone ever read them very much in the first place. They were a bit lame, and what with the Internet and all of the computer games on the market, kids just aren't going to read any old crap these days."

Sam smiled wolfishly, an incongruous look on his normally kind face. "Forgive me for asking, but who was this detective of yours?"

"Oh, he wasn't a detective; my boss was a superhero."

"You've crossed genres then, coming to the club today; that takes a lot of guts."

Jan felt anything but brave. In fact, she wanted nothing more than to go straight back to bed and fade away like her boss, self-determination be damned. "It's not really crossing genres; superheroes are sort of like detectives—even the unions are affiliated, like Doctor Johnson said."

"You shouldn't sell yourself short; it still takes guts for a fictional character to control their own destiny. You'd be surprised how many give in and fade away, never to be heard from again."

She grinned as she returned the compliment. "You ought to know, dating a fairy tale princess."

To her astonishment, Sam began to laugh hysterically, flopping back into his chair as tears of mirth ran down his face. Jan looked askance at the good doctor, who simply smiled and shrugged as if to tell her to wait and see.

Eventually, Sam struggled to control his giggles, wiped the tears from his eyes, and explained, "She might belong in the realm of fairy tales, but no one in their right mind would ever call my lover a princess, least of all herself. In fact, I think that any bluebird that had the audacity to land on her shoulder would find itself blasted into a thousand smithereens!"

"She sounds interesting," Jan said uncertainly.

"That's certainly one way of putting it," Johnson murmured under his breath.

"I think so," Sam said enigmatically, ignoring Johnson's comment. "But you didn't tell me who your late boss was?"

"Oh." It was Jan's turn to blush furiously; she had sincerely hoped she was going to get out of this without having to admit her former allegiance. Sinking as deep into her chair as it was possible to go, she murmured, "Librarian Man."

"Sorry, I didn't catch that; what did you say?" Sam demanded.

"Speak up; there's a good girl," Johnson added encouragingly.

"Librarian Man," she announced with considerable resignation.

To give him credit, Sam did his best not to laugh out loud, but despite his best efforts, the corner of his lip still twitched in a decidedly suspicious manner. "Librarian Man? Really? He sounds…erm…interesting."

Jan rolled her eyes and concluded that she might as well just get the embarrassing part over and done with. Perhaps, she thought, it was like ripping a plaster from your knee—something best faced up to and done in one short, sharp shock. "He wasn't interesting at all. We were created by a committee with the sole intention of getting kids to use libraries by making them seem," she winced at the word, "cool."

Sam winced, too, but pressed on with his line of inquiry, presumably from some kind of morbid fascination. "So, what superpowers did he have?"

"He could fly…"

"Of course," Sam agreed, "every superhero worth his ink can fly."

"And he knew the Dewey Decimal System so well it was almost obscene, especially the numbers that catalogue obscene publications."

"That must have come in handy at parties," Sam agreed wryly. "What else?"

"Erm, nothing really, that was about it."

"No ninja fighting skills?" Sam suggested hopefully. "Or laser vision?"

"Not really, no; he just sort of tended to bore our opponents into a stupor by reciting the Dewey Decimal System from beginning to end, which normally gave me time to sneak up behind them and smack them over the head with *The Complete Works of Shakespeare*."

Sam eyed the heavy volume poking out of her handbag with considerable suspicion. "So what powers do you have—apart from your head-smacking abilities, of course?"

She hurriedly kicked *The Complete Works of Shakespeare* back under her chair, silently cursing the paranoia that wouldn't let her leave the house without her weapon of choice. It wasn't that bad really; okay, so she tended to get terrible backache due to the weight of the Bard's melodramatic ramblings, but at least she always had something to read on the bus. "Nothing really; I'm just a really good researcher."

"Research?" Sam sounded no less confused now that she'd revealed her so-called superpower than he had been before.

She nodded. "Yes, I did all the hard work—finding the villains' hideout by checking the electoral register, researching entry into top-secret hideouts via the drainage system, revealing their secret alteregos and that sort of thing, while the boss recited the Dewey Decimal System and took all the credit."

"Fascinating," Sam said insincerely, before turning back to Johnson. "Care to tell me what Jan's abilities have to do with me, by any chance?"

"Rehabilitation!" Johnson smiled, obviously pleased with his own brilliance.

"Thanks, but I don't need rehabilitating," Sam told him.

"Not you, you buffoon, Jan!"

"She doesn't look like she needs rehabilitating, either," Sam glanced assessingly at her.

"I need a new job," Jan admitted uncertainly, "but I'm not sure how you can help with that."

"Why else would I have invited both of you here today if it wasn't because I thought it might turn out to be mutually beneficial?" Johnson asked merrily as he refilled their teacups.

"But I don't know anyone who runs a library," Sam protested. "It's not like I can put in a good word anywhere."

"Oh, I already have a day job at New Orleans Main Library," Jan added.

"It's a sidekick job she needs, which is where I thought you could help out, Sam, old chap."

Sam shrugged. "I can ask around, but I don't really know any superheroes, Johnson. I would have thought you knew more people than I do anyway."

"I do, which is why I picked you, Sam." Johnson gave Sam a look that made it plain he thought both Sam and Jan were being a bit slow.

"Huh?" Sam and Jan said simultaneously.

Johnson sighed, heavily and melodramatically, and continued in an explanatory tone, "Once a sidekick, always a sidekick, Sam. Not that it's anything to be ashamed of, mind you. Sidekicking is an ancient and honorable profession; ask any of the twelve disciples if you don't believe me; ask the knights of the round table, or even that Puss In Boots chappie that hangs around with your little friend Peaseblossom."

"I wasn't trying to question the value of anyone's status in fiction," Sam pointed out rather anxiously, with the air of a man who has just inadvertently committed a horrendous social faux pas.

"My point," Johnson continued obliviously, "is that Jan here can make the move from the Realm of the Superheroes to over here in the Detective District, but her nature remains essentially that of a sidekick..."

"Sorry to interrupt," Sam asked, "but I just wondered, Jan, why did you come over here from the Realm of Superheroes anyway?"

Jan went bright red, spluttering, "Mr. Stupendous!"

"Beg your pardon?" Sam frowned.

"Mr. Stupendous, he has X-ray vision." She thought the rest was self-explanatory and really didn't want to spell it out for him.

"Yes, I know," Sam said blankly.

Jan sighed heavily, thinking that detectives could be remarkably thick at times. "You really didn't think he just uses his powers for good, did you?"

"Yes, well, that's the general impression one gets from the media," Johnson said as Sam nodded.

"Well, let me tell you," Jan huffed disgruntledly, "the Man of Iron is one hell of a pervert. I'm not the only one who's had trouble with him, but the courts won't listen to any complaints about him. The last time anyone complained, the judge threw the case out of court and asked for Mr. Stupendous's autograph on the latest laudatory article about how he'd saved a bridge from falling down."

"But what did they complain about?" asked both men at once.

Jan went even redder. "He keeps using his X-ray vision to look at women's underwear!"

Sam muffled his giggles behind his hand. "And that's why you want to work over here in the Detective District?"

"Yes," she scowled. "No one over here has superpowers, which is fine by me, because if you ask me, superpowers are a real pain in the ass. If you're not trying to buy lead-lined underwear so no one can use their X-ray specs on you, you're trying to fend off the unwanted attentions of Captain Octopus' tentacles; it's just downright freaking ridiculous, and I've had enough! I'm never working for another superhero ever again; the office Christmas party was a freaking nightmare last year!"

"Yes, well, as I was saying," Johnson coughed embarrassedly while Sam stifled his laughter, "Jan, like myself, will always remain a sidekick, and no amount of self-determination can ever change that fact, so she needs someone to sidekick for, which is where you come in, Sam my friend."

Sam abruptly stopped laughing. "What do you mean, Johnson?"

"Well, since you have already successfully achieved self-determination, as well as crossing genres in a rather spectacular fashion, I was hoping that you could help me out with the sponsorship program. I simply couldn't think of anyone more suitable than you, what with the whole scheme in its infancy and all, of course I'll owe you a massive favor..."

"But," Sam spluttered, looking on the verge of panic, "I've always worked alone; you know that, Johnson. I don't think I'd know what to do with a sidekick, not to mention the fact that, as you yourself pointed out, I've crossed genres these days, and I'm not even doing any detective work anymore."

"And you're afraid that your girlfriend will be jealous if you take on an attractive female assistant?" Johnson suggested with a raised brow.

"Yes," Sam squeaked rather sheepishly.

"Well, that settles it then," Johnson announced with considerable satisfaction.

"Oh good." Sam appeared to have reawakened his interest in breathing.

"Yes, you and Jan can set off on your mission at once," Johnson beamed.

"What?" Jan and Sam chimed in unison.

"Oh, didn't I tell you?" Johnson said with the most unconvincing display of innocence Jan had witnessed since the Joker claimed not to have invented the nuclear whoopee cushion. "My good lady recently had a word with your good lady, and they both think it's a wonderful idea for the pair of us to indulge in a little bit of charity work."

"I'm not sure I'm happy being described as charity work," Jan interrupted, "especially since there's an unspoken implication that librarians aren't threatening."

"You wouldn't say that if you'd ever met some of the librarians over at the Grimm Memorial Library in the Fairytale District," Sam muttered. "I mean who in their right mind puts an eight-foot-tall ogre in charge of children's literature?"

"Presumably someone with firsthand experience of working with children?" Jan suggested.

"Anyway," Johnson said with the air of a man desperately trying to get the conversation back on track, "the ladies think it's a good idea—especially yours, Sam; she thinks it would be a shame for you to lose touch with your roots and thinks you ought to keep your hand in."

Sam, who had, by now, assumed the expression of a man who is happily henpecked, grumbled, "I keep trying to tell her that I was a lousy detective, but she refuses to listen."

"Don't put yourself down, Sam," Johnson said heartily. "You weren't that bad! Perhaps you should think of this mission as much-needed practice; after all, I did say it would be mutually beneficial."

Sam made a rude face in response. "The last time you talked me into something mutually beneficial, Johnson, I ended up being molested, assaulted, and arrested, so your argument really doesn't hold much weight on that account."

"Ah, but you did meet the love of your life, didn't you?" Johnson said with all the smugness of a grand master executing checkmate.

Sam looked grumpy but said nothing.

"So," Johnson continued blithely as he applied verbal thumb-screws, "I'd say that if nothing else, you owe me a bit of a favor."

"Fine!" snapped Sam. "Just tell me what you need me to do."

"Nothing too taxing, old chap. I want you to take Jan here out on one mission, just to get her back into the swing of things and help pad out her C.V.—what do you Americans call it, a resumé?—a bit so I can find her a more permanent position. After that, all I'll need you to do is provide a good reference."

Sam's questioning gaze flickered briefly to Jan, who shrugged as he asked, "What's the mission?"

"It's simply perfect for the two of you and your combined talents," Johnson exclaimed. "I think you'll do just splendidly. You see, over in Science Fiction, they're having a slight problem with some books."

"Books?" Sam asked. "How can books cause a problem? I mean they're not exactly sentient, are they?"

"Ah, well, there's the rub you see," Johnson looked rather pleased with himself. "Some silly moo of an author went and created living books—some kind of school textbook with teeth, if you can believe such a thing! Anyway, there are rather a lot of them, because apparently some fictional bookshop or other ordered far too many copies. The unsold copies all got together and formed a hive mind, which became self-aware, although not exactly intelligent. This book-ge-stalt entity, or whatever it is, chewed its way through the bars of its cage and managed to take over one of the quieter corners of Science Fiction. It calls itself Beastie and is demanding more biscuits than is reasonable. So, since Librarian Man is no longer around, I thought the two of you ought to be able to handle it before it runs out of digestives and actually eats someone."

"You want me to take over for Librarian Man?" Sam seemed distinctly unimpressed. Jan couldn't say she blamed him, since her former employer hadn't exactly been the most exciting individual ever known to fiction.

"Yes," Johnson nodded enthusiastically.

"I can't fly," Sam stubbornly pointed out somewhat desperately.

"That's why I got you both rocket packs," Johnson said with the happy air of a man who has thought of, and trounced, every counter argument.

"Shit!" Sam went pale with what Jan was fairly certain was terror. She didn't blame him either; he wasn't the only one who wasn't keen on the idea of a jet engine in close proximity to his backside. She found herself quietly hoping they wouldn't need to fly on this mission, not least because she had no head for heights.

"Language, Sam—ladies present!" Johnson seemed heartily offended. "Now, the mobile library is parked outside with the rocket packs already in the back as well as a few crates of chocolate digestives with which to open negotiations. Why don't you go and familiarize yourself with the special features whilst I have a quick chat with Jan here?"

Looking like a man condemned to the gallows, Sam slunk out of the room, muttering mutinously under his breath. Once they were alone, Johnson patted Jan kindly on the knee and asked, "Now, my dear, what did you learn from our little tête-à-tête?"

"Erm...that I don't want a job at Grimm Memorial Library?" she suggested tentatively.

"Apart from that?"

Jan felt her mind go uncomfortably blank; it wasn't a pleasant experience for a Know-It-All.

Johnson smiled indulgently. "One of the most basic skills of a good sidekick, my dear, is hero management. Make sure early on in the relationship that he knows who's really in charge, or you'll have no end of trouble. Sam ought to be good practice for you. I'm sure you're going to do just fine. Might I suggest that you start by making sure you get your choice of music playing on the journey, otherwise, you'll never hear the end of that country and western rubbish Sam's so fond of."

Jan suddenly felt much more confident as she made her way out to the car park, pulling her favorite Rolling Stones CD out of her bag as she went; if she could handle a hero, man-eating books would be no problem at all.

Serving the Public
by Gloria Oliver

ou've been reassigned.

Y Even after two weeks, the words still rankled. Chesney Forbanter, head librarian for more than ten years at Trumbles, had been reassigned. And for what? She'd only corrected the district manager on his minor error. Wrong was wrong after all. But it seemed the district manager, and, therefore, her boss, hadn't seen things that way.

Chesney took a deep breath, trying to calm herself, and took a look at her new posting.

Set in Old Town, the area had seen sunnier days. Few remembered it had been the high center of the city once, before it had been moved to the Sallis district—though the information was there for anyone who cared to look.

Low round walls with protective beasts loomed around the library's property. The particular style hadn't been used in generations. The heads were missing on most, but she could still make out what could be a chimera, a manticore, and a sphinx or two.

Reaching into her voluminous purse, Chesney retrieved the large key given into her keeping. It fit into the lock only after she smashed it in several times, dislodging some nesting material and dirt.

The sharp screech of the gate as it moved set her teeth on edge. She wormed in through the tight opening, then stopped to brush her coat and remove the dirt and rust currently streaking her clothes.

The lawn around the building was weed-infested, overgrown, or dead. Chesney raised a brow as a rat the size of a small dog rushed by, something alive and bleeding trapped in its mouth. Not a proper set of library grounds, indeed.

She made her way to the building proper.

The ancient Stylean columns on the porch were cracked and chipped, the tell-tale grooves worn down. Any architect worth his salt would have recognized the style and the top-notch workmanship, even through the graffiti. If that didn't speak of its ancient origins, the two-sided sloped roof, rather than the more modern four-sided style, would have given it away.

Dreading what she might encounter in the interior, Chesney straightened her back and sauntered up the broken steps. This was her station, for good or ill, and all deserved an open library, regardless of their rank. She just needed to see what she'd been left to work with and salvage what she could.

The marred doors stood more than twice her height. Their quiet grandeur peeked out here and there, miraculously having survived the carved declarations of love, diatribes against the establishment, and sexual performance advice, all with a myriad of misspellings. Chesney grimaced. Vandalism was no excuse for poor spelling and a lack of penmanship.

Unlike the gate's lock, the door proved free of debris. The key inserted smoothly and turned without a quibble, a satisfying click stating the door was unlocked. Yet the moment she removed it, another loud click reverberated from the lock. When she attempted to pull the door open, it didn't budge.

Frowning, she placed the key in the lock again and turned it. Once more she heard it unlock. When she removed the key, she heard it lock itself again.

Not one to give up easily, Chesney unlocked the door a third time, but, this instance, left the key in the lock. The moment she moved to pull open the door, the key turned on its own and then spit out onto the floor.

Was this some kind of joke by the Ministry? If so, they needed a reassessment on the meaning of humor.

Gathering the voice and attitude that had sent transgressing citizens running at Trumbles, she said, "I'm sorry, but this *will not do*. I've come to work and don't have time for pranks. So kindly stop this nonsense at once!"

Chesney glanced around but no one jumped out from behind a column, and the door didn't spring open to show a guilty person or two skulking behind it. Her frown growing more pronounced, she retrieved the key and tried the door again. It would open for her no more than it had before.

Hands on hips, she glared her displeasure at the door before putting the key back into her purse. Making sure her hat was still in place, she stomped down the steps.

She was debating on whether to go around the building or go find a voice carrier box to call her superior when something else caught at her attention.

"Madam, oh, madam! Over here, madam!"

She turned around. A man in somewhat threadbare robes and a mashed pointed hat was waving at her with some sort of painted sign from the other side of the gate. Could it be the responsible culprit about to turn himself in? Somewhat doubting things would be that simple, Chesney nevertheless headed in his direction to find out what he wanted.

"Yes?" Though she tried, she couldn't keep a disapproving tone from creeping into her voice. The closer she came to the visitor, the more she disliked him. She held nothing against the poor and impoverished as long as they strove to improve themselves and better their circumstances. Such facilities as were available in a library were most often appreciated by those very people, and could make a librarian quite proud of her small role in helping them advance.

However, the closer she approached, the more it was obvious this man didn't fall into that category. If anything, he appeared to be the type who preyed on the gullibility of others to cheat them and line his pockets. Why else would he be carrying a sign reading "Magic R Us—School of Wizardry and Magic at affordable rates?"

"Madam, would you mind stepping out here with me? It would greatly ease my heart to see you do so."

"What are you talking about?" Chesney stared at the short man, studying his face. Though his clothes were well-worn and his hat a victim of some unimaginable accident, his peppered beard was well groomed and what she could see of his cheeks were a healthy color. His brown eyes could even be called earnest—but then that would be a boon to a hoodwinker, wouldn't it?

"Madam, that place isn't safe. Please, come out of there."

Chesney didn't move. "I ask you again, sir, what are you talking about?" It didn't escape her that he made sure not to get too close to the open gate.

"That building, madam, that old library, it isn't safe."

"I've been assigned here, sir, by the Ministry. Of course it's safe."

He stared at her open-mouthed for a moment then laughed. It

would have been a pleasant enough laugh, if not made at her expense. "The Ministry, you say? Madam, the Ministry has been sending its outcasts to this very spot for near on twenty years. It is more than aware the place is cursed, and it's the easiest means for it to rid itself of undesirables on the payroll."

"What? Are you, sir, implying the Ministry would willingly place one of its employees in danger, and that I, Chesney Forbanter, am an *undesirable?*" If she hadn't already known the gate would move only grudgingly, she would have pushed it shut in his face that instant.

"So you asked to be assigned here?"

This brought her indignation up short. "No, sir, as a matter of fact, I did not."

"Then please, madam, follow an old man's whim and come out here, and I will tell you what I know of the place." If anything, he looked even more earnest than before.

Even as she distrusted this, she couldn't come up with what he could possibly be trying to gain by doing it. She moved closer and hesitated, dreading getting her coat and skirts dirty again.

To her surprise, the man jumped forward to grab the gate and pushed it open farther. Chesney supposed she had no choice but to repay his efforts by stepping outside.

"All right, I have done as you requested. Now please explain yourself." She made sure her tone left no question she would brook no further evasions.

"First off, let me introduce myself, madam." He dragged off his bedraggled hat and bowed. "My name is Moffet Middleguard. I am the Headmaster of Magic R Us, a school of wizardry and magic." He gestured back behind him. "That is my school."

What had at one time probably been an impressive five- or six-story building rose close to the retaining wall of the library. Though ivy clung and thrived on the mortared and likely magicked walls, it was obvious that at some point in time, the top three stories of the building had suffered a devastating catastrophe.

Chesney tapped her foot impatiently. "And?"

Moffet's cheeks darkened with color, his gaze no longer quite meeting hers. "About thirty or more years ago, my Master, the Great Grandal, was laboring on his life's work when something didn't go exactly as planned." He took a deep breath, as if steeling himself. "There was a tremendous explosion, which took the top of the tower. After many years of research and gazing into the waters, it is my opinion Master Grandal forgot to close the door to keep out the cat." He shook his head slowly as if still lamenting the far-off tragedy. "Athos came out unscathed, but my master wasn't quite so fortunate."

Chesney felt sorry for the sad circumstance, but enough was enough. "You've yet to explain what any of this has to do with the library."

"Why it has everything to do with it." Moffet bobbed his head up and down. "The energies released in the experiment rained down upon the library. Can you not see that the explosion aimed itself in just that direction?" He used his sign to point from the gouged side of the tower toward the library and back.

Chesney grabbed hold of her hat, the resulting fanning of air from the sign threatening to dislodge it. She checked the angle of the broken upper stories and the direction of the library itself and saw he was right. "Yes, I do see it, but I still don't understand..."

Moffet cut her off, his eyes shining with awe and fear. "The library was magicked by those showered energies. They brought it to life!"

Chesney blinked, Moffet's words echoing in the air. Surely, he couldn't be serious. "You're saying it's alive?"

Moffet nodded.

"Poppycock! I'd sooner believe it was cursed."

He took her outrage in stride, as if having seen it all before. "That's what most folk believe, madam, as a matter of fact. For soon after, things seemed to move on their own, odd noises sounded among the stacks, doors closed. All manner of strange things happened."

Chesney's lips drew to a thin line. "Next you'll be expecting me to believe the Ministry did nothing about this."

"Oh no, on the contrary, madam! The Ministry sent all sorts of people out here, not only after the explosion but also as the reports of incidents piled up. But they could do nothing. No magics they tried, no prayers, or bribes, would stop the weirdness. One librarian after another left. When they tried to remove the books, it was as if they'd crossed an invisible line, and it became a war zone—there was smoke, lights, noise, howls; it was a total madhouse! Watched the whole thing from the third story from a comfy chair with my glass of iced tea.

"That was pretty much when the place was closed up, all information on it hushed up, and the Ministry started using the place to dump undesirables." He leaned in close. "Personally, I think it remains on the books so some politician can make off with the budget."

"Hmph." Chesney had heard more than enough. "Well, I thank you for your explanation, sir. However, I will not be so easily deterred from my purpose. Libraries are meant to serve. And one way or another, I mean for this one to do so."

Moffet's mention of a budget gave Chesney the idea of where to start her campaign. Neatness, orderliness, research, and knowledge were her life's blood. She knew quite well how to navigate certain levels of the Ministry's bureaucracy. You never spoke to the man in charge; you always went to his secretary instead. As long as it did not require a signature, those who actually did the work could get you whatever was required.

By mid-afternoon she had a copy of the budget for the Old Town Library, had set up several deliveries to be charged against it, and had a plan for the morrow. One way or another, Old Town would have a library again.

The next morning, Chesney made her way to Old Town once more, this time dressed in more serviceable clothes.

First she unlocked the gate then struggled with it to open it wide on both sides. Then she walked up to the building and stood before the doors, key in hand. "I am a librarian. You are a library, regardless of whatever else you might be. We're here to serve the public."

She inserted the key and turned it, then pulled it out. She wasn't too surprised when she heard the lock click itself closed again.

She gave the door an acknowledging nod before turning on her heel and moving back to the open gates. Armed with cleaning implements and a bit of magic, Chesney got to work.

"Good morning, madam. I see you did indeed decide to return."

Chesney pushed away a loose strand of hair as she turned to face her greeter. It was Moffet, bedraggled hat, worn robes, and tacky sign in place. "Good morning, sir."

About that time, a wagon laden with a large assortment of items arrived. Chesney searched the bed of the wagon and brought out a big, wrapped item. She moved it over to the piece of wall she'd cleaned away then took the cover off. The sign was white with gold embossed letters that said "Old Town Library." In smaller letters at the bottom was the following: "Open Mon–Sat 8 to 6."

"You can't get in the building, madam. Surely you're not serious about giving this a go?" Moffet stared at her in genuine bafflement.

"Of course I am. I said I would."

That said, Chesney got back to work. The afternoon was spent painting the gate and oiling its hinges.

The next day, she spoke her declaration just like the day before and turned the lock on the door. After it locked itself again, she got busy with the area around the building, cleaning the interior side of the wall and planting grass seeds. Cantrips helped make short work of the weeds, though cutting back the overgrown grass took the rest of the day.

Moffet checked on her once or twice, staying well on the outside of the gate. A few faces peeped in through the open way, but no one ventured in.

Chesney tackled the outside of the building the following day after once more trying the door. She did the covered front first, a few well-cast cantrips getting rid of most of the graffiti. Elbow grease and collapsible ladders helped take care of the rest.

That afternoon, she noticed Moffet watching her from a lawn chair set in the open third story of his building. When he noticed her noticing, he waved. Though it was uncharacteristic of her, she found herself waving back. He had tried to warn her when he could have just minded his own business. She supposed he might be all right after all, if a little unimaginative.

The delivery wagon came by again. This time with short bookshelves and a few benches and chairs, which she helped place under the awning. Coverings would protect the shelves at night and during any rain.

The driver stacked several boxes of books by the nearest column to the stairs. Some were from her own personal library, others from used book vendors, the rest old copies from a couple of librarian friends whose budgets had allowed them to buy new replacements. Lovingly, she sorted each box and placed the books on the racks.

From her bag, she took out a small sign which she hung from the gates: "Story Hour 4 p.m. Daily."

More passersby took peeks past the gates, yet no one would venture inside. Chesney did nothing to encourage or discourage them. The choice must be theirs and theirs alone.

Promptly at four, she chose a children's book at random and began to read out loud, her practiced voice easily covering the area. She had no audience, yet she didn't feel alone. There was a strange tension in the air, like surprise mixed with excitement. Surely it must be her own.

When she closed the book, she noticed several dirty faces peering from around the open gates. The moment she saw them, however, they ducked back out of sight. Chesney hid a smile.

Saturday had even more faces peering her way as she read. A few brave ones sat out where they could be seen. Chesney made no indication she knew they were there, which suited everyone fine.

She did get one surprise that evening, however, as she unfolded the covers to put over the shelves.

"Can I help you with that, madam?"

Startled, she turned around and found Moffet standing at the steps. "That would be very nice. Thank you."

He took his hat off and looked a little sheepish. "Figured it was about time I saw what there was to see."

They had everything set in short order.

Sunday was a difficult day for Chesney. After all the build up in the last week, the library would be closed, and she wouldn't be there. She was afraid of losing her momentum.

So Monday found her a little anxious as she opened the gates and moved through her usual routine. The fact there was a morning shower didn't help matters. If it rained in the afternoon, no one would come for sure.

Much to her surprise, Moffet stopped to see her at noon and asked if he might join her for lunch. He'd brought a small sack with him. As they moved chairs around and used one of the benches as a table, he started pulling food out of the sack until there was enough for at least four people. Chesney's estimation of Moffet's abilities went up several notches. Maybe his only problem was a lack of literary imagination and not actual skill. She thought she might be able to help him with some of that.

Story time came, and Moffet returned. So did the children, though they stayed past the gates as normal. Chesney realized she'd worried needlessly.

During the middle of the story, she half paused in surprise but then made herself continue. As she described the house of cookies and candies tempting the children, she could swear she could smell them. She risked a glance in Moffet's direction, but he was sitting exactly as before. Curious.

By the time she was done, several children had actually risked the path to the building, sitting quietly. When she closed the book, however, they all scurried away again.

Each day, the children came a little closer, more and more of them braving in passed the open gate. Terribly pleased, Chesney was still somewhat distracted as strange things continued to happen whenever she read out loud.

Just like the scent of cookies and candy, other smells relating to what she was reading would gently tickle the nose. As the days progressed and the children came closer, minute sounds would play as well, very low key, almost unheard, yet noises relating to the story as she told it. As the chirping of crickets rose to fill in the background on Wednesday, she glanced at Moffet and saw his eyes were wide and round, his hands clenched together in his lap.

The children came even closer. Their eyes also wide, but in wonder rather than fear. Chesney just went on, acting as if it were perfectly normal, excited and frightened herself.

Either the flyers or word of mouth did the trick as the next day a few adults came by for story time. Some even lingered afterward to look at the other books. Moffet came by and helped her close again and set a small statue of a dog on the steps.

He scratched at his chin, his gaze not quite meeting hers. "Hope you don't mind. It's only a sound alarm watchdog. More to scare away anyone tempted than anything else. We've no idea what 'it' might do if someone tried to take 'something' without checking it out."

The building's wrath would be the least of their problems if anyone dared do any such thing. Something of this must have shown on her face for Moffet laughed.

"Sorry, madam, that was rude of me. But I am starting to see why the Powers sent you here after all." His disarming grin was strangely infectious.

Yet despite all this, each morning when she turned the lock, within moments she would hear it click closed again—with no increasing hesitation.

More and more people came each day, many now bringing their own chairs. Vendors set up shop outside the walls, selling drinks and snacks to passersby.

Each story brought with it smells and sounds and then thin shimmering pictures that would wisp over her head on occasion.

Then the following day she noticed a book in the children's section she'd not brought. The book was old, the binding in an older style, yet both in perfect condition. She used it to read from that afternoon.

Soon other books appeared or exchanged with hers overnight. She wasn't sure if Moffet noticed and made no mention of it, sure the rest would assume she had made the changes.

By the fourth week, she started a morning class for children and adults on reading. She'd noticed the hungry look on some of their faces and knew they wished to learn to consume the books' contents on their own like she did. With her open library being as small and easy to care for as it was, she welcomed the distraction.

She filed more paperwork, and soon city maintenance actually started coming round to take care of the grounds. They heard of story time and joined to hear and watch as well. The next day people obviously not from Old Town arrived to see the show. She couldn't have been happier.

Chesney should have known things were going too well. It had totally left her how she'd been placed here to be punished and to disappear, not thrive.

She and Moffet had just removed the coverings from the shelves that morning when the small group arrived. She instantly recognized Mr. Parsons, the district manager, the man responsible for placing her there. Behind his heavily jowled form was a thin man with a notebook and two uniformed others that seemed to be there with him merely for effect.

"Good morning, Mr. Parsons."

"Nothing good about it. Nothing at all, I dare say!" He gave her a piercing stare.

"I'm very sorry to hear that, sir." Chesney folded her hands before her, closing her librarian's politeness shield. She had a feeling today it would be sorely tested. "How may I help you?"

"I've been getting reports about you, Miss, Miss…"

His secretary took a small step forward. "Forbanter."

"Yes, quite." Parsons nodded slightly and the secretary stepped back again. "Miss Forbanter. Seems you are making quite a stir around here. It is not the type of thing we wish for in Old Town."

A low growl trickled through the air. No one paid it any attention.

Chesney took a deep breath before making a reply. "I am only doing my job, sir. Serving the public."

"Is that right? More like entertaining the uneducated masses, seems like. Setting yourself up a stage here on government property." He waved at the shelves and chairs, his jowls quivering as he moved. "Collecting some extra wages perhaps, are we?"

"Now hold on there!" Moffet stepped forward bristling on her behalf. The low growl was repeated again. "There's no need to speak to Miss Forbanter that way!"

Parsons seemed to grow taller, looking down his nose at Moffet as if he were less than insignificant. "This is city business, sir. I would suggest you stay out of it or you shall be forcibly removed from the premises." The two uniformed men, appearing half bored before, snapped to attention, looking eager.

"No, please!" Chesney inserted herself between them and touched Moffet on the arm. "Everything is quite all right. I appreciate the...sentiment, but I must handle this." She smiled at him with her eyes, showing the gratitude there for his actions though she could not speak of it.

She felt Moffet relax slightly and saw him nod, though he looked far from pleased.

Chesney turned to face the district manager. "Sir, all the libraries have a children's story hour. I don't understand why there's a problem."

"The problem, *Miss* Forbanter, is the fact you're supposed to be running a library. Children's Hour is conducted indoors, not where everyone can see, like some cheap outdoor stage show."

Chesney felt heat rise to her cheeks. She clasped her hands tighter, her politeness shield badly battered. She half feared Moffet would attempt to interfere again, but a quick glance over her shoulder showed him staring down at the alarm dog. It seemed to be the source of the growling. "I had never meant to give such an impression, sir. I only wished to let the residents know the Old Town Library was once more open for their use."

"Open? Open, you say? Gentlemen, does this library look open to you?"

Chesney's heart skipped a beat. No! She'd inadvertently given them the very opening they'd most likely been hoping for. Though she would be willing to argue that a library was a library whether surrounded by walls or not, she had a feeling it would make little difference here. She had the sudden sneaking suspicion of just who had been misappropriating the funds from the Old Town Library's budget.

"No, sir, I would say it was not," came the triple reply.

"So, Miss Forbanter, what have you to say for yourself?" Parsons' voice dripped with sarcasm. He was a predator clamped onto the scent of blood.

The growling grew louder.

Chesney wished Moffet would muffle the alarm and get it over with. Almost as she thought it, there was silence.

She opened her mouth to say something though she possessed no idea what. It would be for naught. It was over. The work she might have done here. The help she could have given these people. All those possibilities...gone. It was done.

Then in that moment of hesitation, a click echoed loudly around them.

As if it were a signal, the growling started up again, even more intruding than before.

Chesney blinked, not sure if she should believe her ears or think the sound something her imagination conjured out of desperation.

"Actually, sir..." She turned her back on Parsons and stepped to the door, her heart beating faster and faster. Dare she believe? Her cold hand settled on the door's knob and turned it before pulling on the door. It swung out toward her. "I just hadn't gotten to open the library properly yet today."

The growling rose in pitch again.

Chesney turned to face him. "I will take your advice to heart, however, and only have Children's Hour inside the building from now on. Would you care to step inside for a tour?"

Parsons' mouth opened and closed, opened and closed, no words coming forth. His eyes had widened, very much like Moffet's had that time before.

Movement down by his ankles drew his attention before he could rally. Staring up at him, with wicked, glowing red eyes and sharp, exposed teeth, was the stone alarm dog. The growling grew in volume once again.

Moffet glanced at him and the others, a touch of red in his cheeks. "I swear I never magicked it to do that. It's a little past my power level. It's only supposed to be an alarm dog."

The color totally drained from Parsons' face. His assistant and the uniformed men were already starting to back away.

"I don't think he likes you." Chesney's brow went up, her gaze meeting with Parsons'.

"Perhaps, yes, I should take my leave. Everything seems well in hand, yes, yes, well in hand. Just make sure to keep Children's Hour indoors from now on."

The alarm dog barked at him, a booming sound that echoed after it was done.

Parsons half stumbled down the steps, struggling to catch up with the others. As he neared the gate, all the remaining statues on the wall turned in his direction, the same unnerving glowing eyes on them as on the alarm dog. Chesney was sure someone had been reading too many horror tales.

Parsons' yelp as he noticed them rang out all the way to where she stood. He took off after his fellows at a much faster pace than how he arrived.

Chesney hid a smile as she turned away from the sight, and found Moffet standing very still beside her. The alarm dog had returned to his previous spot and appeared as if it'd never moved.

She took his arm in hers. "Very clever, our library."

He looked across at her, the touch of panic in his eyes subsiding. "Y-yes, I suppose you could say that."

"Come, our friend awaits."

Moffet nodded and didn't resist as she turned them around to step into the open doorway leading into the library.

Lights sprang to life around them, shining off the immaculate marble floors. Shelves upon shelves of books stood before them, eagerly awaiting readers.

Chesney stared around her, her eyes bright. "Thank you." She smiled at all she could see. "Together, you and I, we will more than serve."

With Moffet at her side, she strolled deeper into the library to view all the mysteries waiting within.

Dusk
by Nyssa Anne Madison

"Lance, I got the package you sent," a man's voice confirmed on the other end of the line. "I need to talk to you. Now. Call me immediately. I am *so* not joking. If I don't hear from you by tonight, I am flying over there."

Lance snapped closed his cell phone as he entered his office, tossing his briefcase on his desk. Glancing around the room, as he always seemed to do upon entering, he wondered how his life ended up here with him teaching classical studies at Loyola instead of excavating some far-off cavern, discovering treasures of the worlds about which he now teaches. Then he remembered that 99.9 percent of the digs he had been on resulted in sore muscles, sunburned skin, and little else.

The blinking red light on his desk phone seemed to be pulsing out a message in Morse code. Picking up the receiver, he punched in the password to his voicemail. It was Kevin—again. Lance deleted the message without listening to the whole thing, immediately dialing.

"Hello."

"I was right, wasn't I?" Lance asked without preliminaries.

There was a pause. "Yes."

Lance sucked in a breath. He *knew*, but to have it confirmed…He sat heavily on his chair. This was it. This was one of those moments where the Universe shifts, fates are altered, and lives are irrefutably changed. "Fuck. That means—"

"We are, as they say, not alone," Kevin finished.

"Fuck."

"I believe you said that already."

"It bore repeating."

"Come to Nevada."

"Is that an invitation?"

"More like an order," Kevin said, suddenly serious. "That wasn't the first communication, but it was the most in-depth. We're going."

"You're going to Tanali?"

"*We're* going to Tanali."

"Fuck!"

Lance ran farther back into the cave, praying nothing in the abyss before him would stare back, barely keeping his feet as he stumbled over the unknown terrain. He listened for sounds of claws on stone, but nothing could be heard over the tattoo of his own heart and the hard intakes and releases of breath.

Ahead, he spotted a dim shimmer of golden light. He ran toward it, unsure if it would lead to his salvation or his demise. He stopped abruptly, catching himself on the ragged stone edging of an unexpected drop. Peering down, he discovered the source of the light was from a flame issuing brightly in a copper-like urn at the base of a golden sarcophagus bearing an image of a woman, so detailed, that even from his height of 100 yards or so up, her beauty was strikingly real.

In his distraction, he had forgotten about the predators that had chased him into the cave in the first place. Fishing his flashlight from his flap jacket, he illuminated the cavern in a burst of white light.

Before him was a set of steep, narrow stairs leading down into the heart of the chamber. Drawn by his life calling, by his desire to find something that would make sense of his existence, he descended the steps, nearly sliding down them, not thinking about how he would climb back up or what might await him once he did. All that mattered was that tomb and what that human-like woman figure carved into the strange stone might mean.

When he reached the bottom, he was surprised that the tomb was so small, barely five feet long. *Perhaps it belongs to a child*, he thought. The engraving showed differently. It was definitely a woman's body, complete with full breasts and curved hips. The lid was a monument to the most beautiful creature he had seen. Her mere image on stone seemed to entrance him with her flowing hair and large doe eyes. Up close, the subtle differences between her and a human were more noticeable: the shorter, pointier nose; extreme thinness of her limbs that, instead of looking skeletal, looked delicate and right; the way her big eyes dominated her face.

He gently traced the cheek of the image with a forefinger. The stone was smooth and cold, like marble back on Earth, and it felt…

alive, as if it were vibrating under his touch, responding to his caress. He stroked the ridges of hair carved in flowing waves reaching nearly to her knees and could almost feel its silky texture beneath his fingertips. As if reading braille, he closed his eyes, allowing his mind to build a three-dimensional picture of the hills and valleys of the carving's landscape.

He could picture her, petite, yet unmistakably grown, her body half shadowed in the never-ending twilight glow of the planet, her hair wrapping around her like a cloak as her eyes took in all around her. In his vision, she was as splendidly naked as she was on her memorial. As his thoughts turned to the delicate curves of her body, he jerked his hand away, shaking his head.

It had been too long, too many years, hell, decades, since he had seen a woman, let alone touched one. He felt perverse, nearly having a pornographic dream in the middle of a burial chamber of sorts he'd stumbled upon while running from a strange beast. The part sabre tooth, part grizzly had killed Kevin, the only other survivor from the mission that was Earth's exploratory committee to Tanali.

Storms, technical problems, bad radar, the fact space travel of this magnitude had never been attempted before, any number of things could be blamed for the ship veering off course and making a crash landing into a mountain range at the northern part of the planet.

For nearly a week, Kevin and he had tried to send messages back to Earth between vain attempts to salvage the ship and bury the dead in ground that wouldn't give way. The fallen crewmates had been burned on pyres the second day, the day after the predators first came, following the coppery scent of blood hanging in the air.

Once admitting the grand failure of the mission and spending several days coming to terms with their fate—the fact that, in all likelihood, they would never leave this planet—the two survivors had gathered as many weapons and as much food as they could carry and set out to find shelter that wasn't washed in the blood of their companions.

And now Lance was alone, terrified, and wondering if it wouldn't be more humane to just sacrifice himself now rather than face the ongoing challenges of being an alien invader completely unwise to the inhabitants or ecology of the planet on which he was now stranded.

He glanced at the sarcophagus again. Frightened as he was, he wanted to see a live version of the image before him. Sighing heavily, he decided to return to camp to reclaim as many provisions as he could, take care of Kevin's remains, if there were any, and then return to the chamber, where he felt he would be reasonably safe from the predators. As for the other inhabitants of the planet, well, that remained to be seen.

When the screeching of metal against rock, bending and breaking, stopped competing against the screams of the humans doing the same, an unnatural silence fell, and Lance lost consciousness.

As he floated in the darkness, he noticed a soft glow in the distance. It grew as if cresting a hill until he could make out the figure of a woman. Her skin was luminous like a flame flickering behind frosted glass: white, gold, sparkling—utterly dazzling. The hair that draped around her looked spun of fine strands of gold, copper, and bronze. Her eyes, her hypnotically huge eyes, were of the darkest chocolate with pupils so dilated, her irises were nothing but frames around them.

She reached for him, her skin warm against his, as if perhaps it were fire in her veins that gave her such a glow. And when her plump, peach lips met his, sparks danced around their mouths.

Lance jerked awake, adrenaline coursing through him after such a sudden shift in states. Glancing quickly at his surroundings, he spotted no immediate threat. He strained his ears, listening for a growl, a click of claws, but there was nothing. Just the perpetual silence.

He gazed up at the sky and cursed. He wasn't sure if it was the planet as a whole or just this area, so near the top pole of the globe, but the sky remained a constant twilight, never bright, never dark, just perpetually dim, like the pretense of a storm that will never manifest.

Kevin had found it promising, likening it to a forever dawn, a potential waiting to be fulfilled, but to Lance, it was an unyielding dusk that stubbornly refused to give way to the utter darkness of night. It was distorting his sense of time and interrupting his body's natural sleep patterns. But what was worse was that without the natural marking of the end of one day and the start of another, he felt like he was trapped in an endless time loop, some purgatory designed to make him lose all semblance of sanity when he needed his wits the most.

He stood up and stretched with a groan. He was too old to sleep on rocks. Exhaustion had evidently overtaken him—last night, yesterday, some time—as he held vigil over his friend's burning remains. He was surprised the predators hadn't come for him while he slept.

Perhaps the smell had deterred them, he thought. The stench of burning bodies was unlike anything he had encountered before, yet he found no solace in knowing he would never have to smell it again.

He shook such thoughts from his head and began to gather up all that he could carry, making food his first priority since he had seen very little vegetation during his time on Tanali. Deciding that his previous plan of returning to the burial chamber was a good one, he set off.

Time passed—though be it days, weeks, or even months, he was unsure, the relenting twilight offering him no mercy—and Lance developed a routine. He would leave the chamber and scout the surrounding rocky range, a different direction each day, mapping out a circumference with the chamber as its center. When he began to tire, he would return to what he had taken to calling "home," where his Lucy waited. It began as a bad joke in his unraveling mind, when upon his return to the tomb once, he had yelled out in a bad Latino accent, "Lucy, I'm home." Since that point, he had begun to think of the woman resting there as Lucy. As if naming her made her real, he began to talk to her, or at her, as it was. *I guess I know I am still sane, because she hasn't answered back yet*, he often mused to himself. She was still the only native he had encountered, her perpetual flame the only other sign of life in the tomb.

He wondered if such a northern part of this planet was much like the Arctic at home, sparsely inhabited, barren nothingness. It seemed logical enough, given the lack of vegetation and water. He counted himself one lucky bastard when he found a tiny stream of water pooling in one of the "antechambers" to his new residence. One day, out of stupidity, sheer boredom, or a subconscious wish for death, he shot one of the tiny critters he had nicknamed jackalope that often jetted across his path and cooked it in a fire made up of the strange, barklike vines that clung to rock faces here, like ivy on a fencepost back home, and ate it without a thought to his self-preservation. When he survived the night without illness or death, he assumed he found a new source of protein.

He had developed a pattern to life on Tanali, useless as he often thought it was. He walked, he ate, he slept, and he dreamt. He believed it was his strange, wonderful dreams of her, of Lucy, with her glowing body and whisper of a voice that kept him sane, though he wasn't sure sane people had erotic dreams featuring dead alien females in whose burial chambers he was now living. But he refused to dwell on that for too long.

A persistent trickling awoke him, and he groaned, thinking his sink was leaking—again—until he remembered that it had been quite some time since he had been anywhere with indoor plumbing. Crawling out of his bed, which consisted of two sleeping bags and several skins of jackalopes vaguely stitched together with string tied between slits he'd cut in the hide, which, all in all, was fairly comfortable, Lance stumbled toward the source of his wake-up call.

The antechamber puddle was becoming more of a wade pool as water ran down the drainage path carved into the stone from years of rain making the same journey. The steady flow piqued Lance's curiosity. The atmosphere here had been just as bland and uneventful as the ever-present twilight. Deciding to investigate, he clambered up the steep steps, long since learning it was easier to do so on all fours than upright. Meandering the now-familiar path, he was greeted at the exit by a heavy downpour of rain. A childish joy ran through him at the sight before he rushed out, dancing around in the shower like a child splashing in puddles. Stripping off his grimy clothing, he let the precipitation wash over him, cleanse him, renew him. Even long after his skin was freed of dirt and grime, he remained in the rain, rejoicing in the feeling of familiarity as it pulsated against his skin. If he closed his eyes, he could pretend to be home.

After two sleep cycles—the only way Lance could keep track of time anymore—the persistent rain had lost some of its joy. Returning to the chamber, he removed his soaked clothing, spreading it along the floor to dry with "yesterday's" clothing, which was still wet. He only had two sets of clothing; food rations had been a higher priority after the crash. Wrapping his jackalope blanket around him, he pulled out the one non-necessity item he refused to leave behind.

The book was small, about the size of a mass market paperback, but only half as thick. It had arrived inconspicuously on his desk, an anonymous package bearing a FedEx label with no return address. Its cover was, Lance guessed, some sort of animal skin, and the pages were thin and delicate, like sheaves of tracing paper, only less translucent. The text was handwritten, intricate calligraphy in a rust-brown ink, letters swirling and joining in a complicated dance. At first, he thought it was Old English, but it wasn't. Nor was it Latin, or Sumerian, or Roman or any other old language he knew. It was similar, but not the same. Letters and phrases of one language partnered with those of another to form new compounds that left his brain hurting. Intrigued by the puzzle, he spent nearly a year surrounded by his own Rosetta stone of notes as he slowly learned the key to the secret code of the Tanalian language.

He opened the cover and began to read, though the story had long since been memorized. Providing his translation held true, it told the tragic story of a young woman sacrificed for the betterment of her people, much like the Aztecs' ritual deaths in honor of their gods. What set this tale apart was that the priest who wrote this story was also the one responsible for taking the life of the woman. And in true tragic form, the woman was also his only child. But what never failed to capture Lance's imagination was the hastily scrawled addendum to the story in which the priest confesses that he could not kill his daughter, and, instead, bespelled her into a deathlike sleep so she may rest "without bearing harm" for all eternity.

Closing the book, he stretched out on his makeshift bed and closed his eyes, wondering what necessitated the sacrifice of the woman and if the father really was able to suspend her life in some way or if he just gave her another type of death through a poisonous potion or something. *Then again*, he mused, *this could just be fiction.* He allowed his mind to drift until he fell asleep to the sound of the pool in the antechamber swell with new life.

She lay beside him, their limbs still a post-bliss tangle, her body that same glowing wonder it always was. Looking down at her, her big, round eyes intently trained on him, Lance thought himself in love. Part of his brain realized this was nothing more than a recurring dream, a fantasy his mind created to fill the void of human contact in his conscious existence. But mostly, he didn't care. He loved spending time, even if imagined, with this beautiful creature who was as smart as she was luscious. And the sex! He hadn't experienced anything like it in reality or fantasy before. It was as if when they joined, they did so on some level other than just physical, the friction of their bodies creating a fire that burned all barriers between them.

"I wish you were real," he whispered against her neck, relishing the shiver caused by his breath on her skin.

"I am real," his Lucy said, turning her head to give his lips more access to her sensitized skin.

"Real as in physically lying in bed next to me, not in a dream."

"I may not be lying in your bed, but I am lying next to you."

He pulled back, abandoning her collarbone to look into her captivating eyes. "What do you mean?"

"You live in my temple."

"Oh."

"Oh?" She looked amused at his matter-of-fact response.

"Well, yes," he said. "I guess my mind knew that." He leaned down and captured her soft, peach lips in a searing kiss. "But I'd much rather you were alive next to me physically so that we could do this," he positioned himself between her thighs, "somewhere other than my dreams."

There was no more talking, just the sounds of two bodies repeatedly becoming one.

The clacking of stones tumbling to the ground jolted Lance awake. He stumbled into the antechamber to investigate. The constant flow of rain had finally worn the rock away enough for part of it to crumble, revealing a hidden room behind it.

He peered through the small window, shining his solar-powered flashlight's weak beam into the darkness. It was a small area, more like a nook or a closet than a room. It was just large enough to contain a chest and what looked like some personal artifacts: clothing, jewelry, a book.

Eager to have something else to preoccupy himself with while the rainy season continued its tirade, Lance began to excavate the alcove, careful not to pollute his source of drinking water with excess stone and dust. It was a slow process, but as he had little else to do, he didn't mind. Using jackalope bones, he carefully chiseled away the wall, just like he used to do while working on a dig at Pompeii, careful not to disrupt the surrounding area and to preserve any other treasures that may be waiting to be unearthed.

He'd mined until his arms got tired, and then he'd take a nap, or at least close his eyes and allow his fantasy to take over. He likened it to tuning in to watch a soap opera, or if he were honest with himself, a pornographic movie. But as it was the only form of entertainment he had besides the much-read book, he found no reason not to indulge himself.

When he'd finally cleared enough of the stone to remove some items, he reached for the book first. The archaeologist inside him was chastising him for his careless disregard for protocol and the irresponsibility of disturbing findings before they could be properly documented. However, the very bored and thoroughly curious reader inside him overruled any such objections. After all, it wasn't as if he had the equipment to properly document anything nor was there anyone to view such documentation, even if it existed.

Settling down in his bed, he examined the new tome in his hands. It was nearly identical to the one he possessed: same animal-skin cover, same delicate pages, same ornamental writing done in odd-colored ink. He wished for his Rosetta stone to speed up the translation process. After what seemed like several hours had past while he tried to decipher the first page, he gave up in frustration. *I won't be able to do this without writing,* he thought bitterly. Forming an idea, he trekked his way out of the cavern and into the rain-washed world.

Dotting the vines he used to make fires were tiny, red berries. Lance had never been brave enough to taste them; they looked too much like poisonous holly berries for him to risk it. But they would do for making ink. He filled a jackalope skull, its eye sockets plugged with stones, full of the berries before returning to the welcomed dryness of the cavern.

Once stripped of his wet and chilled clothing and bundled in his warm skins, he began mashing the berries, using a bone as a pestle. Adding just enough water to get the right consistency, Lance congratulated himself at his first attempt at making ink. It wasn't the perfect solution as berry juice seeped out the skull, but it would do.

Using his fingertip as a brush, he began to translate the book, word by word, drawing and then crossing out and redrawing letters on the smooth stone floor. It was a slow process as Lance's little-used reasoning skills protested the exercise. By the time he had made sense of the last word on the last page, many sleep cycles had passed, and the floor of the chamber was covered in red letters.

He stood, admiring his success, but was too tired and his eyes too unfocused to read the epic painted on the floor. Choosing to sleep now and look upon his endeavor with fresh eyes tomorrow, he wiped the ink from his hands and snuggled exhaustedly into the pile of skins, welcoming the darkness that would bring her, his Lucy, to him.

His fingers traced the delicate curve of her hip as he cradled her next to him. "Are there others like you here?"

"Why? Am I no longer enough to satisfy you?" she asked saucily.

"More than enough." He kissed her with fervor to illustrate the point. "It's just that I've been on this planet for what must be months now, and I have never seen one of your kind, or any evidence they exist except for your tomb."

She stilled for a moment, a look of deep concentration etched in her features. "I don't know," she finally answered. "It has been a long time since I have been free. You are the only one who has come to visit me."

"Maybe I should go find them."

"No," she said suddenly, sitting up to fix him with a dangerous glare. "You will not go anywhere. You will not leave me."

As if sensing his sudden apprehension, she relaxed her face as she drew her fingers down his bare chest, leaving a trail of harmless sparks behind, as if their passion had a physical manifestation. "If you go, then whoever shall I do this to?"

She lowered her head and her catlike tongue mimicked the movements of her fingers down his chest, lower and lower, until he had forgotten everything but the warmth of her mouth.

Lance paced the length of the room, his trail the gutters between columns of his work, reading and rereading the words that had dried like bloodstains on the stone. He stopped, shook his head as if to clear his thoughts, and resumed his circuit. *It can't be right,* he thought adamantly. *But what if...*

He walked over to the sarcophagus, and with a strenuous push of protesting arm and back muscles, slid the lid off until it crashed on the floor.

There, inside, lay his Lucy, not a shriveled mummy or a pile of former bones reduced to dust, but a beautiful, perfect female Tanalian who looked as though she were merely asleep, resting on a thick cushion.

Lance gasped as he drank in the sight of his imagination made real. Color danced along her frosted skin as if lit from within as waves of bronze, copper, and gold tendrils snaked down toward her knees. She was everything he had pictured, yet more amazing than he could have envisioned himself.

He reached out to brush her silky hair away from her face. Agonizing over what to do, he glanced at the red words on the floor. *What the hell,* he thought.

"Per meus spiritus, Ego liceor vos ago iterum," he whispered against her lips. "With my breath, I bid you live again."

Wishing with all his heart that the spell would work, that his Sleeping Beauty would awake, he did what all princes do: In an act born of love and desperation, he kissed his princess, praying that to do so would breathe life back into her still body.

Slowly he withdrew his lips and waited for his princess to awake. And waited. And waited.

Chastising himself for believing in fairy tales and ancient writings in alien books, he felt like a fool, a fool who desecrated a tomb and molested the body inside.

"I need to get the hell out of here!"

Trembling, he began to disassemble the home he had created in the chamber. But as he did so, his eyes kept stealing glances at the alien woman. Giving up all pretenses, he sighed heavily as he sank onto his bed, and stared at her form until his eyes grew heavy, and he fell back against the skins in a deep slumber.

He screamed her name as pleasure coursed through his body. When he regained control of his senses, he found her licking her way up his sternum, long, sure strokes of her tongue leaving a damp trail up to his throat before her mouth descended on his. She greedily ate at his mouth, feeding at the pleasure she found there.

Suddenly, it was too much; he couldn't breathe. It was as if the air were being forced from his lungs into her mouth. But it was so much more than air; it was something rooted much deeper in him, something much more intrinsic to his Self.

He fought against her; pushing her body off his chest, he scrambled away from her. He tried to talk but could do nothing more than gulp in breaths of air. She reached for him, but he shrank away, confused by what was happening.

"You got your wish," she whispered. "I'm real."

Lance looked at her, eyes wide, and then looked at the surroundings. They were in the chamber, not in the random scenery of his dreams. And in the center of the room stood an empty tomb. His eyes shifted back to hers. "How?"

She pointed to the words on the floor. "You released me."

"It was real?"

"Yes," she said sadly. "My father was to sacrifice me, but he couldn't. Instead he tried his best to stop what was happening by trapping me here."

"Why..." His question died on his lips as she disentangled herself from the skins and stood, baring her nakedness before him. "This is really real?" he whispered, too afraid to move, to even blink for fear she would disappear like his dreams.

She walked to him, wrapping her arms around his neck, pulling his mouth to hers. She traced his bottom lip with her tongue before plunging it inside his mouth, claiming him as her own. When she released him, she slipped her tiny hand in his and led him back to the bed.

Lance's mind was swirling. Perhaps he was still dreaming. Perhaps all the solitude finally drove what little sanity remained from his mind. Or, perhaps, it was all true. After all, it was the book that brought him here, to a foreign planet in the first place. Was it so far beyond reason to believe its contents true?

But if she was the priest's daughter… His eyes flickered over to a smear of red on the floor, the hastily discounted confession deemed unimportant, obviously not real. After all, there was no such thing as—

His thoughts were interrupted by the feel of her skillful hands stroking him while her mouth nipped at his neck before her tongue flicked soothingly against it. It had been so long since he felt another live being naked against him, her heart beating against his, her lungs filling with the same air. He lost himself to the sensation of skin against skin as he lowered them to the floor, her body cradling him between her thighs.

He gasped as their bodies joined, not in pleasure but in fear. Their union engendered an epiphany, a moment of absolute truth, absolute horror, and she laughed, knowingly. "I can see you have solved your riddle."

Lost in his realization, he offered no resistance as she rolled their bodies, pinning him below her with unnatural strength. She slowly rolled her hips, reminding him that they were still locked together. Pleasure rolled through him, chasing away his thoughts. She leaned closer to him, whispering hot breath against his ear. "You know what will happen." Her tongue licked a path from one ear, across his jaw to the other before continuing. "It doesn't have to end in pain. Let me reward your sacrifice with pleasure."

She circled her hips, clenching him tightly inside her, illustrating her point and eliciting a groan from him, followed by a weak "yes." As she kissed him fiercely, his mind went blank as if all thoughts, all intelligence had been erased in the space of a heartbeat, leaving him with nothing but his senses: the taste of her mouth on his, the smell of the alien flowers clinging to her skin, the sight of her abyss-like eyes locked on his, the sounds of their mutual pleasure, the feel of their bodies moving as one.

As he neared his climax, Lance noticed the world rapidly darkening around him.

With a strangled cry, night had come.

Entertaining an Angel Unawares
by Charie La Marr

My name is Kazuko Morelli and I proudly admit to being a New Yorker; born and raised a city girl. I didn't even leave home to go to college. It was just two quick subway stops to FIT, the Fashion Institute of Technology. Like probably all New Yorkers, 9/11 changed my life forever. It's been said that each New Yorker dealt with that tragedy in his or her own particular way. Mine was to vow never to go below Fourteenth Street ever again in my life. I guess never facing that gaping hole in the ground is one way of telling oneself the world is still a safe and happy place. Maybe it was working for me, but maybe it wasn't.

Anyway, that's why it seemed so odd to me that the day after Hurricane Katrina, I felt compelled to stuff as many pairs of jeans and T-shirts as I could fit into my biggest gym bag, borrow my father's car and head south. I'd never been farther south than Washington, D.C. in my entire life, but suddenly I was on the New Jersey Turnpike telling myself I'd always wanted to see New Orleans anyway.

Somehow, the girl whose idea of vehicular navigation was getting on the Long Island Expressway and heading east until she hit parties in the Hamptons found herself in Baton Rouge, Louisiana, in just a little more than thirty hours. I parked in the lot of a strip mall, slipped my arms into the handles of the gym bag like a backpack, and headed out in search of—what, I wasn't exactly sure.

A man and a woman in a pickup truck filled with bottles of water stopped on the road and asked me if I needed help. The next thing I knew, I was trying my best to hold on from my perch atop the cases of water as we rolled over muddy roads at a speed faster than the average New York taxi driver can only dream of. When we reached a Red Cross station, I located some sort of a staging area and volunteered.

The next six days went by in a blur of plastic water bottles, cardboard boxes, and sore muscles. At night, I slept on a cot in a tent with more people than I had slept with in my entire life combined. The gym bag was my pillow, and the terrycloth bathrobe I packed (in spite of the fact I realized there would be very little need for it) was my blanket. Once, I recalled taking something that vaguely resembled a lukewarm shower.

I learned to eat things like grits and okra and other things that had names I don't even care to remember. One night for dinner, a woman with a drawl I could barely understand told me what I was eating was "the part of the pig that went over the fence last." I didn't even ask for any further explanation. As Don Quixote said, hunger is the best sauce in the world.

On my sixth night there, I had a dream, more of a nightmare really. I dreamed I was a tiny droplet of blood lost somewhere in the veins of a giant. I was tired and weak from lack of oxygen and starving to death. I knew I needed to get back to the giant's heart to revitalize myself, but I had lost the way. I woke up before I ever reached the heart, bathed in more sweat than usual on a steamy bayou summer morning and trembling badly. I knew immediately what the dream meant. In Baton Rouge, I was in the life blood of the storm and its victims, but I was burning out quickly. I needed to get to the heart if I was to survive the ordeal and do something that truly mattered. I needed to get to New Orleans.

That morning at breakfast, I found a group of Louisiana National Guardsmen and Los Angeles cops discussing their day's assignment. Hundreds, maybe thousands of people were still holed up in their homes in New Orleans, refusing to leave behind all they had left in the world. Still others had died in their homes. The city was ordered to evacuate, and the guardsmen and the cops would be going door to door taking people forcibly if necessary and searching for the dead.

After all the sorrow and suffering I'd seen already, it seemed like the cruelest thing anyone could do: to tear old people from the only place they'd ever called home and take them away for what would in most cases amount to forever. I tried to imagine someone trying to tell my old Italian grandma Anna she couldn't live on Mulberry Street anymore. In my mind, I could see her kicking and screaming and calling the troops every dirty word she knew in ten different dialects of Italian as she tried to beat them off with her mother's colander in one hand and her grandmother's saucepan in the other.

Before I knew it, I heard my own voice asking to go along. The Guardsman closest to me snorted, almost choking on his grits.

"Now just what good would you be down there in N'awlins, city girl? You think you could handle the stench while wading through water up to the ass of your fancy designer jeans? You ready to look down the barrel of a shotgun some kid looted from Wal-Mart and tell him he has to leave with you? You think you could go one on one with a scared dog that hasn't eaten in over a week and sees you as his next meal? You anxious to kick in a door and discover an entire family dead and bloated almost beyond recognition after floating in that water for over a week? You know what E. coli is? Spend much time up there in the Big Apple treading in raw sewage? Best you stay here where it's safe, city girl. N'awlins ain't no Mardi Gras no more. Nobody is gonna give you no beads for liftin' your shirt now. Nothing's easy in the Big Easy anymore, sister. Trust me, city girl, you don't wanna go."

Somewhere deep inside me, my hot half-Italian blood boiled. I stared him straight in the eye and uttered but four words. "Indulge me, country boy." Two hours later, I was in the back of a National Guard truck on my way into the giant's heart. I was headed straight for New Orleans.

In the downtown area where we ended up, the streets were nearly dry. I won't deny I felt a little relief about that, but I had more than prepared myself for a baptism in the now fetid waters of Lake Pontchartrain. The ground below our feet was slick and slippery though. A layer of sludge squished under my feet, and I didn't need to ask for a chemical analysis of the substance. The stench told me everything I needed to know.

The first three houses we tried were deserted. It was an eerie feeling, watching photos of people I didn't know stare back at me in the empty houses. I walked room to room, surveying the damage and the remnants of life left behind by people fleeing for their lives so fast they had no choice but to leave nearly everything behind. In one house, I bent to pick up a little girl's doll and tried to imagine the child who had left it behind. I said a silent prayer that, whoever she was, she was someplace safe.

I paused long enough to burn each scene into my mind. The photos bothered me the most. My mother is Japanese and when I was a child, her Buddhism was as much a part of my life as my father's Catholicism was. The Japanese have a holiday they call Obon. I remember my mother explaining it to me as a young girl.

She taught me on the first day of the eighth lunar month, the gates of Hell are opened and ghosts are allowed to visit the world for fifteen days. Food offerings are made during this time to relieve the sufferings of these ghosts. The fifteenth day is *Ulambana* or Ancestor Day, when people visit cemeteries to make offerings to their departed ancestors so they will have comfort and feel our respect. There is a ceremony called *Ohaka Mairi* when lanterns are lit at the family tomb. People even visit the tombs of their friends and neighbors to express respect and hear stories of their ancestors.

When my Italian grandpa, Tony, died we even went to Cypress Hills Cemetery in Brooklyn the following year and held *Ohaka Mairi* there for him. We've done it every year since. Nobody loves it more than Grandma Anna.

The irony didn't escape me. Hurricane Katrina hit on August 29. The eighth month, the month the Japanese call *Hachi Gatsu,* the month of leaves. The gates of Hell might have opened a little late this year, but they did open in the form of breaks in the levees that destroyed the once-beautiful city of New Orleans.

Having no more food than a package of Lifesavers in my pocket, I left one in each of the three homes beneath what appeared to be a photo of the peoples' ancestors. It was the best I could do under the circumstances to honor my mother's tradition.

As we approached a fourth house, I could hear the commotion. Clearly this one wasn't deserted. As I got closer, I saw a black version of Grandma Anna. Dressed in a flowered housedress and a clean white apron, her bulk nearly filled the doorway. Her legs were bowed from the weight. She was swinging a broomstick and shouting in a combination of English and a language I vaguely recognized as a form of French. Her white hair looked like plaited, white cotton, and her dark skin was lined with deep creases that resembled an old saddle.

I hurried to the door and stepped between the woman and the grit-eating Guardsman. It took no more than a moment to realize the gist of the dispute. The woman was refusing to leave her waterlogged home, and the Guardsman was threatening to carry her away by force if necessary.

I guess it was her eyes that got to me. Watery and silver and glazed over with the beginnings of milky cataracts, I could see the pain and confusion in them. Suddenly, all I could think of was how warm and wonderful it felt to stand in Grandma Anna's kitchen on a

Sunday afternoon and take in the smell of her homemade sauce simmering on the stove while Caruso played on her old record player and she hummed along softly as she cooked. I could picture this lady doing the same for her grandchildren; only now there was no kitchen left to cook in.

I turned to the Guardsman and pushed him a couple feet away from the frantic woman so she couldn't hear us. "Can I have a few moments alone with her? Really, let me help. I think I can convince her to—"

The Guardsman had little patience for a big-city Amerasian with a heart of gold. "Listen, city girl; we have orders here. And our orders say that we evacuate this quadrant using any means necessary. And if that means hogtying the old lady and tossing her into the back of that truck over there, then so be it. You got that? Now get your city ass out of my way and let me get the job done."

I sighed in exasperation. "But this is her home, soldier. Surely you have a grandma somewhere. Would you appreciate some stranger hogtying her and tossing her into a truck like garbage? Would you like it if someone told her everything that she had ever known in her life was about to be taken away from her? Have a heart, soldier! This is someone's grandma!"

He remained unimpressed. "Sister, I happen to have two grandmas, and if they was living in conditions like this, you bet your sweet, city ass I would want someone to take them away to someplace safe and clean and take care of them. She'll die if she stays here; even you have to realize that. Now get the hell out of my way."

He put his hand on my shoulder and tried to push me aside. I took a deep breath, rose up to my full height of slightly over five feet and stood my ground. "Half an hour, soldier, that's all I ask. You can scout around the other houses in the area while I talk to her. Half an hour. Then if she won't come peacefully, you can hogtie her or whatever you have to do. But please, just give me a chance."

I looked at him with my soft, brown, almond-shaped eyes and silently thanked my mother for giving me eyes that resembled Bambi's. They could be very persuasive, especially when I wanted something. My father always said my eyes were my greatest weapon. He was helpless against them. I turned them up to full capacity. "Think of your grandmas, soldier. Indulge me."

He knew he was beaten; the doe eyes did the trick. He looked at the ground sheepishly and kicked away a splintered piece of wood.

"Twenty minutes, city girl, and not a minute more. If she don't come out with you in twenty minutes, then I go in and carry both of you out forcibly." I started to speak but he wouldn't let me get a word in edgewise. "I mean it, sister, and don't think I won't enjoy hogtying you and tossing you into that truck. Your twenty minutes already started, so get busy."

I glared at him and he grinned in return. Somehow I think he was dreaming up some dirty little fantasy of me roped and slung over his shoulder. "Me Tarzan, you Jane" kind of stuff. However, he could fantasize all he liked because it wasn't going to happen. I walked over to the truck and grabbed two large bottles of water. Then I stuffed a couple packages of peanut butter crackers into my pockets, took a deep breath, and headed back to the house.

The soldier stepped in front of me, and I stopped in my tracks. "What did you just put in your pockets, City Girl?"

I smiled and muttered under my breath, "Cracker."

His eyes opened wide and his nostrils flared. "What? What did you say? I don't think I heard you right, city girl. You got something to say to me, you come out and say it."

I reached into my pocket and pulled out a package of crackers, brandishing them in his face triumphantly. "Crackers. Peanut butter crackers. The lady looks famished. You got a problem with that? Weren't you intending to at least offer her some food?"

He rolled his eyes and stepped aside without so much as another word. I, however, had something more to say to him. The soldier had a little more than a foot on me in height. Standing on the tips of my toes, I stared directly into his eyes and brazenly poked him in the chest as I spoke to him in a lecturing tone. "Soldier? My Grandma Anna always told me that the Bible says to be careful when dealing with strangers because you never know when you might be entertaining an angel unawares. I suggest you remember that." He looked at me with a blank expression that told me instantly he didn't get it. I shook my head and strolled past him.

The black woman had stopped screaming and was eyeing me curiously as she went about the task of sweeping a combination of water, mud, and debris out onto the street. I approached her cautiously, holding the water bottle out as a peace offering. "You look parched. Here, take this. Sorry it's not real cold."

She reached out for the bottle, her eyes never leaving mine. "Go on, it's okay; take it. You need to drink." From close up, I could see she needed more than just water. She was probably severely dehydrated and badly in need of nutrition, but that would have to come later. I could feel the minutes ticking away.

"My name is Kazuko Morelli. I came here from New York City to help out. I don't know if you have a radio inside or if you know much about what's happening, but most of New Orleans is under water. The storm was pretty bad, and then the levees gave out. The city has set up safe places for people like you to get help."

She nodded. "I heared about that, missy. All of it. Never seen nothin' like it in all my days." She took the bottle and opened it, bringing it to her dry lips and drinking so quickly that I feared she would choke. As she drank, I tried to peer inside the house.

I cracked open my water bottle and drank, too. "It's kinda hot out here in the sun, ma'am. I've been up since sunup this morning, and I'm not used to this kind of heat. I'm staying in Baton Rouge; it's my first time down South. It's been a long day so far, and it's not even close to being over. There's just so much to be done. Mind if I come in and sit down for a minute?"

The old woman shrugged and stepped aside. I walked into the ruins of what was once a humble but cozy home. The acrid smell of ammonia mingled with the fetid odors of sewage, death, and decay. "Isn't nothin' much to see in here no more. Most everything down here was under the water till yesterday."

I glanced at the wall in the sodden living room. The high water mark was clearly visible about eighteen inches to a foot below the ceiling. I closed my eyes and shuddered. It was hard to imagine the suddenness of the rising waters and the fear this woman must have felt as she escaped to the upper level, unsure if the water would rise high enough to trap her and drown her in her own bedroom.

My mind wasn't working at full capacity, but I figured she must have been trapped upstairs for six or seven days before the water receded enough for her to come down again. It was inconceivable to me anyone could have lasted that long all alone and trapped without going stark raving mad, and yet I could see the strength and fortitude in this woman. Somehow, she made it when so many had not.

My time was disappearing fast, and I still had no plan for convincing this feisty resident of New Orleans to abandon her home. Frantically, I glanced around the room. I could hear my mother talking to me. *Ancestors, Kazuko. Look for pictures. Maybe there's some family who can take her in.*

I sighed in frustration. There were no photos anywhere to be seen. Either she had time to take them down or the flood waters had washed them all away. And if she did have any family, I figured surely they would have come looking for her. The possibility existed this woman was alone in the world.

I looked around for somewhere to sit. She spoke apologetically, as though the damage in her home was somehow her fault. "There ain't no decent place to sit down here no more, miss. But if you really want to sit a while, you can come upstairs. That's where I been stayin'. Nothin' fancy, but it's dry up there."

I smiled and nodded. She led the way and I followed as she walked into one of the two bedrooms on the second floor. I looked around in awe. The room was immaculate. Lace curtains yellowed with age hung from boarded-up windows and a huge patchwork quilt covered the polished brass bed. Oil lamps glowed on bed stands covered with crocheted doilies. Everything must have been more than 100 years old. This was everything I pictured a proper New Orleans lady's bedroom to be.

She pointed to a Victorian chair covered in threadbare red velvet. "Sit there if you want to. Sorry if it's a little stuffy and dark up here. The neighbor's boy covered the windows for me day before the storm. I 'spect he'll be gettin' around to takin' them down in a day or two more. Meantime, I have the lamps and plenty of oil. Had the radio too, till the batteries wore out two days ago. Had some food and supplies up here, too, but they're just about used up now."

I suddenly remembered the crackers in my pockets. I pulled a package out and held them out to her. She took them eagerly. "You haven't told me your name yet. I'm Kazuko, remember? But most people call me Kassie or Kaz."

She nodded. "I 'member that, Miss Kazuko Morelli. Funny kind of name. Sounds pretty on the tongue though. I like it. My name is Mary. Mary Boucher."

Suddenly, the funny language made sense. Mary Boucher was Creole. I smiled. "I guess Kazuko Morelli is a funny name at that. My father's Italian and my mother's Japanese. They met during the Vietnam war in Tokyo when my father was on leave. Kazuko means "child of peace." I was born after the war when my father brought my mother back to the States and married her. I guess he had enough war and was ready for some peace for a change. Funny thing is, he says I was a miserable baby and have barely given him a moment's peace ever since."

Mary nodded, her eyes suddenly misting over from a distant memory. "My Gervais was there. In Vietnam. He died in 1969. They brought him back here to be buried. Had a big funeral too, we did. Bourbon Street style with the music and everything. Most beautiful thing I ever seen. Got the flag that was on his coffin right over there."

She motioned toward the dresser. A faded American flag folded into the traditional triangle shape rested against the framed photo of a young soldier. At last I had something to go on. There was some family. At least there was at one time. It was a start. "Gervais is a lovely name. Your husband?"

Mary chuckled. "Goodness no! Gervais was my son. He was only twenty when he died; just a baby. I had a daughter too. She was called Maylene. Their daddy run off just after she was born."

"Where's Maylene now?" I regretted the words as soon as I said them. Mary said she had a daughter Maylene. Had. Past tense. Apparently, Mary had lost two children.

"Maylene is gone now too. She got cancer in her breast when she was expecting her second baby. She died about a year later. Beautiful girl, my Maylene."

I noticed the wedding photo on the dresser beside the photo of Gervais. A happy bride with pale brown skin glowed in a white satin gown while standing beside a grinning white man in a black tuxedo. I knew it would be painful to press her for details, but I had to know more. Somewhere out there, Maylene had a husband and children. Mary's grandchildren. If I could get enough information from her, I figured I could try to find them. I had plenty of resources in New York, and I would call in every favor I had in the world if necessary to find Mary's family.

"How long ago was that, Mary?" I could feel my heart beginning to race. Time was ticking away and I knew the Guardsman meant it when he said twenty minutes and not a minute more.

"Maylene's gone now since 1980. I guess her kids would be all growed up by now."

For the first time, I felt truly encouraged. Maylene's children would be in their twenties. If they were still in the New Orleans area, it was likely they had been evacuated to one of the shelters, probably to the Superdome and then on to Houston and the Astrodome. It was a long shot, but a good place to start.

"Do her children live nearby? Do you get to see them much?" I prayed the answer would be yes.

Mary shook her head sadly. "Ain't never seen them. That man she married took her away right after the wedding to live with his people in Seattle. Never did understand that man. My people have lived in N'awlins far back as anyone can remember. This house belonged to my great-grandmother Nettie Dupuis. The Dupuis family been in N'awlins since there was a N'awlins. Anyway, Maylene always wanted more for her life, and I suppose that ain't a bad thing. Me, I worked as a maid at the Fairmont downtown for over forty years and never had no complaints. In fact, I worked three jobs just to pay for Maylene's college. That's where she met Michael. At the Tulane University."

My heart sank. Apparently Mary was truly alone in the world. Her grandchildren were grown up and it was possible that they weren't even in Seattle anymore or that they had married and changed names. Still, I had to try.

"What was Michael's last name, Mary? What are your grandchildren's names?"

Mary laughed for the first time. "Lord, you sure are stuffed full of questions, Miss Kazuko. Maylene married a Woods, Michael Woods. Her first was a boy, and she named him Gervais after her brother. I heared that Michael changed it to Gerry, though. Her daughter was Rebecca Hope. Maylene called her Hope because of the cancer and all. She didn't take no drugs while she was pregnant and by then the cancer was too far gone. Guess hope can only go so far."

I was beginning to agree. Hope, along with my twenty minutes, was running out fast. Woods was a fairly common name, although with some research, it wasn't an impossible task to look up someone named Woods in Seattle. However, even if I could find Mary's family, it might take months, and Mary had to be out of her house in less than ten minutes.

I noticed she finished her crackers and fumbled in my pocket for another package. I handed them to her, and she nodded her appreciation. There was no more time for the soft approach. I had to take a harder line, and fast. There had to be some way to appeal to her better judgment.

Suddenly it hit me. She was a maid at the Fairmont. The upstairs of her house was immaculate, and I assumed the rest looked the same before the storm. She was already cleaning it when I arrived. I recalled the smell of the ammonia.

I swallowed hard and held my breath for a moment before taking the plunge. Mary was either going to listen to me or throw me out in the next thirty seconds, but I had run out of options.

"Mary," I said softly. "You know you have to leave here now. There's no electricity or running water, and no one can say when they might be back on again. Downstairs is a shambles. Everything's soaked, and it'll take weeks for it to dry out. And even if it does, surely you know the water was tainted with raw sewage and other poisons. The mold hasn't even begun to take hold yet, but it will and it'll be deadly for anyone who's very old or very young or has any respiratory illnesses. You know you need to go someplace clean and safe at least for a while, so they can figure out how to clean up this city and rebuild. You need some clean water and hot food. Mary, I know it's not what you want, but you have to know it's the only way to save you. You'll die here, Mary, and no one wants to see that happen, especially me. The storm left this city in ruins. Enough lives have been lost already. Please don't add yours to that total."

I could see the tears well up in her eyes. "I know all about the sewage and the poisons. I already started cleanin' downstairs. I'm old, Kazuko, and I don't know if I got the time to wait for the government to fix things up. I ain't even sure I trust them. I stopped trusting the government when Gervais died. I can take care of my own self, Kazuko. Always have, and always will."

I had to admire her guts. I sure couldn't have handled it myself. I know I would've run for the hills at the first sign of sewage-tainted water. And yet, here I was, sitting on this red velvet chair knowing full well that I reeked of that very same tainted water. I guess at that moment, I found out I was a lot stronger woman than I ever realized.

I glanced at my watch. I had eight minutes left. I couldn't reason with her anymore. "Mary, if you don't leave on your own, they'll take you out by force if they have to. And you just don't strike me as the kind of woman who would sacrifice her dignity that way. So, I tell you what I want you to do. I want you to get me some pillowcases. We're gonna put everything we can inside them as fast as we can, and then we're gonna walk down the stairs and go with the Guardsmen to a safe place where you can be looked over by a doctor and given some food and fluids.

"Don't die here alone, Mary. You're worth more than that. Maybe your grandchildren don't care, but maybe they don't even know about you, I just don't know. One day, one of them might just decide to look up their ancestors the way my mother does. And wouldn't it be awful for them to find out their grandmother died from E. coli or some other disease all alone in a filthy, waterlogged, and rat-infested house? Honestly right now, I don't care whether or not they ever care about you. I care, and that's all you need to know. Now get me those damn pillowcases and let's start packing up before the Guardsmen come back. Mary, they won't wait while you gather your stuff together. They'll just drag you out. Hurry, please?"

I saw her eyes dart around the room as though trying to fix it in her mind one last time. I counted the seconds as she lingered over each and every inch of the room. Finally, she walked slowly over to the bed and pulled the pillows out from under the patchwork coverlet. "I had both my children in this bed, Kazuko. I slept here every night of my life that I can remember. I'm scared now. Don't think I could bear to sleep anywhere else. And my cat Satchmo has been gone since the storm..." Her voice choked with emotion, and she couldn't continue.

I could feel the tears sliding down my cheeks, leaving clean trails where they washed away about a week's worth of dirt and grime. I looked at her pleadingly. "Please, Mary, come with me. I'll go with you to the shelter. In fact, I'll spend the night there with you. We can sit and talk all night if you want to. In a day or two, we'll file the papers for disaster relief, and I'll help you get the house fixed. Everything will be fine, I promise you. We can fix it better than it was before. Please believe me; I won't let you down. Just hurry before they come back."

She looked at me sadly and slipped the blue and white flowered pillowcases slowly off the four pillows. I quickly went to the bureau and took down Gervais' and Maylene's pictures and her flag and laid them on the quilt. Mary added an antique silver dresser set and a small box she retrieved from the bottom drawer. It was tied with a faded red ribbon. I guessed it was probably letters from her son and daughter in the days before their deaths.

It took about three minutes to gather up all the things Mary wanted to take with her. I folded up the coverlet and stuffed it inside a pillowcase, and we began to stuff her clothes in a second one. There was no need for the third or fourth pillowcase; Mary didn't have that many possessions. As I packed, I wondered how many of my possessions I truly valued and couldn't live without. I came to the conclusion that I, too, would only be able to fill about two pillowcases.

When we were done, I checked my watch. I figured we had about three minutes before the Guardsmen would bust in and drag us off, but I wasn't about to let them do that. They could take Mary's home away from her, they could take away the bed where she birthed her two children, they could take away her red velvet chair, but there was no way I was going to let them take away her most precious possession—her dignity.

"Mary? Do you have some special dress? One that you wear to church on Sundays?"

Mary laughed for the second time since we met; it was a bitter laugh. "Ain't been to no church in many years, Kazuko Morelli. I more or less gave up on God when he took my Maylene from me. But if you mean do I have a fancy dress, that I do."

I smiled at her. We could work on the God part later; right now I had to get Mary out of the house with the last shreds of her dignity intact. "Well then, Mary Boucher, I want you to put that dress on. And a hat too if you got one. Me and you are gonna walk down the stairs and out to the truck like two ladies going off on a nice trip. With our heads held high. Now hurry up and get into that fancy dress before the soldiers return."

We beat them by a full two minutes, but I suspect they took their time getting there. When they returned, we were standing in the doorway, me with a moth-eaten old fur stole draped over my shoulders, rhinestone dangle earrings and a dusty hat from about 1940 perched jauntily on my head. Mary was in her best taupe-colored lace dress and a wide-brimmed picture hat with faded ribbons streaming down her back. A bright purple feather boa left over from a Mardi Gras parade was wrapped around her throat. We even found a tube of red lipstick and painted our lips and rubbed some on our cheeks. We must have looked a sight.

The Guardsmen shook their heads at us and tried not to laugh. I slung the two pillowcases over my shoulder and brushed past them with my head held proudly and walking as though I was on my way to my coronation as Queen of the Mardi Gras. Mary followed me. I glanced over my shoulder and giggled at her haughty strut as she passed the soldiers. When I passed Grit Boy, I winked. He busied himself with his rifle, pretending not to notice. His loss; he was kinda cute. I considered giving him a customary New York salute but thought better of it.

A couple of hours later, we arrived at a shelter in a Baptist church not too far from Baton Rouge. Mary seemed frightened and hesitant to enter. I took her by the hand and led her to the Red Cross workers who were processing people as they arrived. They pretended not to notice our outrageous attire. I gave them her name and address. I told them she was a little nervous and asked if it would be all right if I spent the first night with her. They found us two cots in the basement gymnasium, and we stuffed her belongings underneath them and headed off to wash up a little and find the food line.

Mary didn't sleep that night, and neither did I. We talked about everything. We spoke in whispers, even though there were many people like Mary who couldn't sleep. Often we could hear people weeping softly. I tried very hard to keep Mary's spirits up. She laughed when I told her about eating the part of the pig that went over the fence last. She told me her recipe for jambalaya and confided that her secret ingredient in it was Kentucky sipping whiskey. I told her Grandma Anna's recipe for linguine with red clam sauce. Of course, I had to tell her what linguine was first. She told me about her husband, Maurice, and how he left her alone with two small children to fend for herself. She commiserated with me as I told her about my ex-fiancé Devon and how he left me for a schoolteacher from Jersey City with three kids, all by different fathers. Mary was very sympathetic.

When I told her his new romance hadn't lasted six months before the teacher ran off with one of her students, she shook her head and chuckled. "Well, you know what I always say? It goes to show you never can tell. But you know what? You never told me what you do for a living, Kazuko Morelli. Do you work for the Red Cross?"

I smiled. "Oh no. I just came down here because I somehow felt I was needed. I live and work in Manhattan. I design shoes for a large design firm."

Mary snorted. "Oh, so you're the one who designs all them fancy shoes with the high heels and pointy toes that the streetwalkers down in the Quarter wear! Never could stuff myself into a pair of those dang things. My feet just weren't built with no pointy toes."

I laughed. I wanted to tell her the shoes I design sell in large, high-end department stores for several hundred dollars a pair, but somehow it didn't seem appropriate. Mary couldn't relate to the kind of people who wore my shoes, but she could relate to the streetwalkers on Bourbon Street, and that was just fine with me. "Yep, guilty as charged. I guess I do design those shoes."

Mary laughed loudly. The sleeping couple closest to us stirred but didn't wake up. "You know, Kazuko Morelli, when I'm old and living in a nursing home I'm gonna get me a wheelchair to ride around in. Then I'm gonna get me a pair of them red satin shoes with the high heels and wheel myself up and down the halls so all the gentlemen folk can see me in my fancy lady shoes."

I smiled at the image. "Mary Boucher, I'll just have to send you a pair of my best red, satin, fancy lady shoes as soon as I get back to New York. You aren't ready for them quite yet, but when you are, I want you to have them handy."

"I dunno about that, Kazuko. I'm feeling mighty tired and wore out today. Besides, how you gonna find me to send those fancy shoes? How you gonna know where I'm gonna be when I don't even know?"

I got up and sat on her cot beside her, wrapping my arms tightly around her and stroking her hair. "Just don't you worry about that, Mary Boucher. Because I'll know. Trust me; I'll know where you are. I'll make it my business to know where you are. And you have my word on those red satin shoes, I promise you that. You'll be the talk of the nursing home, you wild woman, you!"

It was nearly dawn when Mary finally drifted off to sleep for a while. She awoke late in the morning. I swear she looked like she aged ten years overnight. Her hair looked whiter and the creases in her skin looked deeper; even the cataracts in her eyes looked milkier. For the first time, I noticed she had a deep, rasping cough. I tried to chalk the changes up as my overtired imagination working overtime. But still, as I listened to her cough, I felt an uneasy trepidation.

After lunch, I hitched a ride back to the place where I was staying and took a much-needed shower. I fell asleep and didn't even wake up for dinner. The following day, I was assigned to another area of New Orleans, and after fifteen hours of house-to-house searching, I once again returned to Baton Rouge and fell asleep after another quick shower and a cold dinner standing up in the dining tent.

It wasn't until two days later I found a convoy taking supplies down to the church where Mary was staying. I decided to follow along in my car and check up on her. I thought maybe taking her out for a ride might cheer her up. I remembered seeing a Dairy Queen not far from the church, and I figured I would take her there for ice cream.

When I arrived, I was surprised to find the shelter somewhat less crowded than when I left it, but I couldn't find Mary anywhere. I inquired and was told several people had been picked up by relatives and still more had been transferred to the Astrodome in Houston. I checked the list of people who left and Mary's name wasn't among them. I could feel my heart pounding; something just didn't seem right.

No one seemed to know what had happened to her. I searched frantically. The cots where we slept were now occupied by two small children and their mother. I asked, but she hadn't seen the lady who slept there before. I was about to leave when I noticed two blue and white pillowcases piled up with a few suitcases and boxes in a corner near the Red Cross station. I could barely breathe as I got closer to them. They were Mary's.

Fighting back fear and panic, I stopped a Red Cross worker and asked where the people who owned these items were. Somehow, I already knew in my heart what his answer would be.

"All this stuff here belongs to people who died the last two days. The bags are all numbered. The bodies finally got picked up this morning. They're headed for St. Gabriel where a temporary morgue has been set up. Soon as we have time, someone here is gonna go through these things and look for clues about who the people were so we can notify their next of kin. It's just that no one has had the time right now, and no one over in St. Gabriel will have the time either. It may take weeks or months before we're able to notify everyone's next of kin and arrange burial."

Tears ran freely down my cheeks, and I stood still for a long time and just let them go. Finally the worker touched my shoulder and spoke to me softly. "You her kin, ma'am?"

I shook my head. "No, I'm just a good friend of hers, just someone who cared. We met three days ago in New Orleans. There's no family really. A son-in-law who moved to Seattle over twenty years ago with two kids and lost touch with her. His name is Michael Woods. The children would be grown now; Rebecca and Gervais Woods. They may not even be in Seattle anymore; she didn't know. Other than that, she had nobody."

The man nodded. "I'll fill out a report and send it on to St. Gabriel. No one's sure yet what they're going to do with the bodies. There're too many living people with problems to think about now. The dead'll have to wait a bit longer. Meanwhile, is there anything here among her belongings you would want?"

I knelt and dug my hand into the first pillowcase. I retrieved the photos of her children, the letters, and her flag. "Do you think it would be possible to send these things along with that report to St. Gabriel? I'd like to have them buried with her. She would want that."

He took them from me. "I can't guarantee you, but I'll try. And listen, I'm sorry about what I said about the dead having to wait a bit longer. It was insensitive, I know, but right now we're just trying to do what we can for those who survived..." His voice cracked, and he turned away from me. He didn't have to say any more, but he did anyway. "If there's anything else you want, please take it. I need to go and see about this report now."

After he left me alone with Mary's things, I sat cross-legged on the floor and tried to compose myself. Finally I reached into the second pillowcase and felt for the soft down of the purple feather boa. Holding it, I smiled at the memory of how silly the two of us must have looked when we left her house. It was a memory that I'd hold in my heart forever.

It was in that moment I finally realized why I felt compelled to come to New Orleans. I knew I'd helped many in my days there, but I also knew deep down inside I'd really only made a difference in one person's life and that was Mary Boucher's. And I knew that was enough. It was time to go home.

Wrapping the boa around my neck, I walked out of the shelter and jumped in my car. It was a hot day and I put the top down and cranked up the radio. The voice of Chuck Berry blasted out at me. "*C'est la vie,* said the old folks, it goes to show you never can tell."

I wiped the tears from my eyes and smiled as I looked up at the fluffy pink and white clouds against the powder blue sky. "That's so true, Mary. You never can tell when you might run into an angel unawares. Thank you for being mine."

I threw the car into drive and took off, leaving a billow of dust behind me. The purple boa fluttered happily in the wind like an amethyst Edo-dako kite as I put my foot to the floor and headed north. In two days, I would be back to work and back to my life. Everything would be the way it was before and yet nothing would ever be the same again.

When I returned to New York, we were well into September—*Ku Gatsu,* the long month. It lived up to its reputation. After sleeping for two days straight, I spent three days cleaning my apartment from top to bottom. The purple feather boa now hangs proudly from a place of honor on the coat rack in my living room.

Last week, I went out to an animal shelter on Long Island and adopted a frightened little calico cat rescued from a shelter in New Orleans. I named her Dixie. She keeps batting at the boa. I guess she thinks it's a bird.

And yesterday, I actually went all the way downtown to meet Grandma Anna for lunch at Battery Park. She wanted to find out if Devon and I were going to get back together since his little foray into the world of higher education was over. I said no freaking way; the teacher's pet is history. *C'est la vie.* See? Everything is the same, yet different. At least it seems that way to one five-foot-tall, half Japanese-half Italian shoe designer from New York.

I only wish I knew what was going to become of Mary's body. She would look great entering the Pearly Gates in those red, satin, fancy lady shoes.

How You Can Help

Hurricane Katrina caused nearly $30 million in damage to New Orleans libraries. Eight out of twelve of the Public Library branches were ruined.

To find out how you can help, visit www.nutrias.org and click on NOPL Foundation Rebuilding Campaign. You can make a donation by check, credit card, or PayPal. You can also support RNOPL by purchasing a bookplate or a RNOPL T-shirt.

You can also donate to Friends of the New Orleans Public Library Restoration Fund, which is trying to raise $150,000 to add to the cause. The Friends of NOPL have commissioned local artist Thomas Mann to create a fleur de lis pin in support of the FNOPL Restoration Fund Drive. Each pin is hand-made and one-of-a-kind. Show your support by buying a pin. Visit www.nutrias.org/~nopl/info/friends/friends.htm

New Orleans Public Library Foundation
219 Loyola Avenue
New Orleans, LA 70112

Librarian Prompts

Valencia Hawkins is the head of the African American Resource Center at the Main Branch. She enjoys helping people solve problems they are facing, whether that is with information needed from resources in the library or resources needed from another agency in the community. Some of her favorite authors and works include O'Henry short stories, Langston Hughes biographies and poems, Toni Morrison, Bernice McFadden, and Diane McKinney Whetstone fiction. Her favorite quote is "I am the vine and you are the branches. He that abides in me and I in him will bring forth much fruit; for without me you can do nothing."

Her short story would feature Imani, a hard worker who doesn't mind lightening the loads of others and who loves to see others laugh. She would like her character to be definitive and say something like, "Why shouldn't I be here (or go back)? It's my home."

This prompt is featured in the following works: "We Want"; "Faith"; "Tears of the Phoenix"; "Free to All"; "Lucy Too"; "Zombrarians Attack."

Nancy Van Den Akker, a library associate in Automated Services at the Main Branch, enjoys being able to provide users and staff with a clean database and help train staff to provide good service to the users. C.S. Lewis tops her favorite author list, and her favorite character is Spock. Her favorite quote is "Always try to go through life a little hungry; you never know when you'll meet something edible" by T.J. Bass.

She'd like a comedy featuring Chesney Forbanter, a perfectionist with high expectations of others, impatient with inaccuracies and inefficiency. While suspicious of the motives of others, she is willing to take a stand for what she feels is right. The story would be about a teacher verses a mean library where the library itself is the antagonist and how the teacher manages to pacify it.

This prompt is featured in the following works: "We Want"; "White Wall"; "Tears of the Phoenix"; "Free to All"; "Lost and Found"; "Love Is a One Way Street Out of Hell"; "Zombrarians Attack"; "Serving the Public."

Jan Ezkovich Barnes, an assistant acquisitions librarian at the Main Branch, enjoys the fact that she's as often as not the first person to see the new books and discovering new authors and subjects. "Yeah, for me, it's about the book." Her favorite author is H. G. Wells, and her favorite character is Count Franciscus St. Germain (Yarbro). Her favorite quote is "I may not agree with what you say, but I'll defend with my life your right to say it."

In her story, set in the realm of fantasy, Jan the sidekick would be good-looking, intelligent, shy, prone to depression and anxiety attacks. She would love animals and '60s music. She can be a bit bouncy at times and funny.

This prompt is featured in the following works: "We Want"; "Tears of the Phoenix"; "Free to All"; "Just Another Night at the Drunken Dog"; "Of Blood and Love"; "Zombrarians Attack"; "Otherworldly Conversations"; "And in the Folly of My Mind "; "The New Job."

Kirsten M. Corby, a librarian with the Mid-City Branch, enjoys having access to any book she wants, whenever she wants it, or shortly thereafter. She also likes working with computers and having a profession that is about helping people and not about "filthy lucre, getting and spending—libraries are free to all!" Though she loves too many to name just one favorite author or book, her favorite character is Sherlock Holmes. Her favorite quote is "The truth shall set you free."

In her story, Kirsten, inquisitive and loyal, smart but shy, would be in New Orleans where whatever happens is up to the author.

This prompt is featured in the following works: "We Want"; "Tears of the Phoenix"; "Free to All"; "Le Masque"; "Just Another Night at the Drunken Dog"; "Of Blood and Love"; "Zombrarians Attack"; "No Place Like Home."

Lisa Faulk, a cataloger at the Main Branch, likes being a librarian because of the access to books she gets, and she enjoys working alone. Her favorite author is Virginia Woolf.

She requests a comedy in which a female character is the antihero.

This prompt is featured in the following works: "We Want"; "Tears of the Phoenix"; "Role Models"; "The Caper"; "Just Another Night at the Drunken Dog"; "Zombrarians Attack"; "No Place Like Home"; "And in the Folly of My Mind."

Andrea, a librarian associate at the Main Branch, enjoys reading to children and helping them read, doing arts and crafts with them, and "working with the great people who work with me." Her favorite author is Barbara Kingsolver, and her favorite character is Harry Potter. "When you're going through hell, keep going" is her favorite quote.

Her prompt involves Winn, a man blind in one eye, who joins other handicapped characters in an action/mystery.

This prompt is featured in the following works: "We Want"; "Tears of the Phoenix"; "July 20, 2007"; "Zombrarians Attack."

Tara Cunningham Lombardi, a student library assistant at the Law Library of Louisiana in New Orleans, likes being a librarian because it allows for "shushing unruly patrons and wearing my hair in a bun." Her favorite author is Ralph Waldo Emerson, and her favorite character is Sue from *Jude the Obscure*. Her favorite quote is "I have no response to that" by Meg Ryan in *Joe vs. the Volcano*.

In her comedy, Tara is a sarcastic, stubborn, moody, strong-willed but well-meaning antihero. Things don't usually go her way, and she often puts her foot in her mouth. She doesn't fit in with any particular group, and she's kind of happy on the fringe, but she doesn't have many friends, although she always thought she would. She loves movies and TV shows and has believed their romantic notions of barbecues and dinner parties and brunch on Sundays with a bunch of girlfriends. She hasn't had a lot of friends since college, and she misses that camaraderie, but hasn't found anyone that she likes to be around as much as her old college friends. Tara's thirty-five, and still in library school, and a little wary about finding a job after graduation. She has a four-year-old son named Nate and a husband from Massachusetts named Kevin. Tara lived near the London Avenue. Canal in Gentilly (an area of New Orleans) and lost her house. She now lives in the suburbs, which she hates. She can't wait to get a job and get out of the suburbs and maybe New Orleans.

This prompt is featured in the following works: "We Want"; "Tears of the Phoenix"; "Transcendental"; "Fairy Tale Sundered"; "Zombrarians Attack"; "No Place Like Home"; "Of Blood and Love."

A special collections librarian at New Orleans Baptist Theological Seminary, John T. Christian Library, loves doing different things every day. "Helping people find what they are looking for is nice as well. I work as an archivist, so finding things in old papers and collections that nobody else has seen before is fascinating!" This person's favorite author is J.R.R. Tolkien, character is Treebeard, and quote is "All that is gold does not glitter, Not all those who wander are lost. The old that is strong does not wither, Deep roots are not reached by the frost. Renewed shall be blade that was broken, The crownless again shall be King" from *Fellowship of the Ring*, as written by Bilbo Baggins.

In this short story, a character named Quickbeam, who is hasty, entertaining, valorous, and friendly, appears.

This prompt is featured in the following works: "We Want"; "Tears of the Phoenix"; "Love Is a One Way Street Out of Hell"; "Zombrarians Attack"; "And in the Folly of My Mind."

Beth Patin, librarian at Holy Cross School Library, works at anall boys' school and loves "making the boys excited about reading and books. I love sharing my passion for books!" Her favorite author is D.J. MacHale (the Pendragon series) and her favorite character is Harry Potter. Her favorite quote is "Life is a roller coaster; hold on and enjoy the ride."

In her action/fantasy/mystery flashfic, Creola Dejean, a thirty-year-old beautiful, overweight, Creole woman with long, curly hair and hazel eyes is intelligent, psychic, and sometimes treacherous if crossed. The story is set in New Orleans.

This prompt is featured in the following works: "We Want"; "Tears of the Phoenix"; "Of Blood and Love"; "Breathless"; "Zombrarians Attack"; "No Place Like Home."

Johannah White, a humanities reference librarian at Tulane University, says the best thing about being a librarian is helping people and "being around interesting people engaged in learning about the world and helping the rest of us understand it," not to mention beautiful, wise books and amazing databases. Her favorite author is Joseph Brodsky, and her favorite character is Bridget Jones. Her favorite quote is "Wherever you go, there you are."

In an action/horror/mystery, Grace, a striking, intense, warmly human, brave, wise, but secretly devious and powerful woman, is seen helping people in situations that show her humanity—the best and worst of it. She should be caught in a dilemma and lead herself and others out of it, but does she lead people into the light or the dark?

This prompt is featured in the following works: "We Want"; "Tears of the Phoenix"; "Saving Grace"; "Zombrarians Attack"; "There You Are, Then You Go"; "No Place Like Home"; "The Killer."

Maureen "Molly" Knapp, a reference librarian at John P Isché Library, LSU Health Sciences Center, New Orleans, likes helping people, answering questions, and the ability to shush people with a single raised eyebrow. Her favorite authors include Philip K. Dick, Jonathan Lethem, and Louisa May Alcott. Her favorite characters are Nick and Nora Charles from Dashiell Hammet's *The Thin Man*. Her favorite quote is from Thomas Paine: "We have it in our power to begin the world over again."

Her story would feature Zombrarian. Like any zombie, Zombrarian needs braaaaaaainsss to live (un-live?), but it's only the juicy mental meat of book-lovin' library patrons that gets Zombrarian's gumless lips smackin'! What's that you're reading...Proust? Potter? Pippi Longstocking? Better keep quiet or Zombrarian will give you a shushing you won't forget. Just remember what they say: "Better read...than un-dead!" Zombrarian has some capacity for speech ...especially the word "BRAIIINNNSSSSZZZ" and 'SHHHHHHHHzzzzz' (for shushing unruly patrons, etc.). Zombrarian works in a library at the medical school, so to see her lurking around the anatomy lab cadavers—looking for friends no doubt—or the autopsy books section of the library—where there are many pictures of glorious brains—is quite common. (The call numbers for anatomy lab books are QS 4–QS 17 in the Library of Congress National Library of Medicine cataloging classification, in case you wonder).

This prompt is featured in the following works: "We Want"; "Tears of the Phoenix"; "Lucy, Our New Spirit"; "Zombrarians Attack"; "Binding of the Dead."

Seale Paterson, branch manager of the Hubbell Branch and the Algiers Regional Branch, enjoys helping people, especially kids, find a book they really like. "The thank you after they've read it and enjoyed it really makes me feel like I'm doing my job well. But what I like best: I learn something new every day in every field imaginable!" Her favorite authors include Jane Austen, Carl Hiaasen, Tom Robbins, David Sedaris, and Christopher Moore. Her favorite character is Elizabeth Bennett, and her favorite quotes are: "The road of excess leads to the palace of wisdom" (William Blake) and "It seems to me to show an abominable sort of conceited independence, a most country-town indifference to decorum" (Jane Austen).

In this comedy, the antihero would be witty and unconventional with a dark sense of humor. Though she can be overcritical, she enjoys life (maybe too much sometimes), surrounds herself with interesting and eclectic people, but is still very independent, and tends to get into "situations." She is clumsy, daring, maybe sometimes too impulsive, very self-confident, laughs at her own expense frequently, and, of course, loves New Orleans with a passion. Bonus points if Aunt Tiki's, a dive bar in the French Quarter on Decatur Street (we refer to the area as Lower Decatur) was somehow incorporated. The bartender's name is Brian.

This prompt is featured in the following works: "We Want"; "Tears of the Phoenix"; "Itty Bitty Living Space"; "Love Is a One Way Street Out of Hell"; "Of Blood and Love"; "Laissez Les Bon Temps Rouler Again"; "Zombrarians Attack"; "No Place Like Home"; "And in the Folly of My Mind."

A library associate at the Main Branch in New Orleans' favorite part of the job is his reference work. His favorite author is Charles Dickens and his favorite character is Edmund Dantes from *The Count of Monte Cristo*. His favorite quote is: "It is easier for a camel to go through the eye of a needle than a rich man to enter the kingdom of heaven."

His character's name would be Kevin O'Neal and he would be the hero of the story, a "child" of the '60s who never lost his political fervor. His motto would be "Liberal and proud of it." His story would take place in a court of law where Kevin proves it was the Bush administration's deliberate negligence that caused the city of New Orleans to be flooded and its poorer citizens to be stranded. He donates his contingency fee to New Orleans Public Library for rebuilding, restoring, and restocking purposes.

This prompt is featured in the following works: "We Want"; "The Lady Who Cried and Flooded the Streets"; "Tears of the Phoenix"; "Laissez Les Bon Temps Rouler Again"; "Zombrarians Attack."

BettyLou Strother is a librarian at the Keller Branch in New Orleans. Her favorite part about her job is "guiding children to new authors and titles to expand their worlds." Her favorite author is Andre Norton, and her favorite character is The Star Man's Son.

In her fantasy story, her character's name would be Elizabeth, and she would be dependable, hard working, and a perfectionist who is curious and always trying to keep order. Her story would be a fantasy, but the length and plot would be up to the author.

This prompt is featured in the following works: "We Want"; "Tears of the Phoenix"; "On Order"; "Surviving"; "Of Blood and Love"; "Zombrarians Attack"; "Ghosts."

A librarian at the Children's Resource Center says her favorite part of the job is "seeing kids get really excited about reading a book and getting to learn something new almost every day." Her favorite character (Marvin the Robot) and quote comes from her favorite author's (Douglas Adams) book, *The Hitchhiker's Guide to the Universe*: "In the beginning the Universe was created. This has made a lot of people very angry and been widely regarded as a bad move."

She has always liked the cynical but lovable-despite-themselves characters. They're not overly happy or optimistic but keeping a sense of humor about it all. She'd like the character of her mystery-comedy to be the antihero and be named Crystal Weary. She leaves the plot to the author but would like it to take place in New Orleans if possible.

This prompt is featured in the following works: "We Want"; "Tears of the Phoenix"; "Free to All"; "Staying the Course on St. Charles"; "Lucy Too"; "Zombrarians Attack."

A branch manager at the Alvar Library in New Orleans enjoys answering reference questions and assisting patrons on the computer. "I especially like learning about new authors, titles, and topics of public interest. I also enjoy helping people learn about new information resources. I love to see people empowered with new skills." Her favorite author is Shakespeare, and her favorite character is Mr. Stupendous. Her favorite quote is "What is essential is invisible to the eye."

In her mysterious short story, her character, Melody, would be the hero who is young and smart, seeking answers to life's questions. She would be intuitive and inquisitive; loyal, creative, and dependable, too. She would like her story set at university. Here, the character must live her life consistent with her teaching, although the mystery plot causes her to justify her decision. Her clarity of thought, facts, and persuasiveness wins the day. She would like her character to utter the line: "Life has a life of its own."

This prompt is featured in the following works: "We Want"; "Tears of the Phoenix"; "Solo Refrain"; "Surviving"; "Zombrarians Attack."

Damian Lambert works at the Nix and Mid-city Branch of the New Orleans library as a branch manager. His favorite part of his job is he gets to play and boss people around. Some of his favorite authors are Alan Dean Foster, Gregory Benford, and William Shakespeare. His favorite character is Donald Duck, and his favorite quote is "A good friend will come and bail you out of jail; your best friend sits next to you and says, 'Damn, that was fun!'"

His character's name would be Lance, the antihero in this fantasy where a small colony on a distant world discovers the first alien artifact, and it's deadly. Lance would be reliable, educated, strong, friendly, knowledgeable, and good-looking, in his thirties.

This prompt is featured in the following works: "We Want"; "Tears of the Phoenix"; "Flower Song"; "Zombrarians Attack"; "Dusk."

Sarah Huston is a library associate at the Main Library in New Orleans. Her character's name would be Sarah Truly, and she would be stubborn, clever, funny, and argumentative and would be the antihero involved in a mystery.

This prompt is featured in the following works: "We Want"; "Tears of the Phoenix"; "Zombrarians Attack."

Michele Pope is a serials and government documents librarian at Loyola University Law Library. She loves her job, which deals with the details of published information.

Her character's name would be Lucy, and she'd be shy, funny, and brave in her fantasy story/flash fiction/drabble or poem. She leaves the plot of her story up to the author, but she would like Lucy to secretly enjoy running in mud puddles.

This prompt is featured in the following works: "We Want"; "The Pleasures of Mud"; "Tears of the Phoenix"; "Mud Puddles"; "Lucy, Our New Spirit"; "Lucy Too"; "Zombrarians Attack"; "A Jumbled Shelf."

Henri André Fourroux III is a library associate at the Latter Branch New Orleans Public Library. His favorite part of his job is "being around people who like to read books, helping to promote freedom and sharing of knowledge, and being part of a service which is not partisan, politicized or commodified, something quasi-socialist." His favorite author is Amy Sedaris, and his favorite character is Jerri Blank. His favorite quote is "Is it so different to be new? And is it so strange to be different? Now, I'm not saying that new isn't bad, of course it is. But on this St. Arbor's Day week, we must realize that the new sapling grows into the mighty old oak, which we cut down to make our new ax handles which, in turn, we use to chop down our mighty old oaks."

In his action/mystery/fantasy short story his character's name would be Alex Raclitson, and he would be a hero who has a great deal of learned knowledge, trivial to pop culture, yet elemental and advanced regarding the sciences, cultures, and literatures of the world. This makes him appear aloof and emotionally detached to others. Just on the gay side of bisexual, he knows karate and kung fu and speaks fluent French and Japanese. His family lived in Japan when he was a child, and he studied French in high school. He doesn't suffer fools gladly unless he has to spend time with them at work or such where he tolerates them, yet when he is required to assist someone, he can be accommodating and pleasant—but, of course, with the understanding he doesn't have to go home with that person. He can be mean toward those who've achieved power, fame, influence but find themselves vulnerable (takes joy in the plight of those who perhaps deserved their fall from arrogance and self-importance). He does like to joke around with friends, usually jokes that would offend religious hypocrites (sex, money, interpretation of god, etc.). He will go out of his way to help even coworkers who are vulnerable due to age or health issues. In the end, he really resents the self-righteous rich and will fight for the majority who are poor and working class. He is vegetarian, but will eat meat to not offend humble, simple hosts, but will refuse meat offered by owners of, say, agribusiness slaughterhouses. Having just helped solve a crime, he is on vacation in the Loire Valley in Anjou, Angers.

This prompt is featured in the following works: "We Want"; "Tears of the Phoenix"; "Zombrarians Attack"; "No Place Like Home."

Contributor Biographies

Silvia Barlaam is Italian and trained as an illustrator in Rome, but moved to the U.K. a few years ago. A keen lover of the moving image, she's completing a Ph.D. in film and television studies, meanwhile experimenting with new media and working on a new artistic portfolio to reflect her more recent experiences and the challenges of the British landscape.

Donna Beltz is an award-winning television sound editor and aspiring writer who lives in Topanga Canyon, California, with her husband of—whoa, that's a lot of years—let's just say her husband of many years!

Tanya Bentham and her grumpy cat live in a 200-year-old fisherman's cottage on the North Yorkshire coast, which sounds quite romantic but is, in reality, bloody cold most of the time. She currently earns enough money to keep the cat in the manner to which it feels entitled by telling other people's stories—like *Beowulf*, for instance—but would prefer to earn a crust with her tales of her own devising. *The New Job* is set in the world of *Madame Caravossa's Interdimensional Dating Agency,* and Tanya would like any stray literary agents reading this to know that the aforementioned novel is available for hire like the moderately expensive floozy it was written by.

Moe Biers is a journalist who, some days, feels like he works for *Bizarre Bazaar* and hopes, one day, to be an editor at that fine, upstanding bastion of journalism, *The Onion*. Or a writer for *The Daily Show*. And no, he doesn't actually like beer.

D.J. Black is a librarian living in Missoula, Montana. This is Black's first attempt in the drabble format.

Jason Burger is a collection of auspicious letters from various corners of the alphabet. On paper—among other things—he attends Western Connecticut State University where he is studying literature.

Greta Cabrel is a graduate of the University of Michigan. She has participated in numerous drabble challenges as "Bronze Ribbons."

Rachel Caine is the author of more than twenty novels, including the popular Weather Warden series and the Morganville Vampires young adult series, for which she has sold the film and television option rights. In 2009,

Rachel will launch a new four-book series, Outcast Season, from Roc. She has also written paranormal romantic action/adventure for Silhouette Bombshell. Her most recent paranormal romance novel, *Athena Force: Line of Sight,* is a 2008 RT Reviewer's Choice award winner. She also published an original novel for the television show *Stargate SG-1 (Sacrifice Moon)* under the pseudonym Julie Fortune. She is a contributor to a number of BenBella Books' SmartPop anthologies of nonfiction essays and had short fiction in three best-selling anthologies in 2007, including *My Big Fat Supernatural Wedding, My Big Fat Supernatural Honeymoon* (St. Martins), and *Many Bloody Returns*, which became a *New York Times* best seller. She and her husband, award-winning artist R. Cat Conrad, live in Texas with their iguanas Popeye and Darwin, a mali uromastyx named O'Malley, and a leopard tortoise named Shelley (for the poet, of course). Visit her online at www.rachelcaine.com; www.myspace.com/rachelcaine and http://rachelcaine.livejournal.com.

Gwyneth Cooper is a teacher from New Zealand who has lived and traveled in China, Pakistan, and the Central Asian Republics. She now teaches physics in Northland, New Zealand, but still has itchy feet.

Peg Duthie is a graduate of the University of Chicago. Her poems have appeared in *Boxcar Poetry Review, No Tell Motel, Southern Gothic,* and elsewhere.

Matissa Evensong is a wordsmith who resides in Granite City, Illinois, where she takes care of her grandmother. She's had a few poems published by various publishers, including Noble House. She has been writing poetry and stories ever since she learned how to write. She is an avid reader and loves music.

S.R. Ferguson is a bartender in Glasgow, Scotland. When not serving up spirits to the colorful locals, Ferguson is at home writing the fictional tales of said locals.

C.A. Hiley studied fine art in London, Berlin, and Vancouver. She has never been to New Orleans but is a great fan of libraries everywhere.

Bernadette Joseco is a scientist in her regular life, but during her hours off, she likes to escape into reading and drawing crazy things like bread in libraries.

Julia Katz has a bachelor's degree in English from the University of Connecticut. She lives in New Haven and is working toward a master's degree in teaching. She loves to write and was distressed to find out just how difficult that process is when your computer dies...twice.

Sasha Katz is a jack-of-all trades and a career student. She hopes to become a comedy writer for film and TV, or at least work as a costumer full time. Her livejournal is stupid_drawings.

Robert Kelso is the biggest Harry Potter fan in the world! He is saddened that the University of Alaska, as yet, does not teach Magical Theory or

Transfiguration, but will have to appease himself to finish his forestry degree instead. This is his first published work.

Kim Kiser holds a bachelor's degree in both studio arts and art history and is very fortunate to be working an awesome job at a museum near Pittsburgh, Pennsylvania. She draws and paints on the side, but most recently, her life has been consumed by fiber arts...her mountain of yarn soon threatens to overtake her room. It is all very scary.

Charie La Marr lives in New York with her mother, her son, and three assorted dogs. She is a novelist and ghostwriter who sometimes blogs as The Queen Is A Muse(d) at http://angelsinredhats.com/blog/. She described herself as a "redhead with a redheaded attitude."

Leochi lives in Austria where she is a Waldorfschool teacher. Her hobbies include drawing, painting, photography, and reading. Visit her blog at http://leochisart.blogspot.com.

Nyssa Anne Madison leads a life of intrigue and danger that's full of preternatural creatures...if only in her mind. A slave to her muse, she writes what the fickle creature dictates, which usually involves steamy fantasy tales that have been published in anthologies and e-zines.

Cynthia Maves is a mother of four who lives in Illinois with her children and husband. She is also a shipping/receiving coordinator for a finishing system corporation. This is her first published work.

Diana M. McCabe is a freelance writer and illustrator. She has had short fiction published in Marion Zimmer Bradley's *Fantasy Magazine*, and her art has appeared in the Touchstone Pictures movie *Last Dance*. She has won awards for her artwork in juried exhibitions, including a dragon sculpture made entirely of found objects. She is currently working on a children's book of illustrated verse.

Emily Moreton is a postgraduate student at the University of Bristol in the U.K. She has been writing for as long as she can remember and has had a story published in the literary journal *Chroma*, as well as co-writing a mystery novel as part of a writing group.

N. Apythia Morges is a newspaper editor, freelance editor/designer, and writer. Her articles and weekly literary column have appeared in newspapers in the United States and England, and her fiction has been published in several anthologies and literary journals. She is cofounder of Tears of the Phoenix literary charity organization and coeditor of Tears of the Phoenix Anthologies and Tears of the Phoenix *Ink*. She is pursuing a master's degree in publishing and lives in New York.

Pasquale J. Morrone lives in Maryland on the Chesapeake Bay with his wife, Kathleen. His hobbies include reading, writing, fishing, photography, and cooking. His first novel, *Spook Rock*, was published in 2004.

Born on São Paulo, Brazil, **T.G. Nossack**, also known as Sweet-Lemmon, has always loved the arts and literature. Although she had studied economics, her artistic side was never put aside. However, she had never showed her drawings to anyone until two years ago when she discovered the world of fan art. View her artwork at http://community.livejournal.com/sweetie_art and http://sweetlemmon. deviantart.com.

A.J. O'Connell is a journalist and college instructor who lives and works in Fairfield County, Connecticut. A.J.'s work has appeared in *Citizen Culture Magazine*, on 1up.com, and in various anthologies. She has never been to New Orleans, but were she to go, she would visit the library—but not as her two characters might.

Gloria Oliver lives in Texas. She is the author of *In the Service of Samurai, Vassal of El*, and *Willing Sacrifice*, all fantasy novels. *Cross-eyed Dragon Troubles* will be released in 2008. She is a member in good standing with Broad Universe and EPIC. To find out more, please visit www.gloriaoliver. com.

Eirik Omlie lives in Connecticut where he spends his days as an editor and his nights working on projects like *The Sacrifice*, his first illustration for a book.

Aden Penn is a crocheting file clerk who lives in a small Texas town. She has a penchant for Old Time Radio, *Doctor Who*, and comic books. Her online presence can be found at http://dietpoison.livejournal.com.

Pennswoods, also known as Shannon, is a university professor by day and a self-taught illustrator of fan art and other literary creations by night. She is also a huge fan of the Harry Potter series and devotes far too much of her free time to podcasting about Severus Snape.

Emma Pocock lives on the East Coast of Australia. She is surrounded by her pets, computers, books, and her partner of seven years. She suffers from multiple chronic illnesses and uses art as a great way to escape.

Jennifer Racek lives in Dallas, Texas, with her husband, her daughter, a cat, a dog, and seven hedgehogs. When not programming Web sites at her day job, she enjoys writing, reading, and running one of the top ten largest Harry Potter meet-up groups in the world. This is her first short story. She can be reached via e-mail at jennracek@gmail.com.

Tamela J. Ritter is an award-winning writer, journalist, and editor. Her work has appeared in many literary journals and anthologies across the country. She is the editor of *Whatever Literary Journal* and cofounder of Tears of the Phoenix and coeditor of Tears of the Phoenix Anthologies and Tears of the Phoenix *Ink*. Her novel, *From These Ashes*, is sitting on a shelf, collecting dust.

Theresa Rogers' nonfiction work has been published in T*he Crockett Signal* and *The West County Times*. She has also written a cookbook that will be published in August 2008. This is her first piece of published fiction. She is a fencing practitioner and lives in Northern California with her family.

Jessica Sims is a Canadian interested in travel and the arts. She is pursing a bachelor of arts degree in theater and film at the University of Winnipeg.

Shari Smith is a writer from Dagenham, England. She is an aspiring scriptwriter, solicited by the BBC, and volunteers her time with Habbit Shed, an inclusive theater company in Havering, Essex. The company provides theater workshops for mainstream and special-needs children in the local area.

E.J. Wilson is a college student at University of Massachusetts Amherst, majoring in comparative literature and philosophy who hopes to open a bookstore in the hills of New Hampshire or, you know, become a barista at Starbucks.

Autumn Rose Wood lives with her soulmate in Jackson, Michigan. She is grateful to the Lost Word Writers' Group for their support and to the Tears of the Phoenix for this anthology. Anyone interested in contacting her can e-mail her at autumnrosewood@-hotmail.com.

Yael van der Wouden is a twenty-year-old English major who learned how to draw lines and people by whining and shouting at her mother until she drew it for her, and then Yael copied (though she'd still be doing just that if her mother hadn't stopped complying).

Caitlin Young was born and raised in New Orleans, and recently moved back there after graduating from the University of Mary Washington in Virginia. The daughter of an English-teacher-turned-librarian and having worked in several libraries, she believes strongly in the importance of books and libraries, as well as all those who make it possible for them to exist. She's never found a wardrobe that leads to another world, but that doesn't mean she's given up looking.

Elizabeth S.C. Wu is a graduate of the UCLA English Department, class of 2007, and is currently researching creativity and cognitive function at the UCLA Semel Institute for Neuropsychology and Human Behavior. She will be pursuing a master's degree in public health and community services in fall 2008 at UCLA and wishes ultimately to attend medical school and practice medicine. Among her non-scientific achievements, she is also recognized in fine arts as a California Arts Scholar, and is an alumna of the Ryman Foundation for Fine Artists and the Marie Walsh Sharpe Art Foundation.

Tears of the Phoenix

Tears of the Phoenix, a nonprofit, nonstock corporation, is dedicated to spreading the love of the written word by supporting literary charities and promoting new authors and artists.

Each Tears of the Phoenix anthology benefits a different book-based and/or literary charity. All profits from this book will be donated to the Rebuild New Orleans Public Library project.

To learn more about Tears of the Phoenix and its upcoming anthologies and other projects, please our Web site:
www.tearsofthephoenixink.org
or e-mail info@tearsofthephoenixink.org

Tears of the Phoenix
A book can change a life.

Printed in the United States
131789LV00002B/15/P